Money, History, and
International Finance

A National Bureau
of Economic Research
Conference Report

Money, History, and International Finance: Essays in Honor of Anna J. Schwartz

Edited by **Michael D. Bordo**

The University of Chicago Press

Chicago and London

Michael D. Bordo is professor of economics at the University of
South Carolina and a research associate of the National Bureau of
Economic Research.

The University of Chicago Press, Chicago 60637
The University of Chicago Press, Ltd., London
© 1989 by the National Bureau of Economic Research
All rights reserved. Published 1989
Printed in the United States of America

98 97 96 95 94 93 92 91 90 89   5 4 3 2 1

∞The paper used in this book meets the minimum requirements of
the American National Standards Institute for Informational
Sciences regarding permanence of paper for printed library
materials, ANSI Z39.48–1984.

Library of Congress Cataloging-in-Publication Data

Money, history, and international finance : essays in honor of
   Anna J. Schwartz / edited by Michael D. Bordo.
       p.   cm. — (A National Bureau of Economic Research
   conference report)
     Bibliography: p.
     Includes index.
     ISBN 0-226-06593-6
       1. Money—Congresses. 2. Economic history—Congresses.
   3. International finance—Congresses. 4. Schwartz, Anna
   Jacobson. I. Schwartz, Anna Jacobson. II. Bordo, Michael D.
   III. Conference report (National Bureau of Economic Research)
   HG203.M69 1989
   332.4—dc19   88-39779
                                                                      CIP

Since this volume is a record of conference proceedings, it has been exempted from the rules governing critical review of manuscripts by the Board of Directors of the National Bureau (resolution adopted 8 June 1948, as revised 21 November 1949 and 20 April 1968).

Contents

Foreword

To honor Anna Schwartz for her many years of productive research, the NBER sponsored a conference in New York City on 6 October 1987. At that conference, Anna was presented with a collection of her papers, *Money in Historical Perspective*. This volume is in a sense a sequel to that collection. It includes the papers and comments that were presented at the October conference.

Written by many of Anna's friends and co-authors, the papers reflect the range of contributions that she has made to our understanding of monetary economics by building on her earlier work: her exhaustive study with Milton Friedman of U.S. monetary history, her studies of British monetary history, her analyses of the gold standard, and her research on the effects of monetary policies in other exchange rate regimes. The papers in this volume are filled not merely with references to Anna's work and critical reviews of her findings and analyses. They also are full of affection and respect for Anna as a scholar and a friend.

This book, and the conference on which it is based, are due to the efforts of Michael Bordo. Without his enthusiasm and hard work we would not be honoring Anna in this way. I would also like to thank Mark Fitz-Patrick for his help in publishing these papers. Finally, the Lynde and Harry Bradley Foundation, the Earhart Foundation, and the Alex C. Walker Educational and Charitable Foundation provided financial support for this *Festschrift*.

Martin Feldstein

Preface

The papers in this volume were written for a conference held in honor of Anna J. Schwartz at the Halloran House Hotel in New York City on 6 October 1987. The conference gathered together many of Anna Schwartz's colleagues from the NBER, the academic world, private industry, and government to discuss five papers written on themes related to her lifetime research interests. At a dinner at the end of the conference, Anna Schwartz was presented by Milton Friedman with a copy of *Money in Historical Perspective* (University of Chicago Press 1987), a collection of her articles.

I would like to express my appreciation to the authors, discussants, and invited participants for their contribution to the conference. Above all, I would like to thank Milton Friedman for his help in organizing the conference.

For valuable financial assistance I would like to thank the Lynde and Harry Bradley Foundation, the Earhart Foundation, and the Alex C. Walker Educational and Charitable Foundation.

All the participants express their thanks to Kirsten Foss Davis and her staff for their efficient management of the conference arrangements.

Michael D. Bordo

Introduction

Michael D. Bordo

Anna Jacobson Schwartz began her career over fifty years ago as an economic historian and ever since has continued her interest in historical issues. Over the past close to four decades, she has been closely involved in research on the role of the quantity of money in economy. This focus on monetary issues has given rise to the collection of monetary statistics, the study of both recent and historical monetary developments in the United States, the United Kingdom, and other countries, and the study of international monetary relations.

This introduction begins with a brief biographical sketch, followed by a short summary of the salient themes in Anna Schwartz's research. Then, the main themes from this volume are related to Anna Schwartz's writings. And finally, there is a brief conclusion.

Biography

Anna Schwartz was born 11 November 1915 in New York City. She received her B.A. from Barnard College in 1934, an M.A. from Columbia in 1936, and a Ph.D from Columbia in 1964. She is married with four grown children and resides with her husband, Isaac, in New York City.

Most of Anna's career has been spent in active research. After a year at the U.S. Department of Agriculture in 1936, she spent five years at Columbia University's Social Science Research Council collaborating with A. D. Gayer and W. W. Rostow in a study of fluctuations in the British economy during 1790–1850. She joined the National Bureau of Economic Research in 1941 and has remained at the Bureau ever since. She was appointed Emerita Research Associate of the NBER in 1985.

In 1981–82 Anna served as staff director of the U.S. Gold Commission and was responsible for writing the Gold Commission Report.

Anna served as instructor at Brooklyn College in 1952 and Baruch College 1959–60, and as Adjunct Professor of Economics at the City University of New York, Graduate Division at Hunter College, 1967–69 and New York University, Graduate School of Arts and Sciences, 1969–70.

She has been a member of the Board of Editors of the *American Economic Review,* and is currently on the board of the *Journal of Money, Credit, and Banking* and *Journal of Monetary Economics.* She has also been a regular participant at the Carnegie Rochester Conference Series on Public Policy and is a charter member of the Shadow Open Market Committee.

Elected to membership in Phi Beta Kappa in 1934, she has served as the reviewer of economics books for *The Key Reporter* since 1984. She was a holder of the Murray Fellowship awarded by Barnard College, 1934–35, was a fellow of the Committee on Research in Economic History, 1945, and is currently Adjunct Professor at the Graduate Center of the City University of New York and Honorary Visiting Professor, City University of London Business School. In 1987–88 Anna Schwartz was president of the Western Economic Association.

Salient Themes in Anna Schwartz's Writings

Three themes dominate Anna's writings: economic statistics, economic history, and monetary economics. In the sphere of monetary economics Anna has written extensively on money, income, and prices; monetary policy; and international issues. (See the appendix for a complete bibliography of her writings.)

Economic History and Economic Statistics

In her early career Anna's research was focused mainly on economic history and statistics. Her collaboration with Gayer and Rostow from 1936 to 1941 produced a massive and important study of cycles and trends in the British economy during the industrial revolution, *The Growth and Fluctuation of the British Economy, 1790–1850* (1953). In the two volumes of Gayer, Rostow, and Schwartz, NBER techniques were adopted to isolate cycles and trends in key time series of economic performance. Historical analysis was then interwoven with descriptive statistics to present an anatomy of the development of the British economy in this important period. A legacy of this project is a share price index (originally constructed by Gayer, Jacobson, and Finkelstein 1940) and a legendary Gayer-Rostow-Schwartz commodity price index. Anna, in an introduction to a second edition of *Growth and Fluctuation* in 1975, noted change in her views on the role of monetary forces in British economic history. Reflecting her later research with Milton Friedman on money and business cycles, she no longer accepted the conclusion in the British Study that money passively accommodated the needs of business. Instead she contended that money played a much more active role.

Since Gayer, Rostow, and Schwartz, Anna has written singly or jointly on many aspects of monetary history. Subjects covered range from the origins of competitive banking in Philadelphia (1987, ch. 1 [1947]), to *A Monetary History of the United States* (with Milton Friedman 1963), to a history of world inflation (1987, ch. 2 [1973]).

After joining the Bureau in 1941, Anna turned her attention to the collection of data. In an important collaboration with Elma Oliver she constructed new monthly estimates of currency held by the public, vault cash, and currency held by the Treasury, over the period 1917–44—data free from the defects of earlier money supply series (Schwartz and Oliver 1947). This research would ultimately serve as the basis for the collection of monetary statistics underlying the NBER's money and business cycle project with Milton Friedman and the publication in 1970 of *Monetary Statistics of the United States*. Later, in a painstakingly careful study Schwartz (1960) constructed new monthly estimates of gross dividends and interest payments by all corporations in the nineteenth century. She offered a comment at a recent NBER Income and Wealth conference on the possible explanation of the need to impute bank income (1989).

Monetary Economics

Money, Income, and Prices

In the 1950s Anna began her collaboration with Milton Friedman on the NBER's highly acclaimed money and business cycles project. This collaboration, over a period of thirty years, resulted in three volumes: *A Monetary History of the United States, 1867–1960* (1963), *Monetary Statistics of the United States* (1970), and *Monetary Trends in the United States and the United Kingdom, 1875–1975*, (1982), in addition to Phillip Cagan's *Determinants and Effects of Changes in the Stock of Money, 1875–1960* (1965), and several journal articles including "Money and Business Cycles" (1987, ch. 2 [with Milton Friedman 1963]).

The theoretical background to the project is the modern quantity theory of money (Friedman 1956). Based on the interaction of a stable demand for money with an independently determined money supply, the key proposition of the modern quantity theory is that a change in the rate of growth of money will produce a corresponding but lagged change in the rate of growth of nominal income. In the short run, changes in money growth lead to changes in real output. In the long run, monetary change will be fully reflected in changes in the price level.

Monetary disturbances affect nominal expenditures via the community's adjustment of its actual to desired holdings of real cash balances. The portfolio adjustment affects a wide range of assets and a wide array of explicit and implicit interest rates connecting assets to permanent income streams, but ultimately impinges on total spending. The timing of changes in nominal spending and their breakdown into changes in real output and in the price level depend on factors such as the speed of adjustment of price and wage expectations and the presence of price and wage rigidities (Friedman 1987).

Long-run historical evidence for the modern quantity theory of money is provided in *A Monetary History,* short-run cyclical evidence in "Money and Business Cycles," and long-run econometric evidence in *Monetary Trends*. This evidence and recent literature following it is surveyed in chapters 1, 2, and 3 below.

Monetary Policy

The overwhelming historical evidence linking economic instability to erratic monetary behavior, in turn a product of discretionary monetary policy, has convinced Anna Schwartz of the importance of stable money and of the case for a constant money growth rule. As a consequence she has devoted considerable attention in the past twenty years to the study of monetary policy in the U.S. and in other countries.

As a charter member, with Karl Brunner, Allan Meltzer, and several others, of the Shadow Open Market Committee, Anna has been engaged since 1971 in an ongoing critical evaluation of the Federal Reserve's policies.

The importance of monetary policy and the case against discretion are examined in studies with Phillip Cagan. One shows that the lags in the effects of monetary policy, based on the simulation of recent econometric models, are long and variable (1987, ch. 7 [1976]); another shows that the interest elasticity of money demand has not changed with the advent in the 1960s and 1970s of money substitutes (1987, ch. 8 [1975]). A study co-authored by myself (1987, ch. 10 [1983]) summarizes the recent debate for and against discretion, and links recent economic instability to erratic monetary policy.

Anna has also examined monetary policy in the U.K., arguing that the Bank of England's focus on credit conditions—the legacy of the 1959 Radcliffe Report—rather than on the quantity of money contributed to its poor postwar performance (1987, ch. 5 [1969]). Similar evidence on central banks' choice of inappropriate policy targets is found for Canada and Japan (1969). In addition a recent case study for Canada (and one in progress on the U.K.) show that the use of interest rates as a monetary control technique has produced excessive monetary variability (Bordo, Choudhri, and Schwartz 1987).

Another question Anna has studied is the role of government in money and banking arrangements—whether both outside and inside money should be provided by the free market and whether a central bank is needed to prevent financial crises (1987, ch. 12 and 11). In a recent paper she has examined post–World War II financial market developments in relation to financial stability and the federal safety net (1988).

International Monetary Issues

In the last ten years Anna has been greatly interested in international monetary issues, especially alternative monetary standards. We collaborated on the organization of a 1982 NBER conference on the classical gold standard. The resulting collection of articles (Bordo and Schwartz 1984) summarizes the current state of knowledge on the operation of the classical gold standard from 1821 to 1931. In a recent paper (1987, ch. 15) Anna describes the historical evolution of the gold standard and assesses its performance in providing price level and output stability. She was also a principal collaborator with Michael Darby, James Lothian, et al. in the NBER's *The International Transmission of Inflation* (1983), writing for it a concise and important assessment of the postwar international monetary system (1987, ch. 14).

When Anna was staff director of the U.S. Gold Commission in 1981–82, the Commission was instructed by Congress to assess and make recommendations on the role of gold in U.S. domestic and international arrangements. The Commission's deliberations culminated in its *Report,* volume 1 of which was written by Anna. In addition to the Commission's recommendations, this volume contains an insightful background to the establishment of the Commission—the legacy of fifteen years of inflation—a thorough review of the role of gold in U.S. monetary history, a detailed examination of the merits and demerits of alternative commodity and fiduciary standards, a critical evaluation of existing gold arrangements in the United States with proposals for change, and an appendix containing valuable data.

The Conference Themes

The papers in this volume are directed at the themes in Anna Schwartz's work in monetary economics just discussed: monetary history; money, income, and prices; and international monetary issues.

Monetary History

Two of the papers focus on monetary history. In one, I assess the role of A *Monetary History* as a progenitor of research on this topic. My paper critically surveys the literature on three major themes in the book: monetary disturbances; the domestic monetary framework and monetary policy; and monetary standards.

Much of the recent historical literature on monetary disturbances has focused on the treatment of the Great Contraction of 1929–33 in A *Monetary History*. The consensus has supported Friedman and Schwartz's view of the primacy of monetary conditions as causal forces in the Great Contraction, although evidence of contemporaneous correlation between money and income has been interpreted as supporting significant feedback from nonmonetary to monetary forces. However, evidence of endogeneity of the money supply or of feedback from real forces to the money supply begs the question of whether the Great Contraction had to happen. As Friedman and Schwartz made clear, the Federal Reserve clearly could have stopped the decline in the money supply and the depression with it.

The literature also supports Friedman and Schwartz on the importance of banking arrangements and monetary policy as the setting for monetary disturbances. Of special interest is recent statistical evidence for a regime change that occurred with the advent of the Fed in 1914, and new explanations for Federal Reserve policy failures in the 1920s and 1930s. One reason given for the Fed's failure to conduct expansionary monetary policy during 1929–31 was that based on its indicators—the level of member bank borrowing and market interest rates—it believed conditions were easy.

On monetary standards, recent work corroborates Friedman and Schwartz's interpretation of the greenback episode, of the effects of the agitation over silver, and of the gold standard as a transmitter of monetary disturbances between countries.

In my survey I conclude that "the unique portrayal of the historical circumstances of monetary disturbances and of alternative arrangements as background conditions serve the monetary economist as the closest thing to a laboratory experiment. The book's example has become an important tool of modern macroeconomic research."

Rockoff in his comment on my paper surveys the contribution of Anna Schwartz's writings on pre-1867 monetary history. The collection of data on monetary aggregates, interest rates, and corporate dividends has provided valuable raw materials for future research. Her work on the chartered banks of Philadelphia, on secular inflation through the ages, and on the case against cost-push inflation in the nineteenth century raises questions for future scholars to tackle.

Capie and Wood examine the contribution of *Growth and Fluctuation* by Gayer, Rostow, and Schwartz, to British economic history. They conclude that "the volume remains unchallenged as a source of carefully constructed data for the years it covers," that "it is the pioneering work in British . . . economic history," and that the volume provides an important link between earlier approaches to the business cycle and current real business cycle theories.

Laidler in his comment focuses on pre–World War II business cycle theory. In not attributing a primary role to monetary forces in the cycle, Gayer, Rostow, and Schwartz had followed prevailing views. Of the leading theorists of the day, only Irving Fisher subscribed to a theory with money as the key causal force of the cycle.

Money, Income and Prices

As discussed earlier, a key theme in Anna Schwartz's writings is the short-run influence of monetary change on real economic activity. *A Monetary History* provided ample evidence that although the relationship between money and income was bidirectional, the dominant channel of influence was from money to business activity. Such evidence was based on historical episodes where the sources of monetary change were recognized as clearly independent of business activity and where monetary change could be associated with a change in income in the same direction. Additional evidence for this finding was based on a number of studies using time-series regressions.

Cagan's paper critically evaluates recent literature which disputes this conclusion. His survey criticizes studies by Kaldor and Tobin in 1970 that made the case for an endogenous money supply, the more recent use of bivariate Granger-causality tests, and most emphatically studies employing vector autoregressions (VAR). Though VAR is a valued technique for dealing with the problems of endogeneity, multicollinearity, and spurious correlation which plagued earlier time-series regression studies, Cagan argues that the results of recent VAR studies, which imply a minor role for monetary shocks in explaining changes in real activity, remain largely spurious. These results reflect both the filtering techniques employed, which remove most of the cyclical movements in money, and the masking of monetary influences by innovations in interest rates, in turn a reflection of monetary policy. In lieu of sole reliance on time-series methods, Cagan advocates the use of the type of historical analysis pioneered by Anna Schwartz.

Rasche in his comment on Cagan argues that sole reliance on historical analysis as an alternative to time-series methods presumes that historical analysis itself is not faulty. Instead, he advocates supplementing VAR analysis, which by itself cannot identify effects from money to income, with judgment based on theory and historical analysis.

Capie and Wood address some of the issues raised in the U.K. following the publication of *Monetary Trends*. Of particular interest were the findings by Friedman and Schwartz which indicated a stable, long-run money demand function in over a century of data; the absence of any influence of money on real activity; and the use of phase-averaged data. Capie and Wood's critique of Hendry and Ericsson's (1983) attack which found in effect that the money demand function had been misspecified, cites recent evidence by Holly and Longbottom (1985) that replicates Friedman and Schwartz's results using Hendry's own techniques. Capie and Wood also defend the use of the phase-averaging technique, which Hendry and Ericsson criticized as well, emphasizing its value in capturing the influence of nondeterministic trends.

Laidler comments on the anomalous result in *Monetary Trends* for phase-averaged data (corroborated by Goodhart 1982 using annual data) that monetary change has no effect on output. Laidler attributes the result to foreign price and exchange rate shocks, which influence prices independent of changes in money supply.

International Issues

In Anna's work in recent years on international monetary issues, three themes are stressed. First, the relationship to the money stock of the international monetary standard. Under flexible exchange rates, the stock of high-powered money is an independent variable determined by the monetary authorities. Under the fixed exchange rate gold standard, high-powered money becomes a dependent variable determined by the balance of payments and, at one remove, by the relationship between domestic and foreign price levels. Second, the comparative performance of alternative monetary regimes—the gold standard versus fiat money regimes—in providing monetary, price level, and real output stability. Third, the international transmission mechanism—whether real and nominal shocks are transmitted differently between countries under fixed and flexible exchange rates—and the role of monetary policy in transmission. Two papers in this volume deal with these issues.

For seven countries, Meltzer and Robinson use a multistate Kalman filter procedure to compare forecast errors (as measures of variability and uncertainty) in the level and rates of change of real output, and the price level for the classical gold standard, Bretton Woods, and the recent fluctuating exchange rate regime. The Kalman filter distinguishes permanent and transitory errors in the levels of series as well as permanent changes in growth rates. Because it is a Bayesian forecasting technique, in generating the forecast it revises the probability weights given to recent and past observations, depending on the past history of shocks. The results show that for most countries the variability of both levels and growth rates of real output were lower in the post–World War II period than under the classical gold standard; in some countries the variability of real output was lower in the recent period of fluctuating exchange rates than under Bretton Woods. Accounting for the changing mix of production between agriculture and manufacturing explains only part of the reduction in variability over time.

Meltzer and Robinson also find price level and inflation variability to be lower in the post–World War II period, especially under fluctuating exchange rates, than under the gold standard in the majority of countries, with the principal exception of the United Kingdom. The latter set of results is contrary to the widely held view that the gold standard fostered long-run price stability and predictability.

Poole in his comment notes that the results on the price level are biased against the gold standard because the period comprises a subperiod of deflation followed by one of inflation. He also suggests that errors in the data in the earlier period would be responsible in part for the greater forecast errors.

To determine whether the advent of fluctuating exchange rates in 1973 led to increased monetary independence, Darby and Lothian compare the behavior of a number of variables (money supply, interest rates, price levels, and real output) under the Bretton Woods system and the subsequent period of floating exchange rates across a sample of twenty OECD countries. The greater variability of, and lower correlation between, long-term measures of nominal variables under floating rather than under fixed rates implies increased monetary independence in the long run. The key finding is that a positive and significant correlation under fixed rates between a measure of desired real cash balances and the nominal money supply is not significantly different from zero under floating rates.

In the short run, there is evidence for the persistence of international linkages under flexible rates in the correlation between the United States and each of the other countries of annual changes in the nominal variables. However, these results can be better explained by the reaction functions of monetary authorities to foreign developments than by the operation of the traditional transmission mechanism.

Stockman in his comment notes that interpretation of the correlation between desired real money balances and money supply is ambiguous if the demand for real balances is correlated across countries. He suggests that cointegration is a better method to reveal common trends in the data than the methods used in this study. Furthermore, evidence that real exchange rates are close to random walks suggests that price movements across countries may be explained by real rather than monetary forces.

Conclusion

The papers in this volume pay tribute to the fine tradition of scholarship Anna Schwartz has followed throughout her career. Her research in economic history, in monetary economics, and international finance have all made an indelible mark on our profession. Each of the papers underscores the legacy of Anna's scholarly endeavors to important fields of research.

Karl Brunner and Milton Friedman paid tribute to Anna Schwartz in remarks presented at the end of the conference. Brunner praised her scholarly attitude, the attention to substantive issues of the real world, the clarity of her views, and the carefulness of her scholarship. Friedman described the remarkable collaboration he has had with her over the years.

The contributors to this volume and many others have learned a great deal from working with Anna Schwartz, from her writings, and above all from her example as a true scholar. We hope this collection is a fitting symbol of our admiration.

References

Bordo, M. D., E. U. Choudhri, and A. J. Schwartz. 1987. The behavior of money stock under interest rate control: Some evidence for Canada. *Journal of Money, Credit and Banking* 19, no. 3 (May):181–97.

Bordo, M. D., and A. J. Schwartz. 1984. *A retrospective on the classical gold standard, 1821–1931*. Chicago: University of Chicago Press.

Cagan, P. 1965. *Determinants and effects of changes in the stock of money, 1875–1960*. New York: Columbia University Press.

Darby, M. R., J. Lothian, et al. 1983. *The international transmission of inflation*. Chicago: University of Chicago Press.

Friedman, M. 1956. *Studies in the quantity theory of money*. Chicago: University of Chicago Press.

———. 1987. Quantity theory of money. *The new Palgrave: A dictionary of economics*. London: Macmillan Press.

Friedman, M., and A. J. Schwartz. 1963. *A monetary history of the United States, 1867–1960*. Princeton: Princeton University Press.

———. 1970. *Monetary statistics of the United States*. New York: Columbia University Press.

———. 1982. *Monetary trends in the United States and the United Kingdom: Their relations to income, prices, and interest rates, 1867–1975*. Chicago: University of Chicago Press.

Gayer, A. D., A. Jacobson, and I. Finkelstein. 1940. British share prices, 1811–1850. *Review of Economics and Statistics* (May):78–93.

Gayer, A. D., W. W. Rostow, and A. J. Schwartz. 1953. *The growth and fluctuation of the British economy, 1790–1850: An historical, statistical, and theoretical study of Britain's economic development.* 2 vols. Oxford: Clarendon Press; 2d ed. 1975, Hertfordshire: Harvester Press.

Goodhart, C. A. E. 1982. Monetary trends in the United States and the United Kingdom: A British review. *Journal of Economic Literature* 20(4):1540–51.

Hendry, D., and N. Ericsson. 1983. Monetary trends in the United Kingdom. · Bank of England, Panel of Academic Consultant Paper no. 22.

Holly, S., and A. Longbottom. 1985. Monetary trends in the U.K.: A reappraisal of the demand for money. London Business School EFU Discussion Paper 147.

Kaldor, Nicholas. 1970. The new monetarism. *Lloyds Bank Review* 97 (July):1–18.

Radcliffe Committee on the Working of the Monetary System. 1959. *Report* Cmnd 827. London: H.M.S.O. (August).

Report to the Congress of the Commission on the Role of Gold in the Domestic and International Monetary Systems. 1982. Vol. 1 (March).

Schwartz, A. J. 1960. Gross dividends and interest payments to corporations at selected dates in the 19th century. In *Trends in the American economy in the nineteenth century.* Studies in Income and Wealth, vol. 24, National Bureau of Economic Research, 407–45.

———. 1969. Short-term targets of some foreign central banks. In *Targets and indicators of monetary policy,* ed. K. Brunner. San Francisco: Chandler Publishing Company.

———. 1987. *Money in historical perspective.* Chicago: University of Chicago Press.

———. 1988. Financial stability and the federal safety net. In *Restructuring banking and financial services in America,* eds. William S. Haraf and Rose Marie Kushmeider. Washington, D.C.: American Enterprise Institute.

———. 1989. Comment on Rymes. In *The measurement of saving, investment, and wealth,* eds. R. E. Lipsey and H. S. Tice. Studies in Income and Wealth, vol. 52. Chicago: University of Chicago Press. Forthcoming.

Schwartz, A. J., and E. Oliver. 1947. *Currency held by the public, the banks, and the Treasury, monthly, December 1917 - December 1944.* Technical Paper 4, National Bureau of Economic Research.

Tobin, James. 1970. Money and income: Post hoc ergo propter hoc? *Quarterly Journal of Economics* 84 (May):301–17.

I   Historical Perspectives

1 The Contribution of *A Monetary History of the United States, 1867–1960* to Monetary History

Michael D. Bordo

The long-awaited monetary history of the United States by Friedman and Schwartz is in every sense of the term a monumental scholarly accomplishment . . . . the volume sets, . . . , a new standard for the writing of monetary history, one that requires the explanation of historical developments in terms of monetary theory and the application of them to the techniques of quantitative economic analysis. . . . One can safely predict that it will be the classic reference on its subject for many years to come.

> H. G. Johnson (1965, 388)

The book is clearly destined to become a classic, perhaps one of the few emerging in that role rather than growing into it.

> A. Meltzer (1965, 404)

The transcendent virtue of the *History* is its unerring vision in seeking out important problems and its clear delineation of areas needing further research. The book offers an almost inexhaustible supply of worthwhile conjectures. I have no doubt that it, . . . , will be the focus of a major share of scholarly research on money and income during the coming decade. For this, if for no other reason, the book must be counted a monumental contribution to positive economics.

> R. W. Clower (1964, 380)

This is one of those rare books that leave their mark on all future research on the subject.

> J. Tobin (1965, 485)

Michael D. Bordo is a professor of economics at the University of South Carolina and a research associate of the National Bureau of Economic Research.

For helpful comments and suggestions, the author would like to thank George Benston, Bennett McCallum, Allan Meltzer, Hugh Rockoff, Anna Schwartz, and Geoffrey Wood. Able research assistance was provided by Ivan Marcotte.

1.1 Introduction

Four eminent scholars from different schools of thought all believed over twenty years ago that *A Monetary History of the United States, 1867–1960* by Milton Friedman and Anna J. Schwartz, published in 1963, was destined to become a classic. Their judgment was sound.[1]

Table 1.1 presents a chronological breakdown of references to the book in professional journals. The citation analysis is based on two sources: the *Social Science Citation Index* which covers the period 1969–87, and a sample of ten leading journals in monetary economics and economic history from 1964 to 1987. The second sample is included in the SSCI, but separating it has value because it covers the entire period since the book was published and because it allows us to examine the incidence of citations in journals from different fields.

As can be seen from table 1.1, the number of citations has been increasing, although irregularly, since 1965. This is clearly the hallmark of a classic since the citation rate for most articles and books in science generally peaks within three years and then gradually tapers off.[2]

Also of interest is the pattern of citations revealed by an examination of the articles in the sample of ten journals. In the first ten years after publication, the majority of articles citing *A Monetary History* were in monetary economics, of which a considerable number concentrated on issues raised by the debate between modern quantity theorists and Keynesians. By contrast, in the last decade, the majority of articles, even those in mainstream economics journals, have concentrated on the interpretation of historical episodes in *A Monetary History*. This recent interest in monetary history is the focus of this paper.

A Monetary History is a treatise both in economics and in economic history. In the former role, the book uses history to expound the modern quantity theory of money. In its latter role, the book reinterprets U.S. monetary history in terms of the relationship between the quantity of money and the rest of the economy. The former treatment represents a major component of modern quantity theory research of the 1950s, 1960s, and 1970s; the latter treatment has in itself led to a revolution in monetary history as economic historians and economists expand upon and criticize Friedman and Schwartz's treatment of diverse episodes of U.S. monetary history. This paper examines the second legacy of *A Monetary History*—its role as a progenitor of research in monetary history. Specifically the paper surveys the literature on three major themes in *A Monetary History:* monetary disturbances (section 1.3), the domestic monetary framework and monetary policy (section 1.4), and monetary standards (section 1.5).

As background to the survey in section 1.2, I briefly summarize the contribution of the book to modern quantity theory research and

Table 1.1   Citations to *A Monetary History of the United States, 1867–1960* in the Literature

Year	JPE	AER	JME[a]	JMCB[b]	RECSTAT	JEH	EEH	JF	EJ	QJE	Total	SSCI
1964	0	1			0	1	0	1	0	0	3	
1965	3	2			0	0	0	0	1	0	6	
1966	4	1			1	0	0	2	0	0	8	
1967	4	2			0	0	0	1	0	0	7	
1968	6	0			0	0	1	0	0	0	6	
1969	3	2		3	0	1	0	0	0	0	10	13
1970	2	1		1	0	0	1	1	0	1	6	19
1971	2	0		4	0	3	1	1	0	0	11	14
1972	2	2		5	0	1	0	3	0	0	14	15
1973	1	1		1	0	4	1	0	0	0	9	10
1974	0	2		1	0	1	1	0	0	1	7	20
1975	1	2	0	3	0	1	1	0	2	0	10	19
1976	3	2	3	1	0	3	0	1	0	0	13	33
1977	0	1	1	4	0	2	2	0	0	0	10	33
1978	0	1	3	3	1	1	0	2	1	0	13	30
1979	0	0	4	1	1	0	1	0	0	0	7	19
1980	1	2	1	3	0	2	1	0	0	0	10	28
1981	0	0	0	3	0	3	1	0	1	0	8	40
1982	2	0	4	3	0	2	1	0	0	0	12	30
1983	2	2	4	0	0	1	3	1	0	0	13	38
1984	3	3	1	1	0	6	0	0	0	0	14	35
1985	3	2	4	3	0	3	4	1	1	0	20	35
1986	3	1	2	3	0	0	2	1	0	0	12	47
Total	45	30	29	43	3	35	20	18	6	2	229	478

Note: The citations are from: Journal of Political Economy (JPE); American Economic Review (AER); Journal of Monetary Economics (JME); Journal of Money, Credit and Banking (JMCB); Review of Economics and Statistics (RECSTAT); Journal of Economic History (JEH); Explorations in Economic History (EEH); Journal of Finance (JF); Economic Journal (EJ); Quarterly Journal of Economics (QJE); and the Social Science Citation Index (SSCI).

[a]JME began publication in 1975.

[b]JMCB began publication in 1969.

provide a brief overview of its interpretation of U.S. monetary history. Finally, the paper concludes with an evaluation of *A Monetary History*'s contribution to monetary history.

1.2   Background

1.2.1   *A Monetary History* and the Modern Quantity Theory

In the 1950s, Milton Friedman and Anna Schwartz began their collaboration on the NBER's highly acclaimed money and business cycles project. This collaboration, over a period of thirty years, resulted in *A Monetary History of the United States, 1867–1960* (1963a), *Monetary Statistics of the United States* (1970), and *Monetary Trends in the United States and the United Kingdom, 1875–1975,* (1982), in addition to Phillip Cagan's *Determinants and Effects of Changes in the Stock of Money, 1875–1960* (1965), and several journal articles, including "Money and Business Cycles" (1963b).

The theoretical background of the project is the modern quantity theory of money (Friedman 1956). Based on the interaction of a stable demand for money with an independently determined money supply, the key proposition of the modern quantity theory is that a change in the rate of growth of money will produce a corresponding but lagged change in the rate of growth of nominal income. In the short run, changes in money growth lead to changes in real output. In the long run, monetary change will be fully reflected in changes in the price level. Long-run historical evidence for the modern quantity theory of money is provided in *A Monetary History,* short-run cyclical evidence in "Money and Business Cycles," and long-run econometric evidence in *Monetary Trends.*

A Monetary History is a study of the quantity of money and its influence on economic activity in the U.S. economy over a nearly one-hundred-year span, marked by drastic changes in monetary arrangements and in the structure of the economy. The principal finding is that changes in the behavior of money are closely associated with the rate of change of nominal income, real income, and the price level. Secularly, a close relationship between the growth of money and nominal income, independent of the growth of real income, is found. Cyclically, a close relationship between the rate of change of money and of subsequent changes in nominal income is isolated.

The authors also find a number of remarkably stable relationships between money and other economic variables. These include the findings that velocity exhibits a steady secular decline of a little over 1 percent per annum until after World War II, and that the relationship between U.S. prices and prices in other countries, adjusted for the exchange rate, changed little over the period, which is evidence of the strength of the purchasing-power-parity theory.

However, of most interest are the findings from history that the money-income relationship is invariant to changes in monetary arrangements and banking structure. These changes are captured in the arithmetic of the proximate determinants of the money supply. Over the long run, high-powered money (H) is the key determinant, supplemented by the deposit-reserve ratio (D/R) and the deposit-currency ratio (D/C); over the cycle the ratios become more important, especially in severe contractions, when the D/C ratio dominates.

The different monetary arrangements since 1867 include: (1) the greenback episode, 1861–78, when the United States had flexible exchange rates with the rest of the world and the money supply became an independent variable; (2) the gold standard period, 1879–1914, when the quantity of money became largely a dependent variable determined by the country's trading relationship with the rest of the world; (3) the gold exchange standard, 1919–33, when the quantity of money, though partly determined by external conditions, was also heavily influenced by Federal Reserve monetary management; (4) the period since 1934 described as a "discretionary fiduciary standard," with gold just a commodity the price of which was fixed by an official support program.

In addition, there were several important changes in the banking structure. These include the establishment of the national banking system (1864) and the Federal Reserve (1914), and the institution of the Federal Deposit Insurance Corporation (1934), which removed the threat of banking panics.

Identification of unique historical and institutional circumstances, it is argued, provides the closest thing to a controlled experiment in which the direction of influence from money to income can be isolated. Thus the authors demonstrate that in many cases changes in money were independent in origin from and temporally preceded changes in economic activity—the most notable examples being the gold discoveries in the 1890s, wartime issues of fiat currency, and the restrictive actions of the Federal Reserve in 1920–21 and 1937–38. Although they identify an influence from income to money over the business cycle, they argue that the main influence, both secularly and cyclically, runs from money to income.

Of special importance is the evidence on monetary disturbances: sharp declines in economic activity were precipitated by sharp reductions in the money supply, while episodes of sustained inflation were invariably produced by monetary growth in excess of the growth of real output. For both types of disturbance the historical record provides instances where inappropriate actions by the monetary authorities were to blame. Thus the Great Depression of 1929–33 was a consequence of an unprecedented reduction in the quantity of money that the Federal Reserve System could have prevented, while episodes of inflation during the Civil War and World Wars I and II were the product of wartime issues of fiat currency.

The historical evidence in *A Monetary History* is complemented by evidence on business cycles reported in "Money and Business Cycles" and in Cagan's *Determinants*. That is, specific cycles in money growth precede reference cycle turning points, the amplitude of cycles in money growth is closely correlated to business cycles, and the identification of major cycles all leads to the conclusion that "appreciable changes in the rate of growth of the stock of money are a necessary and sufficient condition for appreciable changes in the rate of growth of nominal income" (Friedman and Schwartz 1963b, 53). The evidence argues against the view that cycles in monetary growth are merely a lagged response to the business cycle.

Long-run econometric evidence for the modern quantity theory of money is based on reference cycle phase-averaged data to remove the influence of the business cycle, provided by *Monetary Trends*. The study examines the relationships among the money stock, nominal and real income, the price level, and the interest rate for the United States and the United Kingdom for the century from 1875 to 1975. The key finding of this work is a stable long-run money demand or velocity function for each country, with the money demand function for each country affected in similar ways by a common set of determinants. A second important finding is parallel movements between money and nominal income which, given the stability of money demand and variability in conditions of money supply, primarily reflect an influence running from money to income.

A third and related finding is the neutrality of money. For the United Kingdom and the United States (with one exception) a sustained one-percentage-point change in money leads cumulatively to a one-percentage-point change in the price level. Only for the interwar period in the United States does monetary change have a major influence on real income in the same direction, and a positive relationship exist between changes in prices and output—a relationship consistent with a negatively-sloped Phillips curve. The idiosyncrasy of the interwar period derives, it is argued, from two severe monetary contractions in that period.

Thus *A Monetary History* is an integral part of modern quantity theory research. Recent research in macroeconomics on the natural rate hypothesis, the importance of monetary regimes, and the case against discretionary monetary policy, builds on its foundation.

1.2.2   Overview of Friedman and Schwartz's Interpretation of U.S. Monetary History, 1867–1960

As a backdrop to the literature survey to follow, I will briefly sketch some of the salient points of the authors' reinterpretation of the monetary history of the United States from shortly after the Civil War to after World War II.

A Monetary History begins in 1867 during the greenback episode that ended 1 January 1879. In that period, when the United States had a flexible exchange rate with the rest of the gold standard world, the principal concern was to resume specie payments at the previous parity. Friedman and Schwartz demonstrate, based on earlier work by Kindahl (1961), that despite active public debate over the pace and methods to achieve the required deflation, resumption was achieved by the economy growing up to a constant money stock rather than as a consequence of any explicit government policies.

The succeeding seventeen years, after the United States successfully returned to the gold standard, were characterized by deflation, monetary instability, and political agitation over the monetary standard. The advocates of silver wanted injections of silver to offset the ravages of the worldwide gold deflation. Instead of inflation, Friedman and Schwartz demonstrate, the silver movement produced more deflation than would otherwise have been the case, as capital and gold fled the United States because of a fear that the U.S. would abandon the gold standard. Fear of deflation and silver agitation diminished once new gold supplies from South Africa and Alaska swelled the world monetary gold stock. The gold discoveries, the authors argue, were no accident but were induced, with long lags, by secular deflation under a commodity standard.

The national banking system from 1863 to 1914 was characterized by periodic banking panics. The panics of 1893 and especially 1907 precipitated a movement for banking reform which aimed to establish an agency to satisfy the public's demand for high-powered money in times of distrust of bank solvency. Friedman and Schwartz argue that the Aldrich Vreeland Act of 1908, which was successful in preventing a panic in 1914, and the occasional resort by clearinghouses to restrictions of convertibility of deposits into currency under the National Banking System, proved superior to the actions of the agency designed to prevent panics—the Federal Reserve System established in 1914. The Fed failed to act as a lender of last resort. Had the clearinghouses restricted convertibility during the panics of the early 1930s, as they would have done in the absence of the Fed, the massive bank failures and monetary collapse of 1929–33 would have been averted.

The newly established Fed, after a serious blunder in 1920–21 when it delayed too long to stem the post–World War I commodity price boom and then raised the discount rate too sharply, subsequently developed the tools to provide monetary stability in the 1920s. The authors argue that had the architect of Fed policy in the 1920s, Benjamin Strong, lived beyond 1928, the disaster of 1929–33 would have been avoided. A vacuum of leadership after Strong's death is held to be responsible for the failure of the Fed to curtail the banking panics and its passive acceptance of a one-third decline in the money supply. Power shifted from the New York Federal Reserve Bank, an agency tuned to the needs of the money market and adept at the operation of policy, to the Federal Reserve Board and the other reserve banks, neither of which had the experience or understanding of monetary policy required to deal with the crisis.

The New Deal introduced legislation which radically altered monetary arrangements in the United States. Of key importance, according to Friedman and Schwartz, was the adoption of federal deposit insurance in 1934. By eliminating at the outset a loss of confidence by the public in convertibility of deposits into currency, it solved the problem of banking panics, which the Fed had failed to prevent.

In addition, prohibition of private gold holdings, the gold purchase program, and revaluation of the price of gold, converted the United States from the gold exchange standard to a managed fiduciary standard, with gold relegated to the status of a price-supported commodity. Legislation allowing the Fed to alter reserve requirements led to a disastrous monetary contraction in 1937–38 after the Fed doubled reserve requirements in a mistaken attempt to soak up excess reserves to restrict future credit expansion. According to Friedman and Schwartz, the banks held reserves in excess of requirements because their demand for liquidity had increased as a result of their traumatic experience of the panics of the early 1930s. The increase in required reserves just locked up their precautionary balances, forcing the banks to reduce earning assets to restore their reserve holdings to the desired level.

During the next two decades, monetary policy was subordinated to fiscal policy and thus the Fed played a role subservient to the Treasury. This passive policy culminated in the bond-price-support program of World War II. By pegging the interest rate to short-term treasury bills at ⅜ percent and pledging to maintain the rate on long-term securities at 2½ percent, the Fed was converted into an "engine of inflation" providing whatever high-powered money was required to maintain the fixed pattern of interest rates.

The threat of renewed inflation during the Korean War led to the Accord of March 1951 and the restoration of monetary independence to the Fed. During the remaining years of the study, according to the authors, there was remarkable monetary stability—a stability which in hindsight was quite unique.

1.3   Monetary Disturbances

The ninety-four-year span covered by *A Monetary History* was characterized by a wide variety of monetary disturbances. Of the twenty-four NBER-designated cyclical downturns, six are designated severe, each of which Friedman and Schwartz document to have been preceded by a sharp downturn in the money supply. Two of the monetary contractions, in 1919–21 and 1937–38, were the result of monetary policy actions, and the others, including the Great Contraction of 1929–33, were marked by banking panics. In addition to monetary disturbances that produced declines in economic activity, the book documents one period of sustained inflation—from 1897 to 1914, a consequence of the gold discoveries—and two world war periods of fiat-induced inflation.[3]

A key theme in *A Monetary History* and the subsequent literature is the role of monetary institutions and monetary policy in producing monetary and economic contraction. In consequence, the survey of the literature on monetary disturbances focuses on two issues: banking panics and the Great Contraction.

1.3.1   Banking Panics

Monetary Instability

Friedman and Schwartz devote considerable attention to the role of banking panics in producing monetary and economic instability in the United States.

Bernanke (1983), contrary to Friedman and Schwartz, argues that banking panics have direct effects on economic activity over and above their effects on the money supply. To the extent that banking panics produce losses in the financial sector of the economy, the cost of financial intermediation is increased and the efficiency of resource allocation reduced. Bernanke tests this hypothesis on the banking panics of 1930–33 by incorporating several measures of the cost of financial intermediation—real deposits and liabilities of failing banks, and the spread between the Baa and the Treasury bond rate—into a Barro-Lucas-type regression equation (which explains changes in output by unexpected money growth, unexpected changes in the price level, and lagged output). The statistically significant results that he obtains for the equation lend support to his hypothesis.

However, according to Vaubel (1984), Bernanke's results may imply that bank failures led to a risk-induced rise in the demand for money or else were associated with an anticipated decline in output. If the cost of financial intermediation reduced income, it could only have done so because the monetary authorities allowed a large risk premium to develop. The risk premium was not the inevitable consequence of bank failures, but rather reflected the public's uncertainty about how the authorities would react.

Brunner and Meltzer (1988) do not accept Bernanke's treatment of the debt crisis as a separate and independent exogenous shock. They view the debt crisis as an induced response to the major deflation of asset and output price levels consequent upon the failure of the Fed to act as a lender of last resort, in a system with many holders of nominally fixed debt. Major shocks to the banking system affect the money supply and bank credit multipliers simultaneously.

Bernanke's interpretation of his results, moreover, suggests that financial intermediation skills would be irretrievably lost as a result of bank failures. In fact, however, those skills continued to be available once the banking situation stabilized.

Also contrary to Friedman and Schwartz on the role of banking panics in producing monetary and real contraction, DeLong and Summers (1985) provide evidence that removing panics, and the quarters immediately surrounding them, from the data reduces the variance of income during 1896–1914 by only 20 percent as against a 40 percent reduction in the variance of monetary growth. They therefore conclude that monetary shocks are an inadequate explanation of shocks to real output. DeLong and Summers find that severe economic contractions before World War II were produced by deflationary real shocks which raised the real interest rate in the face of sticky nominal rates.[4] Such an interpretation, however, is inconsistent with evidence of a high degree of international capital mobility during this period.[5] High real interest rates should have attracted capital inflows which would have halted severe economic contractions.

Rational Expectations

In recent work by Garber (1981), Garber and Flood (1982), and Blanchard and Watson (1982), bank panics are viewed as based on the rational expectations hypothesis that rational agents will not systematically make forecast errors. Bank panics are the contagious effects of "runs." According to Garber (1981):

> A run is defined as a speculative attack on an asset price fixing scheme which causes a discontinuous asset shift in private agents' portfolios. The run occurs because of agents' belief that the nature of the price fixing regime will change, thereby causing a discontinuous shift in asset rates of return. (p. 4)

In the case of a bank run, the price under attack is the price of deposits fixed in terms of currency. In a world of perfect foresight, the required asset exchange will be carefully arranged in an orderly manner far in advance of the event, as, for example, in the case of a run on a banking system insured by a central bank as lender of last resort. In that case the run will end through the sudden acquisition of bank assets by the central bank. A "panic" characterizes a run whose timing was not perfectly foreseen. In such a case there may be discontinuous shifts in asset prices and unanticipated capital gains or losses on some assets.

According to Diamond and Dybvig (1983), in a world of asymmetric information, banks are able to transform illiquid financial assets into liquid ones by offering liabilities with a different, smoother pattern of returns over time. Banks provide efficient risk sharing which the private market cannot provide. However, the illiquidity of bank assets also subjects banks to the vulnerability of runs. A run can be triggered by any random event because rational depositors not wishing to be last in line will rush to convert deposits into currency.

Waldo (1985) develops a model in the Diamond and Dybvig mold which explains two empirical regularities associated with banking runs observed by Friedman and Schwartz: a rise in short-term interest rates and a fall in the deposit-currency ratio in anticipation of a possible run. The rise in short-term interest rates occurs because banks attempt to meet withdrawals by selling long-term securities before maturity. Yields on short-term assets rise in concert. The fall in the deposit-currency ratio in anticipation of a possible run occurs because, in the event of a run, the banks' losses on the premature sale of their long-term securities eventually force them to default on some of their deposits. Savers shift from deposits to currency in anticipation of possible runs to partially protect themselves against this risk.

Smith (1987) also constructs a model of nationwide banking panics in the Diamond-Dybvig vein, which captures many features of the national banking system. Key features of the model are the assumptions of geographically dispersed unit banking, nationwide linkages of unit banks through the inverted pyramid of reserves held in reserve and central reserve city banks, and interest payments on deposits and loans not state contingent.

Based on these assumptions, Smith demonstrates how exogenous shocks that caused unit banks to withdraw interbank deposits could produce panics. According to Smith, the key reason for a nationwide panic was the holding of bankers' balances by a central reserve agent. The absence of this feature, he argues, explains why nationwide banking panics did not occur in the free banking era. Moreover, following Friedman and Schwartz, Smith argues that the added severity of the panics of 1930–33 can be explained by the existence of the Fed. Banks did not consider suspending convertibility of deposits into currency as they had done during the national banking era.

Smith's interpretation of history differs from the record in two important respects: there were panics in 1819, 1837, 1839, 1847, and 1857, and interbank balances were a feature of the pre–Civil War banking system. His model implies that nationwide branch banking systems will not be subject to panics, notwithstanding the contrary experiences of Austria, Germany, and other central European countries in 1931.

In a slightly different vein, but on rational expectations lines, Gorton (1984b) argues that banking panics are not unique events, as described by Friedman and Schwartz, but represent a rational response by depositors who wish to smooth their consumption flows over time. Rational depositors plan to dissave in periods of expected low consumption, such as at business cycle troughs. The likelihood of suspensions of convertibility would also be highest in mid-contraction, so depositors will rush to convert their deposits to currency when they expect a trough to occur.

To provide evidence that rational depositors will increase the currency-deposit ratio (precipitate a banking panic) when they expect a business cycle trough to occur, Gorton (1984b) regresses the currency-deposit ratio during the national banking era (1873–1914) on measures of the expected return on deposits, the variance of that return, and a variable acting as a signal of the covariance of consumption and capital losses on deposits—the unexpected shock component of failed business liabilities.[6] His finding of a significant and positive coefficient on the failed liabilities variable is consistent with his hypothesis. Moreover, findings that panics coincided with dates of the largest values of the shocks in the liabilities of failed businesses, and that the shocks came after business cycle peaks and before troughs in all panics except 1895, lead him to conclude that the failed business liability shock was a cause of panics. Friedman and Schwartz's hypothesis is that panics were due to unanticipated failures of financial institutions, often holding assets of failed nonfinancial firms.

A problem with Gorton's approach is that if depositors could predict a panic, should there have been panics? If depositors could predict panics, why could banks, equally vulnerable during panics, not predict them? In addition, panics did not necessarily occur in all situations that were otherwise equivalent. In some, predictable signals to market participants of institutional readiness to provide additional funds promptly nipped an incipient panic in the bud, as in 1884 (Schwartz 1986). In others, no such signals were forthcoming and panic erupted. Finally, Gorton's approach implies that a panic may be optimal for private arrangements but it will not necessarily be socially optimal.

Restrictions of Convertibility

Friedman and Schwartz (p. 698 and elsewhere) argue that restrictions of convertibility of deposits into currency by the banking system during the national banking era had therapeutic effects by alleviating a banking panic and facilitating speedy recovery. Had such an option been available to the banks in the early 1930s, the banking panics would have ended before producing the massive fall in the money supply.

Dewald (1972) disputes Friedman and Schwartz's interpretation, instead following Sprague (1910), who opposes restriction because of the high costs imposed on the payments system. According to Dewald, the New York banks could have reduced their reserves to handle withdrawals in emergencies such as the panics of 1893 and 1907, even if it meant violating reserve requirements. Furthermore, he alleges that Friedman and Schwartz's advocacy of restriction in 1907, and suspension during the Great Contraction in 1930 rather than 1933, contradicts their approval (on p. 698) of the issue of emergency currency in 1914 under the Aldrich Vreeland Act.

In reply, Schwartz (1972) doubts that the New York banks would have been willing to run their reserves below the legal limit without a change in the law. Moreover, even if the New York banks had been willing to run deficits, what mattered was their own preference for liquidity in a panic. For Friedman and Schwartz (1963a) suspension was a second-best solution if no institutions existed to increase high-powered money.[7] In 1914, Aldrich Vreeland currency was available. In the 1930s, the Fed could have created high-powered money but did not do so; therefore, early restriction was preferable to deflation.

According to Gorton (1985b), in a world of rational expectations but limited information, restriction of convertibility represents an optimal arrangement between banks and customers to allay an incipient panic. With limited information, bank customers monitor a noisy signal of banks' investments, e.g., the failures of important nonfinancial firms or the liabilities of failed companies. A panic is then a rational response to movements in this indicator because depositors fear capital losses on their deposits. Restriction is a way in which banks indicate to customers that their investments are sound.

Clearinghouses

Friedman and Schwartz (chapters 3 and 4) discuss the private market lender-of-last-resort role of the New York Clearing House and other clearinghouse associations in issuing clearinghouse loan certificates during panics. Timberlake (1984) and Gorton (1984a) describe how the New York Clearing House evolved ways to restore confidence in bank deposits during financial crises. Issuing clearinghouse loan certificates in 1873, based on the discounted collateral of member banks' earning assets, released the greenbacks that otherwise would have been tied up in interbank settlements to satisfy depositors' demands. Later, in the crises of 1893 and 1907, clearinghouse currency was issued in exchange for loan certificates. The system provided depositors insurance that individual bank failures would not impose a liquidity squeeze on other banks.

For Gorton (1985a) the development of the clearinghouse on the lines of Coase (1937) was a response to the idiosyncratic, agent-specific nature of demand deposits. Unlike bank notes, these instruments do not possess the information qualities requisite to developing a market. During a panic, according to Gorton, the clearinghouse association, by quickly organizing all member banks into one firm, established a coinsurance scheme that made it difficult for the public to focus on the weakness of an individual member. The clearinghouse could also allay the panic by issuing loan certificates which acted as close substitutes for high-powered money.

In sum, Friedman and Schwartz's treatment of banking panics has spawned interesting theoretical research. A key integrating element in these papers is the assumption of asymmetric information, an assumption implicit in Friedman and Schwartz's treatment. A second element is the importance of real world institutional features—the absence of a lender of last resort, unit banking, the inverted pyramid of credit, and restrictions on the interest that banks can pay on deposits and charge on loans—all features stressed in *A Monetary History*. The third element that emerges from this approach is the asserted predictability of panics in sharp contrast to Friedman and Schwartz's view of them as unique events.

1.3.2   The Great Contraction, 1929–33

The Great Contraction of 1929–33, characterized by a one-third decline in the stock of money, prices, and output, was the most severe and prolonged contraction in U.S. history. It quickly became worldwide in scope. For Friedman and Schwartz (chapter 7) monetary forces were paramount in explaining it. The key ingredient of the monetary collapse was a series of banking crises which led to the closing of one-third of the nation's banks. In terms of the proximate determinants of the money supply, the decline in M was produced by declines in the deposit-currency and deposit-reserve ratios.

Friedman and Schwartz highlighted several episodes during 1929–33:

(a) *The stock market crash of October 1929 and the year succeeding it*. Concern with stock market speculation, combined with a conflict between the New York Fed and the Federal Reserve Board (see section 1.4 below), had led to a rise in the discount rate in 1928; too little to stem speculation, but sufficient to reduce money growth below trend and induce deflation. The resultant sharp decline in output from October 1929 to September 1930 marked the contraction as a severe one.

(b) *The first banking crisis, October 1930 to March 1931*. A series of bank failures in the south and midwest led to an attempt by the public to convert their deposits into currency. This attempted conversion produced "a contagion of fear" that spread through the corresponding banking system to the whole country, culminating in the collapse of the Bank of United States in December 1930.

(c) *The second banking crisis, March to June 1931*. This crisis was similar to the first banking crisis but, because of the weakened capital structure of the banks, the effects were more severe.

(d) *Britain's departure from the gold standard in September 1931*. An external drain, to which the Fed reacted by raising the discount rate, ignored Bagehot's rule to lend freely but at a penalty rate, thereby exacerbating the internal drain.

(e) *The $1 billion open market purchase the Fed conducted, under congressional pressure, from April to June 1932*. The policy succeeded in offsetting the effects of the fall in the money supply but was short-lived.

(f) *The banking holiday of March 1933*.The cumulation of previous banking panics weakened the banking system. Internal drains plus rumors of departure from the gold standard led for the first time to a domestic demand for gold combined with an external drain, precipitating the nationwide banking holiday. (According to Friedman and Schwartz, the banking holiday was much worse than restriction of payments under the national banking system. Then only some types of payments—those involving the conversion of deposits into currency—were restricted. In the banking holiday, all payments were restricted, throwing the economy into paralysis.)

The survey that follows examines the literature on the Great Contraction that *A Monetary History* stimulated, which includes new interpretations of the origins of the contraction: Peter Temin's (1976) critique of the monetary approach and the subsequent debate, a reiteration of the position taken in *A Monetary History* by Schwartz (1981), a reinterpretation of the banking holiday of 1933, and recent studies of the recovery.

Origins of the Great Contraction

Hamilton (1987a) provides evidence consistent with Friedman and Schwartz that the contraction started with tight monetary policy beginning in 1928. He stresses two factors: policy to stem stock market speculation and a gold drain in 1929 to France after it returned to the gold standard at a parity that undervalued the franc.

According to Meltzer (1976), expansionary monetary policy from 1927 to 1928 raised U.S. prices relative to those of other gold standard countries (i.e., prices in the United States declined less than in other gold standard countries). This produced a current account deficit, a gold outflow, and a decline in the money supply in 1928–29.

Field (1984a) contends that the increase in the volume of asset exchanges associated with speculation in the stock market markedly raised the transactions demand for money in the 1920s. Using monthly data over the period 1919–29, he finds that the level of trading on the New York Stock Exchange, holding constant income and interest rates, had significant effects on the demand for narrow money (currency plus demand deposits). A dynamic simulation of the model shows an upward shift of 17 percent in demand deposits in New York City due to asset exchanges. Had the Fed been aware of the effects of this upward shift in the demand for money in raising interest rates, according to Field, it would not have engaged in as contractionary a policy to offset the speculative boom as it did. Because it ignored the effects of stock exchange transactions on the demand for money, the Fed tolerated high interest rates, with devastating effects on the construction and automobile industries. Both industries turned down before the stock market crash, precipitating the Great Depression (Field 1984b).

The Temin Debate

In *A Monetary History,* Friedman and Schwartz attribute the massive decline in prices and real output in the U.S. from 1929 to 1933 to an unprecedented decline in the quantity of money.[8] The fall in the money stock, attributable to a shift to currency from deposits, was largely caused by bank failures in 1930–31 and 1933. Temin (1976), however, counters that the bank failures could not have caused the fall in the quantity of money since there was no evidence of a rise in short-term interest rates during 1929–31 (in fact, short-term rates fell). In his view, a fall in income produced by a decline in autonomous consumption expenditures led to a fall in the demand for money which, interacting with an interest-elastic money supply function, produced the fall in the money stock and in short-term interest rates.

Against Friedman and Schwartz's money hypothesis, Temin first propounds reserve causality. Because changes in the money supply affect interest rates and income, but money demand is also determined by interest rates and income, it is possible that nonmonetary forces that reduced the level of income could have reduced the demand for money, in turn causing a fall in the money supply.[9]

Three sources provide evidence for the money hypothesis: Anderson and Butkiewicz (1980), Schwartz (1981), and Evans (1985). Estimates of a structural model for 1921–33 showed bank failures had a greater effect on money supply (via their influence on the currency-deposit ratio) than on money demand (Anderson and Butkiewicz). Moreover, bank failures were explained not by income but by lagged bank failures (suggesting the Fed might have been at fault). Money Granger-causes income but not the reverse, based on monthly data for 1919–39 (Schwartz). According to estimated vector autoregressions also using monthly data, demand deposits during the Great Depression were not related to past output, prices, or interest rates (determinants of money demand), but were related to bank reserves and were a proxy for the marginal cost of funds (determinants of money supply) (Evans).

Two sources provide evidence for significant contemporaneous feedback from income to money and a passive money supply: Gordon and Wilcox (1981) and Boughton and Wicker (1979). According to Gordon and Wilcox, who used both quarterly and monthly data for 1920–41, lagged money significantly caused income (GNP), lagged income had no effect on money, but the correlation between money and income was significant contemporaneously.[10]

Evidence against Friedman and Schwartz's view that bank failures were a key cause of the unprecedented rise in the deposit currency ratio was that they accounted for only about a third of the 1930–33 rise (Boughton and Wicker 1979, in a regression using quarterly data for 1921–36). Moreover, the substantial fraction of the variation in the currency-deposit ratio due to interest rates and income suggested to these critics that there must have been important feedback from income to money.[11]

Temin's second argument against the money hypothesis is that bank failures in 1930 could not have been the precipitating cause of the Great Depression because they had themselves been caused by a previous decline in economic activity. Friedman and Schwartz attribute the initial bank failures in U.S. agricultural regions to poor loans and investments in the 1920s. Temin concludes, however, based on a regression explaining bank failures across states for the years 1929, 1930, and 1931, that previous bank suspensions were not significant whereas a measure of agricultural income (cotton income) was. Thus, according to Temin, a depression-induced decline in agricultural income was a key cause of bank failures, not previous bad loans.

Temin's view is not sustained by Wicker (1980), who demonstrates forcefully that the banking panic in the autumn of 1930 was triggered by the collapse of Caldwell and Company in Nashville, attributable to its "weak and precarious financial state on the eve of the depression," and not to the decline in agricultural income. The collapse of Caldwell quickly led to the suspension of numerous Caldwell-related banks across the South. According to Wicker, the collapse of the Caldwell financial empire represented an autonomous disturbance to the currency-deposit

ratio as postulated by Friedman and Schwartz, which in turn contributed to the spread of confusion and fear that produced the panic of
October 1930 to March 1931.[12]

Temin's view that the 1930 bank failures were not explained by previous bank failures is also not sustained. Significance tests by Stauffer
(1981) show that the trend of state bank failure rates, 1928–29, did
carry over into 1930. Moreover, for twelve states where cotton production was important, rank correlations between measures of bank
failures, farm income, and measures of weakness of the banking system, suggest that the banking structure of the rural states rather than
income was the key determinant of bank failures.

Finally, micro data on national banks, assembled by White (1984),
explains the bank failures of 1927, 1928, 1929, and 1930 by the structure
of the banking system. The results of a logit model show that the
increase in the number of bank failures did not represent a radical
departure from the 1920s. In the 1920s, many rural banks carried assets
whose expected future value had declined. The coincidence of tight
money and the weakening of asset positions due to deteriorating conditions in agriculture led to the failure of many small unit banks in
sparsely populated rural areas, a result consistent with both Temin's
and Friedman and Schwartz's positions. However, the key cause of
bank weakness, according to White, was the prohibition of branch
banking in most of these states. The case of Canada, which experienced
a similar decline in agricultural income but had nationwide branch
banking and no bank failures, makes the point.

Temin also argues that the value of banks' portfolios reflected a
depression-induced increase in the riskiness of bonds (measured by the
differential between Baa and Aaa corporate bond yields for a fixed
sample of bonds). Mayer's (1978a) criticism of this point is that, although the yield on high grade bonds did not increase significantly
between July and December 1930, it is unlikely that banks held many
risky Baa bonds on which yields did increase by one percentage point.
In sympathy with Temin, White (1984) finds that the portfolios of state
banks in Vermont, which held only small portions of U.S. government
securities, were susceptible to a decline in value.

Temin has been further challenged for holding that the money multiplier was sufficiently interest-elastic that it would have fallen in response to a fall in money demand. Mayer (1978a) finds little evidence
of response of the deposit-reserve ratio to a fall in interest rates, and
only moderate evidence of a response by the deposit-currency ratio—
for semi-annual periods of low interest rates from 1913–30—confirming
Cagan's (1965) earlier evidence of interest inelasticity of the money
multiplier.[13] Mayer also argues that, as declining income reduces the
demand for money, this would create an excess supply of money that

would have the effect, after some lag, of raising income and, hence, money demand.[14]

Temin's third argument against the money hypothesis is that the short-term commercial paper rate, which declined in 1930, should have risen. He explains the rise in other interest rates by an increase in risk rather than a scramble for liquidity. In his view, the fall in nominal interest rates could not be masking a deflation-expectation-induced rise in ex ante real rates because contemporary evidence suggests that expectations were sanguine until mid-1931.[15]

Schwartz (1981) criticizes Temin's (and other Keynesians') use of short-term interest rates as a measure of the price of money. She shows that monthly data for the inverse of the price level—a true measure of the price of money, according to monetarists—over the interwar period mirrored all monetary events. She attributes the decline in the short-term commercial paper rate in the face of bank panics to increased demand by banks for commercial paper as collateral for borrowing to meet their need for reserves. However, for Mayer (1978a) the evidence is unclear, even though the decline in short-term rates likely reflected a shift into short-term securities for liquidity motives, outweighing a shift from short-term securities to money. He concludes that the monetary explanation is vulnerable on this issue.

Gandolfi and Lothian (1979) find Temin's use of interest rates misleading because of the procyclical pattern of the rates that tends to mask the liquidity effect of monetary change. Moreover, they argue that the 12 percent decline of the wholesale price index that occurred between August 1929 and August 1930 was substantial enough to have created expectations of a continued decline in prices in the short run.

For Meltzer (1976), Temin neglects, as did the Federal Reserve System during the Great Depression, the distinction between nominal and real interest rates, misinterpreting the fall in interest rates as indicating monetary ease.

It should be pointed out that, had Temin started his analysis in April 1928 when the Federal Reserve sharply reduced the rate of monetary growth, instead of in August 1929, he would have observed a rise in short-term interest rates between March 1928 and September 1929. As the lagged effects of monetary change affected prices and output in 1929, interest rates then declined.[16]

Temin's final argument against the money hypothesis is that the real money supply did not fall. Monetary forces, it follows, could not possibly explain the massive decline in real income that occurred.

According to Gandolfi and Lothian (1979), Temin confuses desired and actual real cash balances. They estimate a money-demand function, using annual data over the periods 1900–29 and 1900–41, that shows an increase in predicted real balances during 1929–31 and a fall during

1931–33, by magnitudes similar to the movements in actual real balances. They conclude that both the initial rise and the subsequent decline were due to changes in the determinants of money demand, offering evidence suggesting that movements in actual real balances are a poor measure of the degree of monetary ease or restraint.

In place of the money hypothesis, Temin substitutes a modified version of "the spending hypothesis." According to the original Keynesian version, a fall in income and prices was produced by the multiplier effects of a fall in autonomous spending (consumption and investment), supposedly caused by an oversupply of housing and the stock market crash. In Temin's view, however, though the crash reduced consumption through adverse effects on the community's wealth, it was not crucial. He does not find evidence of a massive decline in investment expenditures, but judges that an unexplained decline in autonomous consumption expenditures was the likely cause of the decline in economic activity during 1929–31. The judgment is based on an unusually large negative residual for 1930 from a consumption function for the interwar period (1919–41). After 1930, following Kindleberger (1973), Temin regards international forces as dominant.

Mayer (1978b) replicates Temin's consumption function regression—excluding 1919, a transition year from war to peace—and finds the 1930 residual is no longer negative.[17] Using estimates of a consumption function he judges to be superior—the MPS model—over the period 1921–41, in both levels and first differences and including a dummy variable to account for the 1930 shift, Mayer finds he is unable to establish Temin's hypothesis of an unusual downward shift in the consumption function in 1930. Gandolfi and Lothian (1979) show that the change in the residual for 1930 was far from unique compared to all contractions in the longer period, based on a permanent income consumption function for the period 1889–1941.

In sum, the Temin debate leaves monetary forces as the key cause of the Great Depression. The evidence on causality is generally in favor of the money hypothesis, but the contemporaneous correlation between money and income also allows scope for nonmonetary forces. The evidence does not sustain Temin's view that the bank failures of 1930 were caused by the depression-induced decline in agricultural income and depression-increased riskiness of bank portfolios. However, the Stauffer and White studies that attribute the bank failures to weak bank structure in agricultural regions are consistent with both the Temin and Friedman and Schwartz accounts. Temin's contention that the decline in short-term interest rates during 1929–31 is inconsistent with the money hypothesis has also been rejected, but why short-term nominal rates declined has not been definitively answered. Finally, neither Temin's claim that the failure of real balances to decline during 1929–31 contradicts the money hypothesis nor his suggestion of an unexplained decline in consumption as the source of contraction has won acceptance.

A Reappraisal by Anna Schwartz

According to Schwartz (1981), the Great Depression was started by two unexpected shocks of monetary origin: a contractionary monetary policy in 1928, initiated by the Federal Reserve to halt the stock market boom, and the stock market crash of October 1929. Unexpected declines in aggregate demand would lead employers to hire fewer workers at each real wage perceived by them, and workers to refuse offers of employment at lower nominal wages on the basis of no change in expectations. But eventually, on the assumption of rational expectations, a new equilibrium would be reached as expectations were revised. Other things being equal, the result would have been a severe contraction similar to earlier contractions. But instead, the consequence of inappropriate Fed policy generated a further series of monetary shocks—most notably the banking panics of 1930, 1931, and 1933—which in turn led to further declines in output and the demand for labor, and a shift in demand for securities to both short-term instruments and high grade long-term securities.[18]

The Banking Holiday of 1933

Wigmore (1987) challenges the view espoused by Friedman and Schwartz that domestic factors were the primary cause of the banking holiday of March 1933, and instead posits rumors of devaluation as the key factor. Though Friedman and Schwartz discuss the role of rumors of devaluation in converting the internal drain into a demand for gold, they do not view it as the primary cause of the panic. Wigmore argues that rumors of devaluation appearing weeks before the banking holiday—events such as bills in Congress proposing to devalue the dollar, statements by leading financial figures, and FDR's unwillingness to commit himself to the current exchange rate—triggered the run on the dollar. The run manifested itself in both an internal and foreign demand for gold by individuals and central banks.[19] Furthermore, he argues that though the increase in currency was three times the amount of gold reserves lost by the New York Fed, the fact that gold losses threatened to reduce the Fed's reserves below the legal limit—while at the same time it had a virtually unlimited ability to meet demands for domestic currency—was crucial.

Wigmore also attributes the calm which immediately followed the banking holiday to the Roosevelt administration's international policies: the embargo on gold ownership and export, and restrictions on foreign exchange dealings. The former cut off the domestic channels for a speculative run on the dollar, and the 60 percent devaluation of the dollar in the ensuing three months removed the source of the speculative pressure.

The Recovery

The recovery from 1933 to 1937 was marked by rapid money growth (53 percent) and rapid inflation (50 percent for the wholesale price index). Friedman and Schwartz (chapter 9) attribute the monetary expansion to an increase in the monetary gold stock in response to the devaluation of the dollar, the gold purchase program, and capital flight from Europe. At the same time, they argue, rising prices and wages represented in part a rare case of cost-push inflation, the consequence of the National Industrial Recovery Act (NIRA) and other policies that encouraged unionization and monopolization. These policies, with the gold-induced monetary expansion acting as an accommodating force, encouraged inflation at the expense of real growth.

In support of Friedman and Schwartz, Weinstein (1981) finds that the New Deal NIRA codes (1933–35), which encouraged the formation of labor unions and the cartelization of industry, reduced output and raised unemployment more than would have otherwise been the case. First, by increasing wages relative to prices, the codes increased unemployment by 2 percent. Second, by raising the price level by an amount responsive to the 14 percent increase in the money supply that occurred during 1933–35, the codes prevented output from rising 8 percent and unemployment from declining 3 percent. Third, the codes-induced rise in the price level, by reducing the real value of financial assets, led to an additional 6 to 11 percent decline in output.

However, McCloskey and Zecher (1984) deny that the inflation of 1933–34 can be attributed to a wage-price-spiral induced by the New Deal NIRA codes since the majority of the codes were enforced after the price level rose. Based on an examination of weekly data, they contend that the key cause of the price burst was the devaluation by the Roosevelt administration.[20]

Friedman (1984) in rebuttal cites statements from *A Monetary History* (pp. 465–66) which attribute considerable importance to the gold policy as a causal factor in the inflation, emphasizes that Friedman and Schwartz's concern was with the entire period of 1933–37, and demonstrates that McCloskey and Zecher's factual evidence involved the inappropriate use of arithmetic scales in comparing weekly movements in wholesale prices and the exchange rate—a logarithmic scale would give a more accurate picture, and would portray narrower movements in the wholesale price index (WPI) than the exchange rate.

The literature on the Great Depression spawned by *A Monetary History* suggests varied explanations of its causes, duration, and severity. The upshot of the Temin debate and other literature on the period is the primacy of monetary forces. However, contemporaneous correlation between money and income has been interpreted as evidence for significant feedback from nonmonetary to monetary forces. In addition, nonmonetary forces, especially institutional factors such as the regulations governing banking structure, emerge as having considerable importance, and some authors such as Bernanke (1983) (see section 1.3.1 above) stress the disruption of the financial system as an important independent cause.

Evidence of the endogeneity of the money supply or of feedback from real forces to the money supply begs the question of whether the Great Depression had to happen. As Friedman and Schwartz point out, the Fed clearly could have stopped the decline in the money supply and the depression with it. A comparison of the Great Depression with previous and subsequent experience suggests that monetary contraction was the sine qua non that made the depression great. Other explanations do not detract from the importance of monetary contraction which has been a crucial part of all severe cycles. Given the importance of a decline in the money supply, other influences—including the disruption of the financial system—became, in most cases, endogenous rather than causal.

1.4   The Domestic Monetary Framework and Monetary Policy

A key theme in *A Monetary History* is the role of banking arrangements and monetary policy in providing a setting for monetary disturbances. In this section, the literature is surveyed for both the pre-1914 period when the United States did not have a central bank, and the period since 1914 when monetary policy has been conducted by the Federal Reserve System.

1.4.1   The National Banking Era

Inelasticity of High-Powered Money

A key problem that faced the national banking system, which ultimately led to its replacement by the Federal Reserve System, was the inelasticity of high-powered money; that is, the inability to convert deposits into currency during banking panics. This problem was exacerbated by "the inverted pyramid of credit"—interbank deposits held in New York and, to a lesser extent, Chicago and St. Louis. In times of financial stringency, country banks would recall deposits from the central reserve cities to meet local demands for currency, in turn exacerbating pressure on the reserves of those banks.

Cagan (1963) agrees with Friedman and Schwartz that the main defect of the national banking system was inelasticity of currency and that the problem was solved by the creation of emergency currency through the Aldrich Vreeland Act. In addition, he argues that minimum reserve requirements did not reduce monetary instability because banks viewed these reserves as locked up. For Cagan, the inverted pyramid of credit was not as serious a situation as commonly believed because the call loan market, in which interbank deposits were invested, would have attracted the funds anyway. The central problem with the inverted pyramid was that it raised the money multiplier, thereby allowing a greater monetary contraction than would otherwise have occurred in the face of an attempt by the public to convert its deposits into currency.

Dewald (1972) contends that the United States had virtually all the elements of a central bank in place with the national banking system. The New York City national banks, by serving as a depository for other banks, acted as a central reserve. In addition, they acted as a lender of last resort by providing interbank loans, by channeling specie from abroad and from the Treasury to other banks, and by banding together and issuing clearinghouse certificates. Schwartz (1972) denies that the New York banks functioned as a central bank since they could not issue high-powered money at will. Furthermore, interbank loans and clearinghouse loan certificates did not represent additions to high-powered money, but rather substituted for it.

The National Bank Note Puzzle

National bank notes representing liabilities of the national banks were issued by banks depositing government securities with the U.S. Treasury equal in face value (before 1900) to 111 percent of the value of the notes issued. The amount of the notes issued depended on the market prices of the securities serving as collateral. As long as bonds sold at or above par, it was profitable to issue notes. Based on calculations in Cagan (1965), Friedman and Schwartz note that, except for the period from 1884 to 1891, eligible U.S. securities sold above par for the entire fifty years before establishment of the Fed.[21] The amount of notes issued varied with their profitability, yet the amount was well below the maximum. Friedman and Schwartz view this as a puzzle: "[e]ither bankers did not recognize a profitable course of action . . . or we have overlooked some costs of issue that appeared large to them" (p. 24).

Goodhart's (1965) explanation for less than the maximum possible note issue for the period 1907–13 is uncertainty over the possibility that circulation privileges would be terminated in forthcoming reform legislation, which reduced the value that banks attached to bonds serving as collateral. For James (1976), the reason for the less-than-maximum note issue in the last quarter of the nineteenth century was that the rate of return on loans was sufficiently high to make it more profitable to make loans through creating deposits, rather than buying government bonds and then issuing notes (in the form of loans) on the basis of 90 percent of par value. Local loan rates were higher in the south and the west than in central reserve cities, accounting for the lower fraction of the maximum note issue in these regions. As loan rates converged towards the end of the nineteenth century, national banks in the interior increased their note issue.

1.4.2   Founding of the Federal Reserve System

A Change in Regime

The beginning of operations by the Fed in November 1914 marked a "major watershed" in U.S. monetary history. According to Friedman and Schwartz (p. 9), the change in internal monetary arrangements coincided with a loosening of the external link to the gold standard. These two changes created the potential for the new central bank to exercise deliberate control over the stock of money and to promote monetary stability. Yet, the record of subsequent events and greater variability of money after 1914 than before, led them to conclude that "[t]he blind, undesigned and quasi-automatic working of the gold standard turned out to produce a greater measure of predictability and regularity—perhaps because its discipline was impersonal and inescapable—than did deliberate and conscious control exercised within institutional arrangements intended to promote monetary stability" (p. 15).

Mankiw, Miron, and Weil (1987) demonstrate that a significant change in monetary regime actually occurred when the Fed began to operate, as evidenced in the behavior of interest rates, and that market agents rationally anticipated the change. They show that the stochastic process of the 3-month time loan rate at New York City banks changed from mean reversion with a strong seasonal from 1890 to 1910, to close to a random walk from 1921 to 1933. This, they argue, reflected the Fed's role in offsetting seasonal and panic-induced fluctuations in interest rates. Evidence of low posterior odds ratios (the ratio of subjective probabilities of different switch dates conditioning on the data) before December 1914, according to the authors, casts doubt that abandonment of the gold standard in August 1914 explains the change in stochastic process. Moreover, they found that the relationship between 6-month and 3-month rates changed in a manner consistent with the expectations theory of the term structure. Regressions of the long rate on the short rate revealed the former to be less responsive to shocks in the latter in the earlier subperiod. Switching regressions revealed the change in stochastic process to have occurred between December 1914 and February 1915, and the change in expectations to have preceded the regime change by one month.

A Change in the Seasonal Pattern of Interest Rates

The seasonal in short-term rates under the national banking system reflected autumnal crop moving and Christmas demands for currency which put pressure on bank reserves and hence on interest rates. The Fed reduced the seasonal in short-term interest rates, altering its outstanding credit to offset seasonal fluctuations in bank reserves, and at the same time, increased the seasonal in currency outside the Treasury and the Fed and in high-powered money (Friedman and Schwartz, 191–96).

More recently, evidence for a significant decrease in nominal interest rate seasonality after 1914 was found by Shiller (1980), who used the X-111 seasonal adjustment program, and by Mankiw and Miron (1986) and Mankiw, Miron, and Weil (1987), who used time-series methods.

According to Miron (1986), financial panics in the United States before 1914 generally occurred at seasonal peaks in nominal interest rates. This reflected the tendency of seasonal demands for credit to raise interest rates, increasing the ratio of loans to reserves and deposits to reserves. Panics precipitated by exogenous shocks occurred at times when banks were least prepared. After 1914, however, the Fed extended reserve bank credit to accommodate seasonal credit demands, thereby considerably reducing the amplitude of the seasonal interest rate cycle and preventing any panics from occurring between 1914 and 1929. On grounds similar to Trescott (1982) and Field (1984a), Miron associated banking panics after 1929 with a shift to a restrictive policy and the reduction of seasonal accommodation.[22]

Because a similar reduction in seasonality occurred in a large number of countries at the same time, Clark (1986) is skeptical of the Friedman and Schwartz view that it was the advent of the Fed that accounted for the reduction in the seasonal in short-term interest rates. Moreover, the disappearance of the U.S. and U.K. interest-rate seasonal occurred three years before a significant seasonal appeared in total currency and high-powered money in each country. Though the reduction in the U.S. interest-rate seasonal from 1914 to 1916 might be explained by the liquidity effects of reduced reserve requirements and gold inflows, Clark doubts that U.S. seasonal policy could explain a similar phenomenon in other countries. Instead, he attributes the timing of the change in the seasonal pattern of interest rates in 1914 to the breakdown of the gold standard.

Clark's view, however, is challenged by Barsky, Mankiw, Miron, and Weil (1988). Evidence that the seasonal pattern of interest rates did not change after the U.S. and U.K. left Bretton Woods in 1973, and that the correlation between U.S. and U.K. interest-rate levels and changes did not vary before or after 1914, makes their case that the reduction in the seasonal was unrelated to the change in regime. Instead they construct a hypothetical model in which a central bank, committed to interest-rate smoothing and avoiding gold flows, is introduced into a world already containing a central bank dedicated to the same policies (the Bank of England). The two central banks, each pursuing its own policy but taking the other's actions as given, smooth interest rates without gold flows. This is in contrast to the case of a single central bank whose attempts to smooth interest rates will always be offset by gold flows. Based on this model, the authors argue, it is plausible that the 1914 introduction into the world monetary system of the Fed, dedicated to smoothing interest rates, can explain the reduction in the interest-rate seasonal in the United States, the United Kingdom, and other countries.

A fundamental problem with Barsky et al.'s explanation is that in 1914 all countries (except the United States) had left the gold standard. Consequently they would not be worried about gold flows. In addition, the question of why the Fed was so special remains. Why could the Bank of England and the Bank of France, each of which represented large gold standard countries, not have initiated the reduction in the seasonal before 1914? Possibly the answer lies with the populists in the United States, who influenced the constitutional structure of the Fed and who were strongly opposed to the seasonal.

Founding Principles versus Reality

The Fed was established to provide elasticity to the money supply, specifically to provide easy convertibility between deposits and currency and to prevent a recurrence of the banking panics of the national banking era. This goal, according to Friedman and Schwartz (chapter 5), was to be achieved by the expansion and contraction of Federal Reserve notes and deposits. Two key principles lay behind the establishment of the Fed: the gold standard and the real bills doctrine.[23]

West's (1976, 1977) reading of archival material and contemporary sources lead him to support Friedman and Schwartz's interpretation that the two principles behind the Federal Reserve Act were obsolete before the Fed opened its doors. The real bills doctrine reflected early nineteenth century reality: the widespread use of bills of exchange and commercial bills. However, after the Civil War the market for commercial bills, especially two-name bills, declined. Furthermore, the classical gold standard principle was based on a stylized model of observance by the Bank of England of "the rules of the game" and its use of the discount rate to facilitate gold flows. According to West, the

Bank had difficulty making Bank Rate effective and frequently violated "the rules" through the use of policies such as the gold devices (Sayers 1936). Thus the Fed was designed to follow a policy which had never existed.

The Fed's First Policy Failure, 1920–21

According to Friedman and Schwartz (p. 238), if the Fed had raised the discount rate earlier in 1919, this would have moderated post–World War I inflation and the subsequent contraction. Fuel was added to the fire by further raising the discount rate in 1920 and keeping it there until May 1921. Thus, the years 1920–21 were the first important test of Fed monetary policy and its first failure.

Friedman and Schwartz (p. 234) interpret the Fed's reluctance in 1920 to reduce the discount rate after prices and output had declined as concern over its gold reserve ratio. Wicker (1965; 1966, ch. 3), however, based on his reading of Federal Reserve records, regards domestic considerations as more important. In his view, Fed officials feared that lowering the discount rate before member bank borrowing had been reduced to desirable levels would encourage further speculative borrowing. The Fed did not understand the harmful effects of deflation, believing that, with declining prices and activity, member bank borrowing would be quickly liquidated. Not recognized by the Fed, according to Wicker, was that much of the buildup in bank credit financed inventories which took several months to liquidate. Wicker's reading of the archives suggests that a reinterpretation of Friedman and Schwartz's view of 1920–21 may have merit.

1.4.3 Was the Federal Reserve System's Policy Consistent from 1923 to 1933?

Friedman and Schwartz (chapter 6) describe the 1920s as the "high tide" of the Federal Reserve System. Though the real bills doctrine still strongly influenced Fed policy, and despite an ongoing conflict between Governor Benjamin Strong of the New York Fed and the Federal Reserve Board that affected all policy discussion, the Fed successfully conducted countercyclical stabilization.[24] The contraction of 1929–33 could have been prevented if the policies developed in the 1920s had been consistently applied (chapter 7). Friedman and Schwartz attribute the policy failure to a "shift of power within the system and the lack of understanding and experience of the individuals to whom the power shifted" (p. 411).

The only episode that took place when the system united was the decision to raise the discount rate after Britain left the gold standard in September 1931. The experiment with expansionary open market policy in 1932 did not reflect a change in policy but rather just a temporary reaction to congressional pressure.[25] The final banking panic in 1933 demonstrated a complete lack of leadership as each reserve bank acted to protect its own reserves. According to Friedman and Schwartz, none of this would have happened had Benjamin Strong not died in 1928 or had the pre-Fed set of monetary institutions, including restrictions of payments and the Aldrich Vreeland Act, been in place.

Wicker (1965) denies that Fed policy deteriorated dramatically after Strong's death. Based on his reading of the minutes of the Open Market Policy Committee (OMPC), unavailable to Friedman and Schwartz when they wrote their book, he concludes that the Burgess-Riefler-Strong doctrine of open market operations predominated both before and after Strong's death.

According to this doctrine, commercial banks were reluctant to borrow from the Fed, doing so only if in need. By engaging in open market sales, the Fed could induce banks to borrow. When member bank indebtedness rose, rates were raised and loans reduced. Through open market purchases, the Fed could reduce member bank borrowing. Interest rates then fell and banks increased their outstanding loans and investments.

The decision to conduct open market purchases depended on the level of member bank indebtedness in the reserve districts of New York and Chicago. In 1924 and 1927, member bank borrowing in these cities was sufficiently high to induce open market purchases, whereas in 1930 it was comparable to or below that of 1924 and 1927. Consequently, there was no need seen for action. Moreover, based on the voting record of the executive committee of the OMPC in 1930, three of the four members who voted against purchases had been on Strong's Open Market Investment Committee (OMIC) in the 1920s, suggesting to Wicker that Strong might not have carried the day.[26]

Brunner and Meltzer (1968a) support Wicker's claim that the Burgess-Riefler-Strong doctrine remained in place after Strong's death. According to their interpretation of statements by the Fed staff and members of the OMPC, and of reports sent to each board member and reserve bank president, policy was consistent over the whole period. Based on the Burgess-Riefler-Strong doctrine, the Fed had two policy indicators: the level of borrowed reserves and short-term market interest rates. According to Brunner and Meltzer, market interest rates were the key policy indicator during the Great Contraction. The reason the Fed failed to increase high-powered money after 1929 was that market interest rates had fallen to levels lower than those reached in earlier contractions.

Meltzer (1976) explains the majority of decisions by the Fed to purchase or refrain from purchasing in the period September 1929 to April

1931, by the level of borrowing, the change in borrowing, and the level of short-term interest rates. Focus on nominal interest rates as measures of ease and tightness, according to him, ignores the distinction between real and nominal variables. Thus low market interest rates, which may actually reflect deflationary expectations and a high real rate, were misinterpreted as evidence of ease.

Trescott (1982), on the other hand, claims that Fed policy after 1929 represented a radical departure from its policy over the period 1924–29. He estimates a monthly regression to explain Fed holdings of open market securities for the 1924–29 period by variables determining defensive operations and dynamic operations. He then generates levels of open market securities for each month in 1930–33 on the counterfactual assumption that the Fed continued its 1924–29 policy regime through 1933. Beginning December 1929, actual federal open market credit increasingly fell below its estimated value. Trescott attributes the changes in monetary policy after 1929 to a change in the structure of the OMIC. Before 1929, as Friedman and Schwartz argue, it was dominated by the Federal Reserve Bank of New York. In January 1930, the OMIC (which consisted of the five key reserve banks) was replaced by the new OMPC, which included all twelve banks. This produced two blocks to effective decision making: (1) some of the new banks were hostile to expansionary policies, and (2) as the size of the necessary interventions increased, there was greater likelihood they would require the approval of the entire OMPC and the Fed Board, rather than just the discretion (as in the previous regime) of the New York Fed.

Finally, to determine whether Fed policy changed in 1929—as argued by Friedman and Schwartz, and Trescott—or whether the Fed followed the same flawed strategy in the early 1930s as it did in the 1920s—as argued by Wicker, and Brunner and Meltzer—Wheelock (1987) tests whether policy reaction functions over the 1919–33 period for different policy tools changed significantly in 1929. In support of the Wicker-Brunner-Meltzer view, he finds that the Fed's policy tools responded to the same indicator variables over the whole period but that they responded less vigorously in the 1929–31 contraction than in earlier periods.[27] Again, in agreement with the above authors, he concludes that the Fed did not conduct expansionary open market purchases because the low values of its key policy indicators—member bank borrowing and market interest rates—indicated monetary ease. Estimated demand functions for member bank borrowing for the system as a whole and for each Fed district suggest that the Fed's strategy was flawed. It ignored the influence of declining economic activity and financial crises on the demand for member bank borrowing.

In defense of Friedman and Schwartz, however, Wheelock notes that the redistribution of power away from the New York Reserve Bank might have locked the system into a more restrictive monetary policy than otherwise. It did so by increasing the influence of officials who opposed expansionary open market policy relative to those who consistently advocated expansionary policies and who possibly understood the basic flaw in Fed strategy.

In sum, evidence from archival sources and from econometric reaction functions is not entirely in favor of *A Monetary History*'s interpretation of the reason Fed policy failed during the Great Contraction. The revisionist view suggests that the Fed failed because it followed a flawed policy strategy developed in the 1920s. It ran into trouble in 1929–31 because its principal policy indicator—short-term market rates—was misinterpreted as a signal of ease. During the contractions of the 1920s, the decline in activity was so moderate that neither member bank borrowing nor short-term interest rates fell sufficiently for the Fed to refrain from an expansionary policy. This is not to say that superior leadership might not have jettisoned the strategy. But such an explanation places perhaps too much emphasis on the personality of one individual prevailing against institutional tradition.

1.4.4.   New Deal Regulation of the Banking System, 1933–35

The emergency legislation of 1933 and subsequent bank acts created a package to insure the stability of the banking system and prevent a recurrence of bank panics (Friedman and Schwartz, chapter 8).

For Benston (1982), the New Deal legislation package of the Federal Deposit Insurance Corporation (FDIC) and regulation of commercial banks—specifically the prohibition of interest payments on demand deposits and the separation of investment from commercial banking—represents a horse trade between the small unit banks and large money market banks. The small unit banks wanted deposit insurance to protect them from runs, and they also continued to oppose branch banking.[28] The big city banks were not interested in deposit insurance but wanted a prohibition of interest payments on demand deposits as a price-fixing arrangement.[29] At the same time, the investment bankers wanted protection from commercial bank competition.[30] New Deal legislation was an arrangement whereby small unit banks received FDIC plus continuation of the McFadden Act prohibition against branching, large banks received the prohibition of interest payments on demand deposits, and investment bankers received freedom from commercial bank participation in their business.

Recently the contribution of federal deposit insurance to monetary stability has been questioned. Schwartz (1988) argues that it was price level stability until the mid-1960s, rather than federal deposit insurance, that was responsible for financial stability. During this period other countries without deposit insurance also experienced financial stability. Given price stability, an effective lender of last resort can insure stability with or without deposit insurance. Moreover, the flat insurance premium FDIC charges on deposits, regardless of risk, has in recent years—as a consequence of reduced regulation of the financial sector in the face of inflation—increased the incentives for risk taking and hence the potential for monetary instability (Short and O'Driscoll 1983, Kane 1985).

1.4.5   The Increase in Reserve Requirements, 1936–37

In chapter 8 of *A Monetary History,* Friedman and Schwartz document the consequences of a major policy error by the Federal Reserve System—the doubling of reserve requirements between August 1936 and March 1937—which led to a sharp monetary contraction and recession in 1937–38. They dismiss as incorrect the Fed's liquidity-trap explanation of the excess reserves. According to their interpretation, two shifts occurred in the liquidity preferences of the banks: an increase in the reserve deposit ratio from 1933 to 1936 in response to the 1929–33 collapse; and then a second increase from 1937 to 1940 as the banks, viewing their increased required reserves as unavailable to them in the event of a liquidity crisis, restored their desired holdings of excess reserves to the previous level. Thus Friedman and Schwartz conclude that the adjustment of the actual deposit reserve ratio to a change in the desired ratio takes up to three years.

Horwich (1963, 1966), based on a lack of correlation between effective reserves and bank earning assets in the mid-1930s, argues for the liquidity-trap interpretation of excess reserves, although Brunner (1965) correctly criticizes Horwich's methodology as flawed in its specification. Morrison (1966) provides evidence in favor of Friedman and Schwartz's view. Against the liquidity-trap hypothesis, he provides evidence, first, that Canadian banks did not have excess reserves despite similar movements of interest rates and real income (see also Friedman and Schwartz, p. 458); second, that country member banks' reserve deposit ratios quickly restored their original relationship to those of nonmember banks after the reserve requirement doubled in 1936–37; and third, that the elasticity of demand for excess reserves showed little evidence of increase as interest rates fell.[31]

More recently, Wilcox (1984) estimates a demand function for excess reserves, based on the Tobin-Brainard model of bank asset demand and supply and on quarterly data for New York City member banks. In addition to the traditional interest rate and wealth variables, he includes a proxy variable to capture Friedman and Schwartz's shock hypothesis (that the demand curve shifted as a reaction to the liquidity crisis and the doubling of reserve requirements). Both the interest rate and the shock variable are found to be significant. Moreover, the interest elasticity of demand for excess reserves rises as the interest rate falls, a result which Wilcox interprets as evidence of the liquidity-trap view. In accordance with Brunner's (1965) critique of *A Monetary History,* Wilcox finds the adjustment period to a liquidity shock to be somewhat shorter (two years) than that reported by Friedman and Schwartz. Finally, simulations of the model over the 1933–40 period reveal changes in interest rates to explain much more of the increase in excess reserves than the financial shock proxies, especially after 1935.

Wilcox's use of a log linear demand function biases the case towards finding a liquidity trap. Also, omitting nonmember banks and member banks outside New York biases the case against the Friedman and Schwartz view. Since most bank failures occurred among smaller banks outside New York, one would expect the New York banks to be more interest-sensitive and less affected by financial shocks, given their larger size and more diversified portfolios.

For at least a decade, Friedman and Schwartz's interpretation of excess reserves was accepted, although the portfolio-adjustment mechanism of the banking system was questioned (Brunner 1965, Tobin, 1965, Johnson 1965). Wilcox's recent study, despite some problems, suggests that the topic is worth a deeper look.

1.4.6 Treasury Dominance of the Federal Reserve

Friedman and Schwartz (chapter 9) document a major shift in policy responsibility from the Fed to the Treasury in the aftermath of the Great Contraction. The Fed switched to a passive policy (with the exception of the 1936–37 doubling of reserve requirements) because it believed the traditional tools of monetary policy to be ineffective since they could not reduce the excess reserves accumulated by the banking system.

Toma (1982) applies the theory of bureaucracy to explain some aspects of Fed policy in the 1930s and 1940s. According to this theory (see Niskanen 1971, Acheson and Chant 1973), the Fed acts to maximize its discretionary profits—the revenue from its open market portfolio—all of which it was allowed to keep after 1933.

The model Toma constructs predicts that the Fed will try to increase its share of inflation tax revenue—at the expense of the commercial banks and the Treasury—by following policies to reduce the ratio of the total money stock to Federal Reserve credit. But at the same time it will attempt to forestall potential intervention by the Treasury and the Congress by transferring some of its resources to the Treasury. Thus, according to Toma (pp. 181–82), the Fed's acceptance of the Treasury's gold sterilization policy in 1936 rather than conducting the open market sales itself, did not represent acceptance of Treasury dominance over monetary policy, as Friedman and Schwartz argue (p. 532), but rather represented a policy designed to preserve its share of inflation tax revenue at the expense of the Treasury. For Toma, gold sterilization was a way of preventing the Treasury from continuing to capture the capital gain from monetization of gold inflows.

Evidence for the bureaucratic model is based on an observed positive association between the Fed's expenditures and its open market wealth.[32] A key implication of this approach is that the Fed has sufficient independence to produce whatever rate of monetary growth is required to maximize its profits. This assumes the central bank operates in a vacuum, completely removed from the underlying political realities. The record indicates, to the contrary, that the Fed's overall policy stance is clearly related to the desires of the elected government (Weintraub 1978). The scope for the type of independent action suggested by Toma is indeed limited.

1.4.7   The World War II Bond-Price-Support Program

During World War II, the Fed followed a bond-price-pegging program to assist Treasury bond financing of the war at favorable interest rates. Wicker (1969) holds, contrary to Friedman and Schwartz (ch. 10), that the Fed did not give up its independence to the Treasury by agreeing to the bond-price-support program in March 1942. Based on his reading of the record, both the Fed and the Treasury were in favor of preventing interest rates from rising, but disagreed on how to do it, with the Treasury favoring reductions in reserve requirements to provide excess reserves and the Fed favoring open market operations. As a compromise, the Treasury accepted a Fed plan to peg the short-term interest rate at ⅜ percent.

Rather than being an "engine of inflation," Toma (1985) construes the bond-price-support program as a solution to the time-inconsistency problem faced by the wartime monetary authorities, following Barro and Gordon (1983). According to the Barro-Gordon hypothesis, as long as the public rationally expects the monetary authorities to produce monetary surprises, they will reduce their real cash balances, and hence the authorities will capture less seigniorage than long-run revenue maximizing would predict. To solve the problem a preannounced rule is needed. The 2½ percent ceiling on long-term yields was a rule to allow the authorities to rearrange the time path of inflation, to satisfy the government's intention to shift consumption from the future to the present, and to assure the public that, while money growth might increase during the war, it did not represent a long-run policy. For long-term interest rates to stay below the pegged level for extended periods of time, and long-term expectations to stay low, open market operations had to keep the long-run inflation rate low. The support program thus implied that anticipated rapid money growth during the war would be followed by a long period of restraint.

Toma's arguments in favor of this view are: (1) if the public did not believe in the government's commitment, it would have shifted into short-term securities; (2) money growth declined after the war; (3) real cash balances were abnormally high even after price controls were lifted, reflecting expectations of postwar disinflation; (4) based on the 35 percent greater increase in interest rates that occurred during World War I, seigniorage collected in World War II without the bond-support program, because of reduced real cash balances, would have been 3.5 to 10 percent lower each year.[33]

An alternative interpretation to that of Toma's, which also stresses the role of expectations yet is consistent with that of Friedman and Schwartz, is that long-term price expectations were anchored by a strong belief in a return to the gold standard. The experience of rapid deflation after World War I in the United States and in other countries committed to a return to the gold standard, would still have been in the memories of investors. Moreover, investors would have been aware of the negotiations leading to the Bretton Woods Agreement in 1944. In addition, Toma fails to mention the wartime unavailability of consumer durables and the role of wartime price controls. These were two factors which, according to Friedman and Schwartz, raised the level of real cash balances (see also Rockoff 1981), in turn generating more inflation tax revenue than otherwise, and at the same time reducing inflation expectations.

1.5 Monetary Standards

The ninety-four years spanned by *A Monetary History* were characterized by several distinct relationships between the U.S. economy and the rest of the world. Friedman and Schwartz devote considerable attention to the role of the monetary standard in influencing the relationship between monetary and other variables.

1.5.1 The Greenback Episode, 1862–78

The greenback period was a unique episode of freely floating exchange rates between the United States and the rest of the world. The literature stemming from Friedman and Schwartz's treatment of this episode focuses on three themes: the conditions required for resumption, the role of news, and Gresham's Law.

The Conditions Required for Resumption

Timberlake (1975) argues, contrary to Friedman and Schwartz, that the Treasury acted directly to reduce the money supply and foster resumption. His interpretation of the Resumption Act of 1875 is that it allowed the secretary of the Treasury to retire U.S. notes equal to the gross amount of national bank notes issued without accounting for voluntary retirement by the commercial banks. Successive secretaries of the Treasury took advantage of this provision to reduce high-powered money.

Based on Berry's (1978) GNP deflators rather than the wholesale price series used by Friedman and Schwartz and by Kindahl (1961),[34] Officer's (1981) calculation of the real exchange rate between the United States and Great Britain in the greenback era suggests that considerably less than the 54 percent deflation Friedman and Schwartz calculated was required to resume specie payments. In addition, Officer finds that the use of Berry's GNP data corroborates Friedman and Schwartz's conclusion that deflation was a result of rapid real growth and a virtually constant money stock.[35]

The Role of News

According to Friedman and Schwartz, news affects the exchange rate to the extent it affects the demand for and supply of foreign exchange and, at one remove, the determinants of the price level. Some studies, however, have found evidence to support Mitchell's (1903) emphasis on the importance of news as an exchange rate determinant. Roll (1972), using the capital-asset-pricing model, demonstrates that the Civil War bond markets were efficient in that bond prices quickly reflected changes in the premium on gold, as well as all information on military events.

McCandless (1985) tests Mitchell's (1903) hypothesis that short-term movements of exchange rates during the Civil War could be explained by war news. Based on a time-series model using semi-monthly data of the gold prices of the currencies of both the Union and Confederacy, he finds that a "news" variable, consisting of information on battles and major political events, systematically affected the exchange rates of the belligerents in accordance with Mitchell's hypothesis.

For Friedman and Schwartz, the money stock is an independent variable with the price level and exchange rate strongly influenced by monetary forces. According to Calomiris (1986), the exchange rate is determined primarily by fiscal news—news about the size of the government's budget deficit and the speed of retirement of debt—which influences the probability and timing of resumption. In turn, the price level is anchored by movements in the exchange rate. Given the price level and the exchange rate, the money supply passively adjusts to equate real money supply and demand. Vector autoregressions provide evidence for this view. They show that innovations in the exchange rate and price level precede innovations in the money stock, and that innovations in several proxies for fiscal news precede those for the exchange rate and the price level. Unfortunately, Calomiris, like McCandless, does not explain how fiscal and war news affects the fundamental determinants of the exchange rate. Moreover, Calomiris' model of an endogenous money supply implies an unstable money multiplier, an implication inconsistent with ample evidence that it is stable and predictable.[36]

Phelps (1985) compares Friedman and Schwartz's approach to resumption to that of the finance approach (Sargent and Wallace 1983). According to Phelps, Friedman and Schwartz imply that the behavior of the greenback price of gold should vary inversely with expectations of future money growth. In the finance approach (also followed by Calomiris), it should vary inversely with the probability of resumption, which in turn depends on announcements of a fiscal policy compatible with gold convertibility and an announcement of the date of resumption. Phelps devises a chronology of thirteen key financial events in the greenback era, which he uses to show that the exchange rate responded in the direction predicted by events suggesting future changes in money growth in only seven cases, whereas it responded to fiscal news in all thirteen.

A major difficulty with the finance approach is that ex ante news is virtually impossible to identify. The events deemed important from today's perspective may not have been so deemed by market participants at the time.

Gresham's Law

Despite Gresham's Law—which Rolnick and Weber (1986, 198) define as the claim that "when the par price of [two monies] is out of line with the market price, the money overvalued at the mint drives out the undervalued money,"—the issue of greenbacks did not drive both gold and silver coins out of circulation. Instead, though small denomination silver coins disappeared, in the eastern part of the country gold coins circulated at a premium. The authors explain this paradox as follows. If two types of money are coined and made legal tender, and the market and legal prices differ, the money which is overvalued at the mint becomes the unit of account and the undervalued money, if of large denomination, circulates at a premium, while small denomination coins are bundled and used as a store of value. The reason is that the transactions costs of paying a premium will likely be higher for small than for larger denomination currency.

Furthermore, in the west, gold remained the unit of account and medium of exchange while greenbacks circulated at a discount, but this does not, according to these authors, contradict the hypothesis that the overvalued currency becomes the unit of account. The reason they give is that in 1863 California passed legislation which effectively divested greenbacks of legal tender status so they did not have to be accepted for payment at par.

This approach is based on a misinterpretation of Gresham's Law. Friedman and Schwartz clearly state that Gresham's Law "applies only when there is a fixed rate of exchange" (fn. 16, p. 27). According to them, the simultaneous circulation of gold coins and greenbacks simply reflected the operation of a flexible exchange rate. The reason subsidiary silver disappeared was that the market value of silver was bid up to the point at which it became useless to facilitate low value transactions.

To sum up, Officer, using better data, confirms Friedman and Schwartz's explanation for resumption and its timing. Several articles suggest that news may be a more important factor in exchange rate determination than Friedman and Schwartz accept, but this literature does not explain how news affected the fundamental determinants of exchange rates. Finally, Rolnick and Weber view the greenback episode as a denial of Gresham's Law, but their reinterpretation itself does not make clear the distinction between fixed and flexible exchange rates among types of money.

1.5.2 The Classical Gold Standard, 1879–1914

The U.S. restored specie payments on 1 January 1879, and returned to the gold standard. According to Friedman and Schwartz, the way in which adjustment to both external and internal disturbances took place under the standard was via the classical (Hume) price-specie-flow mechanism aided by capital flows. By contrast, in the monetary approach to the balance of payments (MABP) prices and interest rates are rigidly linked together through the force of arbitrage in commodities and capital markets, and gold flows are the equilibrating mechanism by which excess demands (or supplies) of money are cleared (Frenkel 1971; Johnson 1976; Mundell 1971).

McCloskey and Zecher (1976) test a model of the monetary approach to the balance of payments that assumes arbitrage in world commodity and capital markets to explain movements in the U.K. and U.S. balance of payments under the gold standard, 1880–1913. The authors assess the key assumption of commodity arbitrage by examining correlations among price changes between countries, and among regions within countries under the gold standard. For traded goods such as wheat, they found synchronous correlations equally high among regions as among nations, unlike the case of nontraded goods such as labor services and bricks. For overall price indices they found a significant correlation between the wholesale price indices of the United Kingdom and the United States, less so for GNP deflators and even less for consumer price indices. The larger share of traded goods in the WPI undoubtedly accounts for its higher correlation. Evidence in favor of capital market arbitrage was less conclusive.[37] They also compare gold flows—predicted by a simple demand for money function minus the money supply produced by domestic credit expansion—with actual gold flows, and found a very close relationship.

According to McCloskey and Zecher (1984), Friedman and Schwartz base their interpretation (p. 99) of the cyclical expansion from 1879 to 1892 on viewing it as an excellent example of the operation of the classical gold standard on annual data. An examination of monthly data on gold flows and changes in the price level revealed no tendency for price rises to follow gold inflows; instead, price rises preceded gold flows, evidence McCloskey and Zecher find to be consistent with arbitrage and the monetary approach.

Friedman (1984) in reply argues that the relationship between changes in money supplies and price levels is more pertinent than that between gold flows and price levels. Moreover, if one examines semi-annual data, the evidence for that episode suggests that changes in money preceded changes in the price level. In addition, when account is taken of the proximate determinants of the money stock, it turns out that a rise in the money multiplier enabled a rise in the money supply after resumption despite no initial gold inflow, and a large gold inflow in 1879 to be absorbed by a rise in the gold–high-powered money ratio rather than in the money supply. Thus for him, the episode still remains an example of the classical mechanism in operation.[38]

The brief literature cited here on the classical gold standard adjustment mechanism for the United States could be supplemented by earlier articles on both the pre–Civil War period and the classical period by Macesich (1960), Williamson (1961, 1963), and Willett (1968). Pertinent recent evidence for other countries includes Jonung (1984) for Sweden, Fratianni and Spinelli (1984) for Italy, Rich (1984) for Canada, and Drummond (1976) for Russia.

The upshot of these studies is that whether the Hume mechanism or the monetary approach better explains the operation of the classical gold standard remains unresolved. The evidence is consistent with the existence of a number of adjustment mechanisms—commodity price arbitrage, interest rate arbitrage, changes in relative prices, gold flows, money supply changes, and changes in the underlying structure of the international economy—each operating within different time horizons. Thus, running a race between the classical and monetary approach models has only limited value because of the complexity of the issue.

1.5.3 The Silver Agitation

Shortly after the United States successfully returned to the gold standard, maintenance of the standard was threatened by political agitation for free coinage of silver. The free silver movement achieved some of its aims with the passage of the Bland Allison Act of 1878 which created a silver trading dollar, and the Sherman Silver Purchase Act of 1890 which instructed the Treasury to purchase 4.5 million ounces of silver per month. According to Friedman and Schwartz (p. 131), the ensuing issue of silver certificates in itself would not have increased the money supply sufficiently to force the country off the gold standard because of the offsetting effects of other sources of change in high-powered money. The real threat to the gold standard created by the silver purchases was the adverse expectations created that these purchases would lead to even more. The resultant capital outflow led to more deflation than would otherwise have occurred. The deflationary pressure in turn was an important contributor to the banking panic of 1893 and the depression of the mid-1890s. Between 1893 and 1896, threats to the Treasury's gold reserves were allayed by direct measures it took, including the formation of syndicates of bankers who used their credit abroad to engineer offsetting capital inflows.

Garber and Grilli (1986) interpret the Belmont-Morgan syndicate of 1895 as a successful attempt to prevent a speculative attack on the fixed-exchange-rate gold standard. Their model posits an increased probability of attack on the currency according to the extent the rate of domestic credit expansion generates an exchange rate in excess of parity. From 1890 to 1895, the United States ran continuous budget deficits financed by domestic credit expansion. Of special importance for the deficits were the silver purchases after 1890. The Belmont-Morgan syndicate reduced the money supply by selling government bonds for gold, and succeeded in reducing the probability of speculative attack.[39]

According to Friedman and Schwartz (p. 134), had a silver standard been adopted after 1879, the United States would have had the benefits of a flexible exchange rate along with the rest of the gold standard world. The resultant fall in the monetary demand for gold and the increase in that for silver would have raised the gold price of silver sufficient to offset the deflation that occurred under the gold standard.

In support of this contention, Drake (1985) calculates the hypothetical behavior of the U.S. price level between 1879 and 1914 had the United States not demonetized silver in 1879. Accounting for biases in the market-to-mint ratio due to the hypothetical monetization of silver, and for the effects of releasing gold, a reduction in silver for nonmonetary uses, and the effects on other bimetallic countries, he found that the U.S. WPI would have been more stable than it was,[40] that the United States would have been on a gold standard for most of the period with the exception of 1879–90, and that the gold-silver ratio would not have strayed for long from the 16:1 mint ratio.

1.5.4 The Gold Exchange Standard, 1920–33

The gold exchange standard reinstated in the 1920s was more fragile than its pre–World War I antecedent as countries substituted holdings of foreign exchange for gold, hence reducing the gold reserve base for the world money supply, and as countries adopted gold sterilization policies, thereby preventing the balance-of-payments adjustment mechanism from working.

A number of authors provide evidence in support of Friedman and Schwartz's interpretation of the role of the gold standard and U.S. policies in transmitting the Great Depression.

According to Huffman and Lothian (1984), unexpected monetary shocks that affected real income in one country, were transmitted in turn via specie flows (and short-term capital flows) to the money supplies of other countries, and then to real activity. The gold standard thus served to transmit the business cycle from country to country. Evidence for this view is based on Granger-causality tests over the period 1833 to 1933.

Choudhri and Kochin (1980), in a comparison of the experience of a number of small European countries during the Great Depression (1930–33), find that only Spain, a country which maintained flexible exchange rates with the gold standard world, was successfully insulated from the Great Depression. They divide their sample of countries into: (a) countries which maintained the fixed-exchange-rate gold standard throughout the depression—The Netherlands, Belgium, Italy, and Poland; (b) countries which, with the United Kingdom, left gold in 1931—Norway, Denmark, and Finland; and (c) Spain. Then, regressing real output and the price level for each country on U.S. real output and the price level, the results show a strong influence of the U.S. depression on the gold standard countries, with Spain completely unaffected and the other countries in depression until they cut the link with gold in 1931.

Eichengreen (1988) provides evidence that the national gold policies of the United States and France were a key cause of international monetary contraction. Based on a pooled cross-section, time-series regression of the demand for international reserves for twenty-four countries, he shows that U.S. and French gold policies reduced available gold reserves to these countries by one-half. Furthermore, the effects of these policies on the worldwide demand for reserves far outweighed the effects of a shift in liquidity preferences—in the wake of the international financial crisis of 1931—away from holding reserves in the form of foreign exchange.

However, Fremling (1985) challenges Friedman and Schwartz's view that the Great Depression was transmitted from the United States to the rest of the world during the period 1929–31 as evidenced by an increase in gold inflows and the monetary gold stock. According to her, gold inflows to the United States and an increase in U.S. gold reserves did not necessarily mean that other countries were losing gold. Gold mining, as well as conversions of existing private gold stocks into currency, could have raised total world reserves.

Fremling presents evidence that from August 1929 to August 1931, gold reserves in the rest of the world increased from $6.3 to $6.7 billion versus $3.9 to $4.9 billion in the United States. Furthermore, though holdings of foreign exchange in the rest of the world declined, this was insufficient to offset the increase in gold. Rates of change of the total currency stock and gold reserves in the United States compared with the rest of the world indicate that the latter also engaged in significant sterilization. Thus, to the extent the Great Depression was transmitted internationally, other countries as well as the United States must have played a significant role.[41] However, Fremling's analysis considers only aggregate behavior, not the one-to-one relations of the U.S. acquiring gold and each country losing gold.

Thus, with the exception of Fremling's study, the evidence is over-whelmingly in favor of the contention in *A Monetary History* that the Great Depression was spread internationally by the gold standard. Other forces, both real and monetary, however, also played a role.[42]

1.5.5   The New Deal Monetary Standard

The New Deal produced major changes in the monetary standard. A silver purchase program designed to aid the domestic silver industry was instituted at the same time as the gold purchase program.

According to Friedman and Schwartz, the increase in the price of silver led to an appreciation of the Chinese yuan, a decline in exports, a rise in imports, a fall in the monetary silver stock, a fall in the money stock, and hence falling prices and output. Brandt and Sargent (1987) provide new evidence that though prices fell and the monetary silver stock declined, inside money (private bank notes and deposits) in-creased, so that the total money supply increased. Also, according to them, real output did not fall. They view China as a small open economy under the specie standard following a real bills policy (Sargent and Wallace 1982). As such, China took world prices as given, and by discounting only real bills the private banks ensured convertibility of the currency into specie. Banks issued private notes backed by gov-ernment securities, themselves backed by future taxes, so the authors argue that they can be treated as equivalent to real bills. Because China had a vertical Phillips curve, real output did not contract as a result of the deflation produced by the U.S.-induced rise in the price of silver. The increase in inside money reflected intermediation by private banks attempting to capture the real resources tied up in a commodity money. The reason given for China's departure from silver and conversion to a fiduciary standard in 1935 was that the government wanted to capture the social saving from issuing paper money for itself.

Brandt and Sargent's argument suffers from a number of serious shortcomings. First, the timing of the regime change in 1935 is consistent with Friedman and Schwartz's explanation that it was purely a reaction to the silver purchase policy. Second, a closer examination of the evidence presented reveals that real output did decline from 1931 to 1934. Third, Tamanga (1942) shows that most bank loans were made on real estate collateral, a far cry from real bills. It is not certain that inside money in fact increased, as Brandt and Sargent contend. Some evidence exists that suggests declining operations by native banks. Modern banks, for which they provide estimates, may simply have replaced the issues of the native banks that no longer operated.

1.6 Conclusion: The Legacy of *A Monetary History*

A Monetary History of the United States has spawned a vast literature in economic history, much of which has either corroborated or extended themes raised by Friedman and Schwartz. Their views on the timing of resumption, on the implications of a hypothetical bimetallic standard for price stability in the last third of the nineteenth century, on the defects of the theory underlying the Federal Reserve Act, and on the regime change following establishment of the Fed, have all been reconfirmed by subsequent researchers applying newer techniques and more recently available data sources.

A number of controversies, however, still remain unresolved: the role of news in the greenback era; whether the Hume price-specie-flow-mechanism or the monetary approach better explains balance of payments adjustment under the classical gold standard; whether the Fed really smoothed the seasonal in interest rates and, moreover, whether its establishment explains an observed change in the stochastic pattern of interest rates around the world; the mechanism of banking panics; whether commercial banks in the 1930s faced a liquidity trap in excess reserves or a shift in liquidity preferences; whether the Fed subordinated itself to the Treasury in the 1930s and 1940s or was acting as a revenue-maximizing bureau; and whether the bond-price-support program was an engine of inflation or an example of a Barro-Gordon rule.

On one important issue the literature disagrees with Friedman and Schwartz: whether Federal Reserve policy was inconsistent before and after 1929. The archival evidence marshalled by Wicker, Brunner, and Meltzer, supplemented by Wheelock's econometric evidence, makes a strong case for the position that the Fed followed the flawed Burgess-Riefler-Strong doctrine throughout the 1920s and early 1930s. The reason for the Fed's failure to conduct expansionary monetary policy during 1929–31 was that, based on its indicators—the level of member bank reserves and market interest rates—it believed conditions were easy. However, as Wheelock points out, the shift in structure of the Fed after Benjamin Strong's death likely worsened things, in accord with Friedman and Schwartz's position, as it weakened the influence of individuals who had the ability and understanding to depart from the flawed strategy.

Finally, a number of episodes have not yet been reassessed by a later generation of scholars. One is the post-1951 period, which Friedman and Schwartz regarded as a decade of monetary tranquility in a turbulent era. Why was that period so special?

The legacy to economic history of A Monetary History is not simply that its scholarly and thought-provoking reinterpretation of U.S. monetary history has generated a growth industry of scholarly papers. The legacy also stems from the novel way in which Friedman and Schwartz presented monetary history from the perspective of the relationship between the stock of money and the rest of the economy. This interweave between monetary theory and economic history has changed the way monetary history is approached around the world. The analytical framework of the modern quantity theory underlying the book, modified and expanded to incorporate newer theoretical and empirical techniques, has been applied to the experiences of numerous countries over vast ranges of history.

Before A Monetary History, the study of the development of financial and monetary institutions, the conduct of monetary policy, and the anatomy of financial crises, dominated monetary history. A number of monetary theorists used historical examples to illustrate particular monetary theories, e.g., Fisher (1911), Keynes (1930), and Warburton (1958). Some historians applied the quantity theory to explain episodes of inflation, e.g., Hamilton (1934) and White (1980). Friedman and Schwartz were the first to consistently apply a set of theoretical tools to the monetary history of a major country over a period of close to a century, spanning numerous institutional changes and monetary disturbances.

In addition, the data on the money stock, its components, and other aggregates compiled in A Monetary History and in the two companion volumes, has proved and will continue to prove invaluable to both historical and applied research in monetary economics.

By calculating the hypothetical effects on the money stock of a one-billion-dollar-open-market operation at various watersheds during the Great Contraction, the authors pioneered the posing of counterfactual questions—an important tool of economic history—even before Robert

Fogel's (1964) renowned study of the impact of the railroads on U.S. economic growth.

The unique portrayal of the historical circumstances of monetary disturbances and of alternative institutional arrangements as background conditions, serve the monetary economist with the closest thing to a laboratory experiment. The book's example has become an important tool of modern macroeconomic research.

In the dark age of vector autoregressions where it is no longer possible to identify truly causal relationships, turning to the record of history provides a beacon of light. *A Monetary History* has shown the way.

Notes

1. However, the reviewers all had critical comments to make. Clower criticized their methodology for its opaqueness, Tobin was highly critical of their treatment of the long-run behavior of velocity and of their explanation of excess reserves in the 1930s, Brunner (1965) also criticized the treatment of excess reserves and, along with Meltzer, the lack of an explicit model of the money supply process.

2. See Price (1961). Also see Bordo and Landau (1979) for earlier evidence on the pattern of citations in economic theory.

3. There has been only limited attention paid to the inflation of 1897–1914. See Schwartz (1973) for an excellent summary of worldwide historical evidence consistent with the view presented in *A Monetary History* that sustained rises in the price level are closely associated with money growth in excess of the growth of real output.

4. In a similar type of argument, Calomiris and Hubbard (1986) attribute economic contraction in the pre-1914 period to credit rationing in the face of deflationary shocks.

5. See Calomiris and Hubbard (1987).

6. Based on Granger-causality tests between the unexpected shock component of failed business liabilities and both a proxy for consumption (pig iron production) and a measure of losses on deposits.

7. It also should be pointed out that there were numerous arrangements available short of complete restriction. Thus, for example, in the 1930s banks would pay out part of a withdrawal and then pay interest on the remainder.

8. This section draws on Bordo (1986).

9. Friedman and Schwartz (1963a, 1963b) recognize the possibility of influences running from income to money, but present evidence that for major contractions the influence from money to income clearly dominates.

10. The sample underlying Gordon and Wilcox's simulations covered only a limited number of observations of business cycles, Lothian (1981) notes. In regressions based on annual money and income data over the period 1893–1928, money explained a substantial proportion of the fall in income until 1930 and all of the decline in the decade of the 1930s.

Lothian also compares the experiences of the U.S. and the U.K. in the depressions of 1920–21 and 1929–33, presenting evidence that the cycles in both countries had monetary origins and that monetary factors explained their severity and duration. For money to be passive, he adds, some factor other than monetary growth must have varied in the same way between the two countries to explain their different cyclical performances, yet no one had produced such evidence.

Meltzer (1981) denies that the monetary base could have been caused by feedback from income because (a) banks rarely borrowed from the Federal Reserve, (b) there was little evidence of a strong influence coming through the balance of payments, and (c) Fed open market policy did not respond much to movements in income.

11. Trescott (1984) finds that Boughton and Wicker's demand for currency regression is unstable when divided at February–March 1933 and at January 1924. The first period, according to Trescott (1982), represents a different policy regime, the second is dominated by the Bank Holiday. When the pre-1924 and post-March 1933 periods are removed, the regression shows bank failures to have been the key cause of the rise in the currency-deposit ratio, 1930–33.

12. Wicker regards the failure of the Bank of United States in December 1930 as localized in New York City, contributing little to an increase in the bank failure rate elsewhere in the country.

The banking panic of 1930, according to Wicker (1982), was unique in that it originated outside the New York money market and had no discernible effects on interest rates except in local markets. Its only effect appeared to be a decline in expenditure in the St. Louis Federal Reserve District (the district containing most of the affected banks) that was induced by a reduction in bank debits.

13. Also see Gandolfi and Lothian (1979) and Schwartz (1981). Although Boughton and Wicker (1979) find interest rates to be a significant determinant of the deposit-currency ratio, they are doubtful that the elasticity was large enough to justify Temin's claim.

14. See also Schwartz (1981, p. 20) and Meltzer (1976) who argue that Temin's position implausibly implies that if the economy was characterized by an excess supply of money, goods, and labor, by Walras' Law there would have been an excess demand for securities.

15. See also Temin (1983).

16. See Bordo and Schwartz (1977, p. 102).

17. Anderson and Butkiewicz (1980) obtain similar results using quarterly data.

18. Streefkerk (1983) constructs a rational-expectations-based model of the Great Depression in the U.S. which, following the approach of Brunner, Cukierman, and Meltzer (1980), distinguishes between temporary and permanent shocks. His preliminary results are consistent with the Schwartz account.

19. Hamilton (1987b) reinterprets this episode and the 1931 gold drain as examples conducive to analysis by the speculative attack models developed by Garber and Flood (1982) and others.

20. Bessler (1985) tests George Warren's hypothesis (Warren and Pearson 1935) that leaving the gold standard and allowing the price of gold to rise would immediately raise the price of traded goods and hence the price level. Bessler finds, based on innovation accounting from vector autoregressions with weekly data, that gold prices in 1933 Granger-caused key agricultural commodities prices, with a very rapid response.

21. Cagan (1965) calculates the rate of return on issuing national bank notes as the ratio of the net interest income earned on the bonds purchased with the issued notes (net of the costs of note redemption, cash reserves on the notes at the Treasury, and a small tax on the note issue) to the amount of capital

tied up in acquiring the bonds—the difference between the market price and the amount of notes issued. He finds rates of return comparable to those on other assets over the period 1875 to 1913, except for the late 1880s. By 1900, the rate of return was close to 25 percent. For Cagan, the puzzle is to explain why, at such high rates of return, less than 60 percent of eligible notes were issued.

22. Canova (1987), who uses a model of stochastic seasonality based on spectral methods, finds that the interest rate seasonal was not eliminated in 1914. He attributes the reduction in banking panics after 1914 to the Fed's ability to offset foreign-induced shocks to the money supply. Also see Dewald (1972) for evidence against a reduction in the seasonal, and Wheelock (1987) who finds no evidence of any change in interest rate and bank reserves seasonals after 1929.

23. Friedman and Schwartz see an inconsistency between the two founding principles in that the gold standard effectively limited money issue whereas the real bills doctrine did not. See Mints (1945). Sargent and Wallace (1982) construct an overlapping-generations model for a small open economy under the gold standard, which they argue is consistent with the real bills doctrine of Adam Smith. However, Laidler (1984) sees little relevance of their model to Smith's treatment of the real bills doctrine or the gold standard.

24. However, Toma (1987) demonstrates, based on vector autoregressions and monthly data, that the Fed could not have conducted countercyclical open market operations during the 1920s because such operations were fully offset by changes in member bank borrowing which left Federal Reserve credit constant.

25. Epstein and Ferguson (1984) disagree that the reason the Fed conducted large open market purchases in early 1932 was because of Congressional pressure. They argue it did so because the rise in the discount rate in October 1931, by reducing bond prices, threatened the solvency of many large banks, putting pressure on the Fed to act. The reason for early abandonment of the program was declining short-term yields which squeezed the earnings of many large commercial banks (who had shifted their portfolios from long-term to short-term bonds as a reaction to the preceding liquidity crises). According to the authors, it was no accident that Governor MacDougall of Chicago and Governor Young of Boston were the chief opponents of open market purchases, as these were two key districts whose member banks had the highest ratio of investments to loans and the lowest net earnings.

26. Wicker also disagrees with Friedman and Schwartz's view that domestic rather than international considerations dominated policy in the 1920s. His interpretation of the evidence is that in 1924 the majority of governors voting for expansionary open market policy did so because of a desire to build up the security holdings of the Fed to offset a future inflationary gold inflow. In addition, Governor Strong wanted to reduce the interest rate differential between London and New York to help Britain return to gold. International considerations also predominated in 1927, according to Wicker. By contrast, in 1930, the gold standard was not in danger, hence little need was seen for expansionary policy. Brunner and Meltzer's (1968) interpretation of the record disputes Wicker's emphasis on international factors. Their critique is buttressed by the insignificant influence of several international variables in Fed policy reaction functions that Wheelock estimates (1987).

27. Wheelock uses a longer sample period than Trescott, and constructs separate reaction functions for each of the Fed's policy tools, whereas Trescott

focuses only on the Fed's open market holdings and conducts formal stability tests. His application of stability tests to Trescott's model shows no change in policy in 1929.

28. For a discussion of the influence of the small unit bank lobby on U.S. banking legislation before 1929, see White (1983).

29. See Friedman and Schwartz (fn. 22, pp.443–44) for a similar view. See also Schwartz (1979). For evidence that the paying of interest on demand deposits did not lead banks to engage in riskier investments than otherwise, see Benston (1964).

30. White (1986) effectively argues that investment banking activity by the commercial banks during the 1920s did not impair their balance sheets.

31. There is overwhelming evidence against a liquidity trap in the demand for money during the 1930s. See, e.g., Gandolfi and Lothian (1976) and the studies surveyed in Laidler (1985). Brunner and Meltzer (1968b) provide evidence against a liquidity trap in bank excess reserves.

32. Based on a regression using annual data from 1947 to 1979 of changes in real Federal Reserve expenditures on the Fed's open market wealth, a measure of the Fed's nonmonetary output, and a wage variable.

33. The 1947 agreement between the Fed and Treasury to eliminate the ⅜ percent ceiling on short-term rates was not a reflection of the Fed's concern with inflation, as argued by Friedman and Schwartz, according to Toma (1982). Instead, according to the theory of bureaucracy, it served to eliminate a program which made short-term bonds as good as money. The agreement caused banks to increase excess reserves, reduce the deposit-reserve ratio and hence the money multiplier, thereby raising the Fed's share of inflation tax revenue. Further, according to this interpretation, the Fed's decision in 1947 to turn over a fraction of its open market revenue to the Treasury was in exchange for the Treasury's agreement to eliminate the ceiling on short-term rates. At the same time, the transfer served to prevent an attempt by Congress to capture some of the inflation tax revenue earned during World War II.

34. According to Officer, the wholesale price series Kindahl, Friedman, and Schwartz used is flawed by double counting, the omission of services, and the overweighing of imports.

35. Indeed the annual growth rate of Berry's real GNP series of 4.2 percent from 1869 to 1879 is almost identical to Friedman and Schwartz's refined estimate (1963a, 39, table 3) of 4.3 percent.

36. See, e.g., Cagan (1965).

37. Calomiris and Hubbard (1987) provide further evidence of commodity and capital market arbitrage. They calculate allowable bandwidths between U.S. and British prices of selected commodities consistent with arbitrage, finding the actual price movements fall within the range. Evidence for capital market integration is based on triangular arbitrage between U.S. and British high-grade commercial paper rates and bills of exchange.

38. Aghelvi's (1975) evidence for the U.S. during this period that anticyclical movements of the balance of trade dominate procyclical movements of net capital flows supports the Friedman and Schwartz rather than the monetary approach model.

39. Garber (1986) treats dollar bonds under bimetallism as an option allowing the holder to receive, on maturity, either gold or silver, depending on whichever metal's price had increased relative to the official price. Calculation of the option value of bonds during the period 1818–96 provides evidence on the probability the market attached at various times to a switch between silver and gold.

40. Also see Timberlake (1978a) who makes a similar argument without the simulations.

41. Hamilton (1987a) notes that net gold flows going to the U.S. still supports Friedman and Schwartz. Also, it is not clear from Fremling's argument why it should matter if the sources of gold are private or official.

42. See, e.g., Meltzer (1976), Brunner (1981), and Saint-Etienne (1984) on the importance of the Smoot-Hawley tariff, Eichengreen (1987a) for the counter view. Eichengreen (1987b) assesses various monetary and nonmonetary explanations, downplaying virtually all except the consequences of U.S. and French contractionary gold policies.

References

Acheson, K., and J. F. Chant. 1973. Bureaucratic theory and the choice of central bank goals. *Journal of Money, Credit and Banking* May:637–55.

Aghelvi, B. S. 1975. The balance of payments and the money supply under the gold standard regime: U.S. 1879–1914. *American Economic Review* 65:40–58.

Anderson, B. L., and J. L. Butkiewicz. 1980. Money, spending and the Great Depression. *Southern Economic Journal* 47, no. 2 (October):388–403.

Barro, R., and D. Gordon. 1983. Rules, discretion and reputation in a model of monetary policy. *Journal of Monetary Economics* 12, no. 1 (July):101–22.

Barsky, R. B., N. G. Mankiw, J. A. Miron, and D. N. Weil. 1988. The worldwide change in the behavior of interest rates and prices in 1914. *European Economic Review* 32, no. 5 (June): 1123–54.

Benston, G. 1964. Interest payments on demand deposits and bank investment behavior. *Journal of Political Economy* 72(5):431–49.

———. 1982. Why did Congress pass new financial services laws in the 1930s? *Federal Reserve Bank of Atlanta Economic Review* April:7–10.

Bernanke, B. 1983. Non monetary effects of the financial crisis in the propagation of the Great Depression. *American Economic Review* 73, no. 3 (June):257–76.

Berry, T. S. 1978. *Estimated annual variations in gross national product 1789 to 1909.* Richmond: The Bostwick Press, University of Richmond.

Bessler, D. A. 1985. Agricultural prices, the gold standard, and the Great Depression: The Warren Thesis revisited. Texas A and M University. Mimeo.

Blanchard, D., and M. Watson. 1982. Bubbles, rational expectations, and financial markets. In *Crises in the economic and financial structure,* ed. P. Wachtel. Lexington, Mass.: Lexington Books.

Bordo, M. D. 1986. Explorations in monetary history: A survey of the literature. *Explorations in Economic History* 18, no. 3 (October):339–415.

Bordo, M. D., and D. Landau. 1979. The pattern of citations in economic theory 1948–68: An exploration towards a quantitative history of thought. *History of Political Economy* 11(2):239–53.

Bordo, M. D., and A. J. Schwartz. 1977. Issues in monetary economics and their impact on research in economic history. In *Recent development in the study of business and economic history: Essays in memory of Herman E. Krooss,* ed. R. Gallman. Greenwich, Conn.: JAI Press.

Boughton, J., and E. Wicker. 1979. The behaviour of the currency-deposit ratio during the Great Depression. *Journal of Money, Credit and Banking* 1, no. 4 (November):405–18.

Brandt, L., and T. J. Sargent. 1987. Interpreting new evidence about China and U.S. silver purchases. Hoover Institution. Mimeo.

Brunner, K. 1965. Institutions, policy, and monetary analysis. *Journal of Political Economy* 73 (April):197–218.

———. 1981. Comment. In *The Great Depression revisited,* ed. K. Brunner. Boston: Martinus Nijhoff.

Brunner, K., A. Cukierman, and A. H. Meltzer. 1980. Stagflation, persistent unemployment and the permanence of economic shocks. *Journal of Monetary Economics* 6:467–92.

Brunner, K., and A. H. Meltzer. 1968a. What did we learn from the monetary experiences of the United States in the Great Depression? *Canadian Journal of Economics* 1(2):334–48.

———. 1968b. Liquidity traps for money, bank credit, and interest rates. *Journal of Political Economy* 76, no. 1 (Jan/Feb):1–37.

———. 1988. Money and credit in the monetary transmission process. *American Economic Association Papers and Proceedings* 78, no. 1 (May):446–51.

Cagan, P. 1963. The first fifty years of the national banking system—An historical appraisal. In *Banking and monetary studies,* ed. Deane Carson. Homewood, Ill.: Richard D. Irwin.

———. 1965. *Determinants and effects of changes in the stock of money, 1875–1960.* New York: Columbia University Press.

Calomiris, C. W. 1986. Understanding greenback inflation and deflation: An asset pricing approach. Northwestern University (September). Mimeo.

Calomiris, C. W., and R. G. Hubbard. 1986. Price flexibility, credit availability, and economic fluctuations: Evidence from the U.S., 1879–1914. Northwestern University, (December). Mimeo.

———. The international adjustment under the classical gold standard: Evidence for the U.S. and Britain, 1879–1914. NBER Working Paper no. 2206. Cambridge, Mass.: NBER.

Canova, F. 1987. Seasonality, the creation of the Fed and financial panics: A reinterpretation. University of Minnesota. Mimeo.

Choudhri, E. and L. Kochin. 1980. The exchange rate and the international transmission of business disturbances: Some evidence from the Great Depression. *Journal of Money, Credit and Banking* 12, no. 4, part 1 (November):565–74.

Clark, T. 1986. Interest rate seasonals and the Federal Reserve. *Journal of Political Economy* 94, no. 1 (February):76–125.

Clower, R. W. 1964. Monetary history and positive economics. *Journal of Economic History* 24:364–80.

Coase, R. 1937. The nature of the firm. *Economica N.S.* 4:386–405.

DeLong, J. B. and L. H. Summers. 1985. The changing cyclical variability of economic activity in the United States. In *The American business cycle: Continuity and change,* ed. R. J. Gordon. Chicago: University of Chicago Press.

Dewald, W. G. 1972. The National Monetary Commission: A look back. *Journal of Money, Credit and Banking* 4, no. 4 (November):930–56.

Diamond, D. W., and P. H. Dybvig. Bank runs, deposit insurance, and liquidity. *Journal of Political Economy* 91, no. 3 (June):401–19.

Drake, L. 1985. Reconstruction of a bimetallic price level. *Explorations in Economic History* 22, no. 2 (April):194–219.

Drummond, I. 1976. The Russian gold standard, 1897–1914. *Journal of Economic History* 36, no. 3 (September):663–88.

Eichengreen, B. 1987a. The gold exchange standard and the Great Depression. Harvard Institute of Economic Research Discussion Paper no. 1298.

———. 1987b. Did international economic forces cause the Great Depression? Paper presented at the Western Economic Association International meetings, Vancouver, Canada (June).

———. 1988. The political economy of the Smoot-Hawley Tariff. *Research in Economic History*. Forthcoming.

Epstein, G., and T. Ferguson, 1984. Monetary policy, loan liquidation, and industrial conflict: The Federal Reserve and the Great Contraction. *Journal of Economic History* 44, no. 4 (December):957–84.

Evans, P. 1985. Monetary collapse during the Great Depression: Did the money stock fall, or was it pushed? University of Houston. Mimeo.

Field, A. 1984a. Asset exchanges and the transactions demand for money, 1919–29. *American Economic Review* 74, no. 1 (March):43–59.

———. 1984b. A new interpretation of the onset of the Great Depression. *Journal of Economic History* 44, no. 2 (June):489–98.

Fisher, I. [1911] 1971. *The purchasing power of money*. New York: Augustus M. Kelley Publishers.

Fogel, R. 1964. *Railroads and American economic growth*. Baltimore: The Johns Hopkins University Press.

Fratianni, M., and F. Spinelli. 1984. Italy in the gold standard period, 1861–1914. In *A retrospective on the classical gold standard, 1821–1931*, eds. M. D. Bordo and A. J. Schwartz. Chicago: University of Chicago Press.

Fremling, G. M. 1985. Did the United States transmit the Great Depression to the rest of the world? *American Economic Review* 75, no. 5 (December):1181–85.

Frenkel, J. 1971. A theory of money, trade and the balance of payments in a model of accumulation. *Journal of International Economics* 1:159–87.

Friedman, M. 1956. The quantity theory of money—A restatement. In *Studies in the quantity theory of money*, ed. M. Friedman. Chicago: University of Chicago Press.

———. 1984. Comment on McCloskey and Zecher. In *A retrospective on the classical gold standard, 1821–1931*, eds. M. D. Bordo and A. J. Schwartz. Chicago: University of Chicago Press.

Friedman, M., and A. J. Schwartz. 1963a. *A monetary history of the United States, 1867–1960*. Princeton, NJ: Princeton University Press.

———. 1963b. Money and business cycles. *Review of Economics and Statistics* 45, no. 1, part 2 (February):32–64.

———. 1970. *Monetary statistics of the United States*. New York: Columbia University Press.

———. 1982. *Monetary trends in the United States and the United Kingdom: Their relation to income, prices, and interest rates, 1867–1975*. Chicago: University of Chicago Press.

Gandolfi, A. E., and J. R. Lothian. 1976. The demand for money from the Great Depression to the present. *American Economic Review* 66(2):46–51.

———. 1979. Did monetary forces cause the Great Depression? *Journal of Money, Credit and Banking* (November):679–91.

Garber, P. M. 1981. The lender of last resort and the run on savings and loans. NBER Working Paper no. 823. Cambridge, Mass.: NBER.

————. 1986. Nominal contracts in a bimetallic standard. *American Economic Review* 76 (December):1012–30.

Garber, P., and R. Flood. 1982. Bubbles, runs, and gold monetization. In *Crises in the economic and financial structure,* ed. P. Wachtel. Lexington, Mass.: Lexington Books.

Garber, P., and V. Grilli. 1986. The Belmont-Morgan syndicate as an optimal investment banking contract. *European Economic Review* 30:649–72.

Goodhart, C. A. E. 1965. Profit on national bank notes, 1900–1913. *Journal of Political Economy* 79 (October):515–22.

Gordon, R., and J. Wilcox. 1981. Monetarist interpretations of the Great Depression: An evaluation and critique. In *The Great Depression revisited,* ed. K. Brunner. Boston: Martinus Nijhoff.

Gorton, G. 1984a. Private clearinghouses and the origins of central banking. *Federal Reserve Bank of Philadelphia Review* (January/February):3–12.

————. 1984b. Banking panics and business cycles. Wharton School, The University of Pennsylvania. Mimeo.

————. 1985a. Clearinghouses and the origins of central banking in the U.S. *Journal of Economic History* 45, no. 2 (June):277–84.

————. 1985b. Bank suspensions on convertibility. *Journal of Monetary Economics* 15, no. 2 (March):177–93.

Hamilton, E. 1934. *American treasure and the price revolution in Spain.* Cambridge: Harvard University Press.

Hamilton, J. D. 1987a. Monetary factors in the Great Depression. *Journal of Monetary Economics* 19:145–69.

————. 1987b. The role of the international gold standard in propagating the Great Depression. Paper presented at the Western Economic Association International meetings, Vancouver, Canada (July).

Horwich, G. 1963. Effective reserves, credit and causality in the banking system of the thirties. In *Banking and monetary studies,* ed. D Carson. Homewood, Ill.: Richard Irwin.

————. 1966. Liquidity trap in the thirties: Comment. *Journal of Political Economy* 74, no. 3 (June):286–90.

Huffman, W., and J. Lothian. 1984. The gold standard and the transmission of business cycles, 1833–1932. In *A retrospective on the classical gold standard, 1821–1931,* eds. M. D. Bordo and A. J. Schwartz. Chicago: University of Chicago Press.

James, J. 1976. The conundrum of the low issue of national bank notes. *Journal of Political Economy* 84 (April):359–67.

Johnson, H. G. 1965. A quantity theorist's monetary history of the United States. *Economic Journal* 75:388–96.

————. 1976. The monetary approach to balance of payments theory. In *The monetary approach to the balance of payments,* eds. J. Frenkel and H. G. Johnson, 147–67. Toronto: University of Toronto Press.

Jonung, L. 1984. Swedish experience under the classical gold standard, 1873–1914. In *A retrospective on the classical gold standard, 1821–1931,* eds. M. D. Bordo and A. J. Schwartz. Chicago: University of Chicago Press.

Kane, E. J. 1985. *The gathering crisis in federal deposit insurance.* Cambridge, Mass.: MIT Press.

Keynes, J. M. [1930] 1971. *The applied theory of money: A treatise on money.* Vol. 6, *The collected writings of John Maynard Keynes.* Reprint. London:

Macmillan and New York: Cambridge Univ. Press, for the Royal Economic Society.

Kindahl, J. 1961. Economic factors in specie resumption. *Journal of Political Economy* 59:30–48.

Kindleberger, C. P. 1973. *The world in depression 1929–39.* Berkeley: University of California Press.

Laidler, D. 1984. Misconceptions about the real bills doctrine: A comment on Sargent and Wallace. *Journal of Political Economy* 92 (1):149–55.

————. 1985. *The demand for money: Theories and evidence.* 3d ed. New York: Harper and Row.

Lothian, J. R. 1981. Comments on monetarist interpretations of the Great Depression. In *The Great Depression revisited,* ed. K. Brunner. Boston: Martinus Nijhoff.

Macesich, G. 1960. Sources of monetary disturbances in the United States, 1834–45. *Journal of Economic History* 20:407–34.

Mankiw, N. G., and J. A. Miron. 1986. The changing behavior of the term structure of interest rates. *Quarterly Journal of Economics* 101, no. 2 (May):211–28.

Mankiw, N. G., J. A. Miron, and D. N. Weil. 1987. The adjustment of expectations to a change in regime: A study of the founding of the Federal Reserve. *American Economic Review* 77, no. 3 (June):358–74.

Mayer, T. 1978a. Money and the Great Depression: A critique of Professor Temin's thesis. *Explorations in Economic History* 15, no. 3 (April):127–45.

————. 1978b. Consumption in the Great Depression. *Journal of Political Economy* 86, no. 1 (February):139–45.

McCandless, G. T. 1985. Money, expectations and the U.S. Civil War. Dartmouth College. Mimeo.

McCloskey, D. N., and J. R. Zecher. 1976. How the gold standard worked, 1880–1913. In *The monetary approach to the balance of payments,* eds. J. Frenkel and H. G. Johnson. Toronto: University of Toronto Press.

————. 1984. The success of purchasing power parity: Historical evidence and its implications for macroeconomics. In *A retrospective on the classical gold standard, 1821–1931,* eds. M. D. Bordo and A. J. Schwartz. Chicago: University of Chicago Press.

Meltzer, A. H. 1965. Monetary theory and monetary history. *Schweizerische Zeitschrift für Volkswirtschaft und Statistik* 101(4):404–22.

————. 1976. Monetary and other explanations of the start of the Great Depression. *Journal of Monetary Economics* 1, no. 4 (November):455–71.

————. 1981. Comments on monetarist explanations of the Great Depression. In *The Great Depression revisited,* ed. K. Brunner. Boston: Martinus Nijhoff.

Mints, L. 1945. *A history of banking theory in Great Britain and the United States.* Chicago: University of Chicago Press.

Miron, J. A. 1986. Financial panics, the seasonality of the nominal interest rate, and the founding of the Fed. *American Economic Review* 76, no. 1 (March):125–40.

Mitchell, W. C. 1903. *A history of the greenbacks.* Chicago: University of Chicago Press.

Morrison, G. 1966. *Liquidity preference of commercial banks.* Chicago: University of Chicago Press.

Mundell, R. 1971 *Monetary theory.* Pacific Palisades, Calif.: Goodyear.

Niskanen, W. A. 1971. *Bureaucracy and representative government.* Chicago: Aldine.

Officer, L. A. 1981. The floating dollar in the greenback period: A test of theories of exchange rate determination. *Journal of Economic History* 41, no. 3 (September):629–50.

Phelps, B. D. 1985. *A finance approach to convertible money regimes: A new interpretation of the greenback era*. Ph.D. diss., Yale University.

Price, D. J. 1961. *Little science, big science*. New York: Columbia University Press.

Rich, G. 1984. Canada without a central bank: Operation of the price-specie-flow mechanism, 1872–1913. In *A retrospective on the classical gold standard, 1821–1931*, eds. M. D. Bordo and A. J. Schwartz. Chicago: University of Chicago Press.

Rockoff, H. 1981. Price and wage contracts in four wartime periods. *Journal of Economic History* 41, no. 2 (June):381–401.

Roll, R. 1972. Interest rates and price expectations during the Civil War. *Journal of Economic History* 32 (June):476–98.

Rolnick, A., and W. Weber. 1986. Gresham's Law or Gresham's Fallacy. *Journal of Political Economy* 94:185–89.

Saint-Etienne, C. 1984. *The Great Depression, 1929–1938: Lessons for the 1980s*. Stanford: Hoover Institution Press.

Sargent, T. J., and N. Wallace. 1982. The real bills doctrine versus the quantity theory: A reconsideration. *Journal of Political Economy* 90, no. 6 (December):1212–36.

———. 1983. A legal restrictions theory of the demand for money and the role of monetary policy. *Federal Reserve Bank of Minnesota Quarterly Review* (Winter):1–7.

Sayers, R. S. 1936. *Bank of England operations 1890–1914*. London: P. S. King and Son, Ltd.

Schwartz, A. J. 1972. The Aliber, Dewald, and Gordon papers, A comment. *Journal of Money, Credit and Banking* 4, no. 4 (November):978–84.

———. 1973. Secular price change in historical perspective. *Journal of Money, Credit and Banking* 5, part 2: 243–69.

———. 1979. Discussion. In *Regulatory change in an atmosphere of crisis: Current implications of the Roosevelt years*, ed. G. M. Walton, 93–99. New York: Academic Press.

———. 1981. Understanding 1929–33. In *The Great Depression revisited*, ed. K. Brunner. Boston: Martinus Nijhoff.

———. 1986. Real and pseudo-financial crises. In *Financial crises and the world banking system*, eds. F. Capie and G. E. Wood. London: Macmillan.

———. 1988. Financial stability and the federal safety net. In *Restructuring banking and financial services in America*, eds. W.S. Haraf and R. M. Kushmeider. Washington, D.C.: American Enterprise Institute.

Shiller, R. J. 1980. Can the Fed control real interest rates? In *Rational expectations and economic policy*, ed. Stanley Fischer. Chicago: University of Chicago Press.

Short, E. D., and G. P. O'Driscoll, Jr. 1983. Deregulation and deposit insurance. *Federal Reserve Bank of Dallas Economic Review* (September):11–22.

Smith, B. D. 1987. Bank panics, suspensions, and geography: Some notes on the "Contagions of Fear" in Banking. University of Western Ontario. Mimeo.

Sprague, O. M. W. 1910. *History of crises under the national banking system*. National Monetary Commission. Washington, D.C.: Government Printing Office.

Stauffer, R. 1981. The bank failures of 1930–31. *Journal of Money, Credit and Banking* 13, no. 1 (February):109–13.

Streefkerk, N. 1983. The economics of output changes: The American Great Depression—A rational expectations analysis. Erasmus University, Rotterdam. Mimeo.

Tamanga, F. M. 1942. *Banking and finance in China.* New York: Institute of Pacific Relations.

Temin, P. 1976. *Did monetary forces cause the Great Depression?* New York: W. W. Norton.

————. 1983. Monetary trends and other phenomena. *Journal of Economic History* 43, no. 3 (September):729–39.

Timberlake, R., Jr. 1975. The Resumption Act and the money supply. *Journal of Monetary Economics* 7:343–54.

————. 1978a. Repeal of silver monetization in the late nineteenth century. *Journal of Money, Credit and Banking* 10, no. 1 (February):27–45.

————. 1978b. *The origins of central banking in the United States.* Cambridge, Mass.: Harvard University Press.

————. 1984. The central banking role of clearing house associations. *Journal of Money, Credit and Banking* 16, no. 1 (February):1–15.

Tobin, J. 1965. The monetary interpretation of history. *American Economic Review* 55 (June):26–37.

Toma, M. 1982. Inflationary bias of the Federal Reserve System: A bureaucratic perspective. *Journal of Monetary Economics* 10, no. 2 (September):163–90.

————. 1985. A duopoly theory of government money production: The 1930s and 1940s. *Journal of Monetary Economics* 15, no. 3 (May):363–82.

————. 1987. The policy effectiveness of open market operations in the 1920s. Miami University. Mimeo.

Trescott, P. 1982. Federal Reserve policy in the Great Contraction: A counterfactual assessment. *Explorations in Economic History* 19, no. 3 (July):211–20.

————. 1984. The behavior of the currency-deposit ratio during the Great Depression. *Journal of Money, Credit and Banking* 16, no. 3 (August):362–65.

Vaubel, R. 1984. International debt, bank failures and the money supply: The thirties and the eighties. *Cato Journal* 4, no. 1 (Spring/Summer):249–68.

Waldo, D. G. 1985. Bank runs, the deposit-currency ratio and the interest rate. *Journal of Monetary Economics* 15, no. 3 (May):269–78.

Warburton, C. 1958. Variations in economic growth and banking developments in the United States from 1835 to 1885. *Journal of Economic History* 18:283–97.

Warren, C. F., and F. A. Pearson. 1935. *Gold and prices.* New York: Wiley.

Weinstein, M. 1981. Some macroeconomic impacts of the National Industrial Recovery Act, 1933–35. In *The Great Depression revisited,* ed. K. Brunner. Boston: Martinus Nijhoff.

Weintraub, R. 1978. Congressional supervision of monetary policy. *Journal of Monetary Economics* 4:341–62.

West, R. C. 1976. Real bills, the gold standard, and central bank policy. *Business History Review* (Winter):503–13.

————. 1977. *Banking reform and the Federal Reserve, 1863–1923.* Ithaca: Cornell University Press.

Wheelock, D. C. 1987. *The strategy and consistency of Federal Reserve monetary policy 1919–1933.* Ph.D. diss., University of Illinois at Urbana-Champaign.

White, A. D. 1980. *Fiat money inflation in France.* Washington, D.C.: Cato Institute.

White, E. N. 1982. The political economy of banking regulations, 1864–1933. *Journal of Economic History* 42, no. 1 (March):33–42.

———. 1983. *The regulation and reform of the American banking system, 1900–1929.* Princeton, NJ: Princeton University Press.

———. 1984. A reinterpretation of the banking crisis of 1930. *Journal of Economic History* 44, no. 1 (March):119–38.

———. 1986. Before the Glass-Steagall Act: An analysis of the investment activities of national banks. *Explorations in Economic History* 23, no. 1 (January):33–55.

Wicker, E. 1960. A reconsideration of Federal Reserve policy during the 1920–21 depression. *Journal of Economic History* 26, no. 2 (June):223–38.

———. 1965. Federal Reserve monetary policy 1929–33: A reinterpretation. *Journal of Political Economy* 73(4):325–43.

———. 1966. *Federal Reserve monetary policy 1917–1933.* New York: Random House.

———. 1969. The World War II policy of fixing a pattern of interest rates. *Journal of Finance* 24:447–58.

———. 1980. A reconsideration of the causes of the banking panic of 1930. *Journal of Economic History* 40, no. 3 (September):571–83.

———. 1982. Interest rates and expenditure effects of the banking panic of 1930. *Explorations in Economic History* 19, no. 4 (October):435–45.

Wigmore, B. 1987. Was the bank holiday of 1933 caused by a run on the dollar? *Journal of Economic History* 47, no. 3 (September):739–56.

Wilcox, J. A. 1984. Excess reserves in the Great Depression. NBER Working Paper no. 1374. Cambridge, Mass.: NBER.

Willet, T. 1968. International specie flows and American monetary stability 1834–60. *Journal of Economic History* 28:28–50.

Williamson, J. G. 1961. International trade and United States economic development: 1827–1843. *Journal of Economic History* 21:372–83.

Williamson, J. G. 1963. Real growth, monetary disturbances and the transfer process: The United States, 1879–1900. *Southern Economic Journal* 29:167–80.

A Note on Anna J. Schwartz's Contribution to pre-1867 Monetary History   Hugh Rockoff

There are many distinguished economists and economic historians who would be willing to help honor Anna Schwartz by commenting on Michael Bordo's paper. The reason why I am doing so is rather special. During her career, Anna Schwartz has not had many formal students in the way that a university professor would because for most of her career she has been associated with the National Bureau. But she has had a number of unofficial students whom she has encouraged and

Hugh Rockoff is a professor of economics at Rutgers University, New Brunswick, New Jersey, and a research associate of the National Bureau of Economic Research.

counseled, such as Michael Bordo and myself. So I am commenting here as one of Anna's "students."

I have decided not to try to criticize Bordo's paper in the usual way. Bordo has given us an encyclopedic survey of the current state of research on issues explored in *A Monetary History*. Most of the comments I would make on particular issues would reflect relatively small differences in emphasis. Rather, I have decided to use this opportunity to add an appendix to Bordo's paper by focussing on Anna Schwartz's contribution to pre-1867 monetary history.

There has been a tendency, I believe, for economic historians to concentrate excessively on certain episodes. I have not tried to estimate an exact number, but it is clear from Bordo's survey of the literature that a very substantial percentage of the papers he cites, perhaps a majority, are about the Great Depression. If our aim is to build a useful set of generalizations, it is necessary to move beyond what is, after all, one very atypical episode. Indeed, it simply may not be possible to decide among all the plausible explanations by solely examining events within the Great Depression itself. *A Monetary History,* of course, provides a wealth of other episodes worthy of further research. But I believe that the pre-1867 period, at least until recently, has been relatively neglected.

Pre-1867 monetary history has been a special concern of Anna Schwartz. And what I intend is to briefly review some of her most influential papers in this area, as well as the suggestions for research they contain that have not yet been taken up by other scholars. These papers are well known to specialists. But looking at them en masse may help to stimulate additional interest in the pre-1867 period.

New Data

Monetary Statistics of the United States, the second volume of the trilogy, contains, in addition to a discussion of the construction of the data for the post-1867 period, a table providing the extant raw materials for estimates of the stock of money in the United States, or at least some components, going back to 1775, and a discussion of the existing estimates of the pre-1867 stock of money. Friedman and Schwartz do not offer new totals, perhaps indicative of the basically fragmentary nature of the data. But their data could be used for starting points for studies of a number of relatively neglected episodes, including the Revolutionary War, the War of 1812, and the inflation following the discovery of gold in California.

At the end of their discussion of the pre-1867 monetary data, Friedman and Schwartz note that there does not seem to be any break between the monetary data before and after the Civil War. Some preliminary calculations illustrate this point. The ratio of money to GNP seems little different in the years after the Civil War from the years immediately before, apparently hovering around 15 percent. But if this is so, this is a surprising negative finding. The Civil War was an era of rapid change in the monetary system—the national banking system was set up, the gold standard was suspended, a large federal debt was created, and slavery was abolished. It seems surprising that these changes left little imprint on the money-income ratio. The absence of careful study of this issue is an illustration of the point made by Bordo and Schwartz in a survey of monetary history published some years ago that there is a relative lack of studies of the demand for money given the key role assigned to this function by monetary theorists (1977, 118).

A second major work in the area of data collection for the pre-1867 period was Schwartz's study of dividend and interest payments by U.S. corporations in the middle of the nineteenth century (1960).[1] Here Schwartz put together data from a variety of sources, including a Civil War tax on dividend and interest payments, to draw a preliminary picture of the growth and changes in this component of spending. This study shows how much can be learned about profits and profit rates in this period if the archives are attacked with sufficient imagination and energy, and, as Schwartz is at pains to emphasize, it shows the path toward more detailed estimates.

But even the numbers she brought to light in this paper are extremely interesting. Much has been written about the effects of Civil War inflation, a major issue being the meaning of what appears to be a well-documented fall in real wages. Wesley Claire Mitchell (1903, 380–91), in his original statement of the problem, argued that the fall in real wages implied a substantial increase in real profits. But Kessel and Alchian (1959) argued that real wages fell to reflect lower productivity and a variety of other real factors. There was, in other words, no real profit inflation to correspond to the real wage deflation. Others have since entered the debate. But Schwartz's numbers provide the best direct evidence of what actually happened to profits during the wartime inflation, although her sample, which I interpret as showing a small rise in real dividends, needs to be broadened.

Historical Studies

I want to mention four studies here that have been influential and yet contain important conjectures still to be examined in detail.

One of Schwartz's important historical studies is concerned with a topic that has recently drawn considerable attention: the role of competition in antebellum banking (1947a).[2] In that paper Schwartz showed how banks in Philadelphia, beginning with the lone Bank of North America in 1782, accommodated themselves to the growth of competition. It is a fascinating tale of rent seeking—to use a term that became fashionable later—and wildly exaggerated fears. Too much attention in the recent literature, I believe, has been focussed on so-called free banking. And much more could be learned about the sort of banking system Schwartz describes which is based on legislative charters.

Richard Sylla (1985) has cited Schwartz in the course of an argument that monopoly banking tended to break down and that we had de facto free banking in many localities, even under a chartered system, before the Civil War. But as I read her paper, banks continued to pay a fee for a charter. Implicit is a model in which the legislature weighs the increased fees it could charge for charters against some notion of public welfare, perhaps with a dose of corruption thrown in for good measure. And it is not at all clear in what ways and by how much the Philadelphia system differed in the long run from a competitive one. Obviously, more research into the functioning of the sort of system investigated by Anna Schwartz would help to balance our picture of antebellum banking.

Economic historians of a monetarist bent are fond of pointing to the overwhelming range of evidence for the proposition that money matters. It is an important, but often forgotten, point. Criticism of the monetarist interpretation of the Great Depression, for example, on the grounds that it is merely consistent with what happened, misses the point that the interpretation is based on principles that are consistent with a wide range of other evidence. Perhaps no single paper illustrates the range of that evidence more than Schwartz's famous paper, "Secular Price Trends in Historical Perspective" (1973). There she examined the relationship between long-term changes in money per unit of output and prices, over two-and-one-half millennia. It constitutes a powerful case for the quantity theory because the relationship holds over such a wide range of institutional relationships.

The paper also contains one of those conjectures that one might have expected to generate considerable interest. She notes one exception to the quantity theory: the sixteenth century currency manipulations, beginning with Henry the VIII's debasements and ending with the restoration of the currency under Elizabeth. Prices did not rise in proportion to the stock of money during the debasements and did not fall in proportion when the currency was called down. But as far as I know, no one has risen to the challenge this poses. It may be, as Schwartz suggests, that the expectation of further debasements (in effect, an expected capital gain on currency) increased the demand for money sufficiently to offset a good bit of the increase in the nominal supply during the debasements. During the restoration, expectations of a further calling down of the currency may have reduced the demand for money. Over the whole period of the debasements and restoration, it should be noted, prices rose in proportion to the nominal stock of money.

An important diversion in the paper on secular price trends concerned the role of cost-push explanations of inflation. This theme was taken up again in two papers written with Michael Bordo (1980, 1981). In these papers, Bordo and Schwartz examine the argument put forward by W. W. Rostow and W. A. Lewis that nineteenth century secular price movements could be attributed to changes in relative prices of major agricultural commodities rather than to monetary forces. They examine both the logic of the Rostow-Lewis argument and the evidence. Although their regressions showed some impact from a terms-of-trade variable on the price level, the dominant variable was the stock of money.

These papers, like the others I have noted, contain important conjectures for future research. Bordo and Schwartz note, for example, that for some purposes the monetary constitution itself may be regarded as an endogenous variable (1981, 118–19). Why was there such pressure to convert the world to the gold standard in the late nineteenth century? Was it related to changes in the demand for money that increased the welfare gain from a lower equilibrium rate of price change? No one, alas, has followed up on that suggestion.

Finally, let me mention one last paper that I have found extremely useful. This paper, "Real and Pseudo-Financial Crises" (Schwartz 1986), provides a helpful way of classifying financial disturbances. Real financial crises for Schwartz are those in which the payments mechanism is in danger. Other disturbances, even though painful asset price adjustment may be involved, are only pseudo-crises. Real crises alone, she argues, require central banks to act in the role of lender of last resort. Most of the paper uses this distinction to compare and contrast a number of financial crises, and to explore some current theories of crises. One implication, for me, is that the comparative study of crises, despite the long history of this line of research, is still likely to prove fruitful.

Conclusion

The pre-1867 period remains a fertile area for research. Anna Schwartz's papers are a good starting point for anyone entering this area. They show how a determined and imaginative use of the archives can pull out a surprising amount of data, and they provide a rich set of conjectures for future research.

Notes

1. In addition to the two pieces cited in the text, two others should be mentioned. The monumental study with A. D. Gayer and W. W. Rostow ([1952]

1975) produced a wide range of series describing the industrial revolution in Britain that have since become the mainstays of historical research. An appendix to the first volume of the U.S. Gold Commission *Report* (1982), a commission for which Anna Schwartz served as staff director, brings together an important set of data on gold production.

2. In another paper published in the same year, Schwartz (1947b) provided a detailed critique of Fritz Redlich's famous study of the origins of American commercial banking.

References

Bordo, Michael David, and Anna Jacobson Schwartz. 1977. Issues in monetary economics and their impact on research in economic history. In *Recent developments in the study of business and economic history: Essays in memory of Herman E. Krooss* (Research in Economic History, Supplement 1), ed. Robert E. Gallman, 81–129. Greenwich, Conn.: Johnson Associates.

———. 1980. Money and prices in the nineteenth century: An old debate rejoined. *The Journal of Economic History* 40 (March): 61–67.

———. 1981. Money and prices in the 19th century: Was Thomas Tooke right? *Explorations in Economic History* 18 (April): 97–121.

Friedman, Milton, and Anna J. Schwartz. 1970. *Monetary statistics of the United States.* New York: Columbia University Press, for the National Bureau of Economic Research.

Gayer, A. D., W. W. Rostow, and A. J. Schwartz. [1952] 1975. *The growth and fluctuation of the British economy, 1790–1850.* Oxford: Clarendon Press. 2d ed. Sussex: Harvester Press.

Kessel, Reuben, and Armen Alchian. 1959. Real wages in the north during the Civil War: Mitchell's data reinterpreted. *The Journal of Law and Economics* 2 (October): 95–113.

Mitchell, Wesley Claire. 1903. *A history of the greenbacks.* Chicago: University of Chicago Press.

Schwartz, Anna J. 1947a. The beginning of competitive banking in Philadelphia, 1782–1809. *Journal of Political Economy* 55 (October): 417–31.

———. 1947b. An attempt at synthesis in American banking history. *Journal of Economic History* 7 (November): 208–17.

———. 1960. Gross dividend and interest payments by corporations at selected dates in the nineteenth century. In *Trends in the American economy in the nineteenth century* (Studies in Income and Wealth, vol. 23), 407–45. New York: National Bureau of Economic Research.

———. 1973. Secular price change in historical perspective. *Journal of Money, Credit and Banking* 5, part 2 (February): 243–69.

———. 1986. Real and pseudo-financial crises. In *Financial crises in the world banking system*, eds. Forrest Capie and Geoffrey E. Wood, 11–31. New York: Macmillan.

Sylla, Richard. 1985. Early American banking: The significance of the corporate form. *Business and Economic History* 14 (March): 105–23.

U.S. Commission on the Role of Gold in the Domestic and International Monetary Systems. 1982. *Report to the Congress.* 2 vols. Washington, D.C.: Government Printing Office.

General Discussion

STEIN asked Friedman and Schwartz what substantive changes in emphasis and presentation they would make to A Monetary History in view of the criticisms raised in the past twenty-five years.

M. FRIEDMAN replied that children and books should be treated in the same way—you raise them and they have to live their own life. He (and Schwartz) expressed no interest whatsoever in redoing the book.

Friedman then discussed the criticisms of A Monetary History surveyed by Bordo. He made the point that Temin's attack on the monetary interpretation of the Great Depression was directed at the wrong target. The primary emphasis in A Monetary History was on the 1931–33 period, whereas Temin focussed on 1929–31. He was willing to accept the other substantive criticisms of the book or to believe that they have been amply demonstrated by others not to be valid.

Finally, Friedman reiterated the emphasis placed in A Monetary History on the two-way relationship between money and income. He felt that a major misinterpretation of that conclusion was the view that if income influences money, you do not have to worry about the further influence of money. He criticized much of current economic analysis for overemphasizing the distinction between exogenous and endogenous variables. The key question is the level of analysis engaged in. At a deep enough level, everything is endogenous. At a shallow level, everything is exogenous.

KOCHIN amplified Friedman's comment on the relationship between money and income. For Kochin, the key aim of A Monetary History was to find if the relationship of money to income was pretty much the same regardless of institutional regime, or of movements within the institutional regime. Indeed the overwhelming bulk of the NBER's money and business cycles project was devoted to three questions: does income influence money?; if so, by how much?; and is the influence of money on income independent of the influence that exists from income to money. Kochin expressed amazement that the criticism of A Monetary History ignored the possible influence of income on money.

MARTY asked Friedman and Schwartz whether it would have made a difference if the one-third decline in the money stock during 1929–33 had been inside rather than outside money.

M. FRIEDMAN pointed out that it was inside money that declined, and that outside money, i.e., high-powered money, rose in that period. He then described a research project he had worked on at the Federal Reserve Bank of San Francisco over a decade ago in which he attempted to test the proposition raised by Marty's question—that only outside money and not inside money ought to matter. If outside money should count, then high-powered money not adjusted for changes in reserve requirements should be more closely related to other variables than high-powered money adjusted for reserve requirements, because the adjustment for reserve requirements makes the resulting series a proxy for inside plus outside money. His results indicated the opposite—the inside money proxy was consistently and significantly superior to the outside money proxy. These findings, he felt, were puzzling because from a purely theoretical point of view what should matter is only that part of money on which holders earn zero interest.

POOLE argued that focus on outside rather than inside money seems equivalent to saying that financial intermediaries really do not do anything, whereas in fact they are able to successfully turn illiquid, non-marketable loans into demand deposits. He suggested that greater emphasis should be placed on a theory of intermediation.

M. FRIEDMAN amplified the argument leading him to emphasize high-powered money. It is that a perfect capital market implies a high degree of substitutability among interest-bearing assets. A deposit is a mixture of a non-interest-bearing asset and an interest-bearing asset. Only the non-interest-bearing asset is pure money. In a perfect capital market the interest-bearing asset would be a perfect substitute for others. Poole's point is that intermediaries exist because the capital market is highly imperfect. From that point of view, the appropriate definition of the monetary aggregate would be a weighted average of different asset types, where the weights are the fraction of each asset type that can be considered money as opposed to an asset. This was the type of measure favored by Friedman and Schwartz in *Monetary Statistics*.

CAGAN described recent Federal Reserve research on Divisia Indices to produce such an aggregate.

LAIDLER suggested that this discussion leads to the conclusion that it really matters that money is a medium of exchange.

M. FRIEDMAN agreed that it does matter that money is a medium of exchange. However, he had reservations about interpreting the medium-of-exchange function very narrowly. He emphasized that it also matters that money is an asset. Thus, he would treat money not just as a medium of exchange but as a capacity to discharge debts without creating a corresponding liability.

BRUNNER pointed out that outside money and high-powered money (the monetary base) were not equivalent. The analytic function of the concept is very different. The division into outside and inside money emerged with the specification of the Pigou effect. Outside money is a necessary, but marginal, component of the real wealth effect. The term has on many occasions, however, served a less useful function in money supply theory, particularly when large portions of the monetary base consist of inside money, as was the case during the early 1920s.

He also pointed out that when we discuss interest payments on various forms of money we should remember that the total yield of money is the sum of its marginal productivity plus the interest payment. He argued that whether interest is or is not paid on money makes little difference for explanations of money stock and bank credit and for the quality of monetary control, but it may make a difference in terms of efficiency. It was not immediately clear to him whether this result depends on the regulatory system.

MARTY clarified the question he raised at the conference. He was trying to get Friedman and Schwartz to comment on the position recently taken by Bernanke that the failure of the banks as financial intermediaries prolonged the depression of the 1930s in the United States, and that this failure of the intermediary function produced an effect over and above the reduction in the stock of money.

Marty agreed with Brunner and Meltzer's evaluation of the specific historical episode of the 1930s. Following Friedman and Schwartz, Brunner and Meltzer argued that an increase in high-powered money sufficient to offset the reduction in the money multiplier would have, in the main, eliminated the credit shock. However, Marty took issue with the generalizations made by them in their Mattiolli lectures, that in every case no independent shock to credit exists—rather, all such shocks were due to monetary causes. Postulating a totally outside money world, Marty constructed an example of an independent shock to credit that widened risk premiums and reduced (nonbank) financial intermediation.

M. FRIEDMAN, in a comment on Rockoff's paper, cited another case of an inflation that cannot be attributed to a monetary source—the Korean War inflation. It was the only inflation of substantial magnitude in the United States or anywhere else that was not preceded by a substantial increase in the quantity of money; it was purely a velocity inflation.

HETZEL asked Friedman and Schwartz if they had any further insights into the breakdown of a change in money into a change in real output and a change in the price level.

M. FRIEDMAN replied that they had not come up with a simple way of handling the issue.

ROSTOW described how in the Gayer-Rostow-Schwartz study the proportion of changes in money that supported increases in output and prices varied with the stage of the NBER reference-cycle chronology, in turn depending on the degree of capacity utilization in different sectors.

M. FRIEDMAN doubted the Keynesian emphasis on excess capacity. He stressed the role of price expectations in explaining the decomposition. However, he admitted how little progress had been made in resolving the issue.

2 Anna Schwartz's Perspective on British Economic History

Forrest H. Capie and Geoffrey E. Wood

A word that constantly crops up in a description of the work in which Anna Schwartz has shared is "monumental." It is certainly a word that comes to mind when considering *Growth and Fluctuation of the British Economy, 1790–1850: An Historical, Statistical, and Theoretical Study of Britain's Economic Development,* volumes 1 and 2 (1953), Anna Schwartz's first contribution to British economic history. Co-authored with Arthur Gayer and W. W. Rostow, this work was conceived, and largely researched and written, in the 1930s. It runs to over one thousand published pages and almost as many additional pages available on microfilm. It is a testament to its depth that it is still amongst the first works turned to in any investigation of the British economy in the first half of the nineteenth century. When the book first appeared in 1953 it was accepted as by far the most thorough study of the subject. That is still true. Arthur Gayer was the senior partner in the exercise; the idea grew out of his doctoral dissertation completed at Oxford in 1930. Anna Schwartz was, however, involved in the study from its beginning (1936) and did most of the basic data collection and statistical analysis. Walt Rostow joined the team in 1939 and was responsible for most of the historical narrative in part 1 of volume 1 and the general analysis in part 1 of volume 2. It was originally planned in five volumes, but wartime delays, and probably rises in publication costs, resulted in it appearing as two volumes only, with remaining material available on microfilm.

Growth and Fluctuation unearthed, gathered, and collated every available statistical series on the British economy, and constructed

Forrest H. Capie is a professor of economic history at City University, London. Geoffrey E. Wood is a professor of economics at City University, London.

several new ones—around two hundred series in total, all at least on an annual basis and some monthly: data on output, prices, trade, finance, labor, and other variables. It is an extraordinary work.

Amongst the most notable data contributions were new price series for domestic and imported commodities. The Gayer-Rostow-Schwartz (GRS) indices are still widely used and the names run together so easily in this connection that every student of British economic history is familiar with them.[1]

The data are subjected to the full panoply of the National Bureau techniques (put through the Bureau's "special mincing machine" as one reviewer put it, although it was not a Bureau product), and set within the framework that shaped so much work of the 1930s and 1940s: specific cycles and reference cycles are measured and chronicled. Each cycle is explored on a year-to-year basis. Interest is concentrated on cyclical fluctuations and on price movements. A distinction is made between major cycles—"cycles marked in their expansion phases by large increases in long-term investment" (1953, 33)—and minor cycles, usually associated with monetary changes, and, in the upswing, with export growth.

When the book appeared in 1953, twenty years had elapsed since its conception and more than a decade lay between its completion and its publication. In spite of that it was, as noted above, hailed as the most detailed study of the subject. Arthur Gayer died before the work was published and in an addendum to his preface, Rostow and Schwartz took the opportunity to reflect that if the work were being written in the 1950s, it might well be done differently. (The irony is that the hinted-at revised interpretation would have had a Keynesian slant.) But one good reason for leaving it as it was, they argued, was that the data and the statistical analysis both held and were worth publishing as they stood. Other researchers could then use these and draw different conclusions.

Rostow and Schwartz noted, in a brief survey of the economic history literature of the 1940s, that the general historical interpretation had not changed greatly. In economic theory, though, there had been some major developments, notably Keynes's analysis of short-period income fluctuations, and different approaches to long-run dynamic problems. The authors accepted that the changes in income analysis could well have influenced the character of their interpretation. However, the interpretation that had been written in the 1930s they left alone. In this interpretation they did not distinguish between real and nominal interest rates, and they accepted that central banks could control interest rates and that these in turn could influence private business investment spending, which in turn affected aggregate income.

Interestingly, Sir Alec Cairncross (1954), not noted for his emphasis on monetary explanations, in his review of the first edition was critical of the lack of consideration given to monetary causes:

> These minor cycles of the late 'twenties and early 'thirties seem quite plainly to have petered out because of dear money. Indeed, it may be ventured as a generalization that the surest sign of an approaching depression was a rise in the market rate of discount above the yield on consols. Throughout the entire period between 1834 and 1842 there was only a single year (1838) in which the market rate of discount averaged less than the yield on consols. How then can it be said that the money supply was ample? (p. 562)

Aside from criticisms of interpretation such as this, the work was generally enthusiastically received as a "remarkable work of collaborative scholarship" (Imlah 1953).

Evidence of the continuing demand for the book was the appearance of a new edition in 1975. Rostow and Schwartz again took the opportunity to review some of the intervening literature, though only a fraction of the great explosion in the literature impinged directly on the original themes. Interest had shifted in the 1950s and 1960s, as Rostow and Schwartz had in 1953 predicted it would, to long-run growth.

However, on the interpretation of the facts in the original volumes a gulf, described in the 1975 preface as an "amicable divergence of view," had opened up between the two authors. Anna Schwartz indicated that she had, in the light of recent theoretical and empirical research—much of it her own work with Milton Friedman—revised her view of: the role given to monetary policy, the interpretation of the behavior of interest rates, and the difference between *relative* price changes and changes in the *general* price level. She gives a succinct summary of the state of monetary theory in the mid-1970s, and drawing on empirical findings, mainly from post-1865 U.S. experience, suggests that British experience in the period 1790–1850 should not have differed greatly. However, the lack of aggregate monetary data for the period made it impossible to establish this contention, although the type of evidence already alluded to by Cairncross suggested she was correct.

The emphasis on relative prices and the cost explanation that was offered in the original study by GRS failed, she now insisted, to account for price level movements: "Changes in relative prices tell us nothing about changes in the price level" (p. xii). Rises in costs were associated with poor harvests and other difficulties in supply conditions: "These factors are highly relevant to the price of one item *relative* to the price of others. But, for movements in general prices, the cost explanation begs the question of the source of the autonomous increase or decrease in costs'' (p. xii). Thus, while the views that were offered in the original study were not attributable to Anna Schwartz alone, she wanted, in 1975, explicitly to distance herself from the cost-push explanation. Rostow, however, stated that he held to the views contained in the first edition, and did not accept the distinction between individual and general price analysis. He maintained that the monetary system played a passive role and that this was always true—and, therefore, inevitably so—for Britain in this period.

In spite of these surely substantial differences of view, the preface goes on to say that while the alternative analytical framework would not affect the validity of the basic research, it would alter ''the cast'' of the analysis, and ''would entail revision of some of the conclusions'' (p. xiii). Of course, consideration of the long-run trend in output would not be affected since real output growth is affected only by real factors.

When Anna Schwartz was summing up her reservations in the preface, she effectively threw out a challenge to others to take up the different analytical framework and reinterpret the original data. This has not yet been done in any systematic way, perhaps for reasons set out below in the discussion of business cycles.

The criticisms of the book that would be made today are understandable, and made only with hindsight. First, the data. For a work with ''growth'' in the title we would immediately think in terms of the rate of change of an aggregate measure of output. However, as yet this still does not exist for this period and discussion is limited. Furthermore, there are gaps in the data that have arisen from the change in emphasis. For example, we would invariably seek an export/output ratio in any discussion of Britain's economic experience since the external account was always important. (Though again, the lack of an aggregate output series precludes any such construction.) Secondly, advances in econometrics mean that much of the statistical analysis could now be greatly refined. (It is here that the argument for the publication of the original data reemerges. If they were readily accessible, a lot more work could be done by the young computer historians.) And thirdly, advances in theory would lead to the investigations of quite different lines of enquiry, often along lines indicated by Schwartz in her prefatory remarks to the 1975 edition.

2.1 The Business Cycle

As noted above, one of the reviewers, Cairncross (1954), suggested that money should have been given a larger role in the explanation of business cycles than it had been given by GRS. At first sight it may seem surprising that it was not, surprising not simply in the light of Schwartz's later work, but in view of the possibilities of the time. By

1914 all the principal ideas and most of the data on the trade cycle had been set out.[2] Juglar (1889) had provided the basic information and statistical analysis of time series, estimating periodicity and identifying turning points. And by the 1920s a monetary theory of the cycle was certainly a prominent explanation. For example, Hawtrey (1913) saw the business cycle as "a purely monetary phenomenon." Changes in money were a sole and sufficient cause of changes in income. Furthermore, an inspiration for GRS was Mitchell, and he had set out in his organizing survey of problems and materials (1927) the state of the main lines of explanation, including an extensive discussion of monetary factors.

However, it is important to remember that a prominent view of objective enquiry at this time demanded that the data be gathered first, that measurement should then follow, and that theory be brought to bear later—indeed, in part, was suggested by the first two.[3]

Given the closeness of this project to Mitchell (the authors talked to Mitchell and Burns frequently), it is not surprising that the essential elements of GRS's implicit model are those found in Mitchell's writings. Mitchell's views were essentially eclectic, but the general ideas are as follows.

Beginning in a depression, conditions are produced that are favorable to an upswing: costs have fallen and that allows profit margins to begin to rise, inventories are low and require boosting, banks are more willing to lend as their reserves are rising, and so on. These give rise to a cumulative increase in income, increased investment, bank lending, etc., until finally, under a "slow accumulation of stresses," this process is brought to an end and then there is a downward cumulative process. This account was one that gave the main emphasis to businessmen and their expectations, and emphasized the complexity of business conditions and the inability to see the future at all clearly.

Keynes narrowed the emphasis to a few macro variables: income, consumption, saving, and investment. Mitchell, in contrast, did not accept that the key to fluctuations was to be found in a few aggregate variables; and yet, they were not entirely opposed for, in the end, Keynes believed that incentives to invest depended "on the uncontrollable and disobedient psychology of the business world" (1936, 317). Keynes saw cycles deriving from fluctuations in investment which in turn came from fluctuations in the marginal efficiency of capital, and that depended upon changes in the rate of *expected* future returns on current investment. In booms there is an overoptimistic view of future returns and that leads to investment increasing too rapidly.

In contrast, for those like Hawtrey who stressed monetary factors, the primary actor in the process was the banking system. For Hawtrey it was the banks expanding credit that led to the increased money supply and hence increased total spending. Lower interest rates followed, inducing firms initially to expand inventories, leading to rising income and on, cumulatively, to the point where banks halted lending as their reserves ran down too low.

Work on money and the cycle has of course now been done by Anna Schwartz (in collaboration with Milton Friedman in, for example, "Money and Business Cycles" [1963a]), but for many years the role of money in business cycles was the subject of little attention. This has changed recently. There has been a flood of literature on business cycle theory.[4] Much of this theory has been rather different from that which was general, although certainly not universal, at the time Gayer, Rostow, and Schwartz were at work.[5] But GRS inclined rather, as indicated above, to the competing line in cycle theory, when they did come to theory, that derived from overinvestment. The central idea, arising from the fact that producer goods industries were more affected by the cycle, was that changes in the production of consumer goods (which came from changes in demand) gave rise to greater changes in production of producer goods: "the acceleration and magnification of derived demand." It is worth commenting here that it was changes in demand that were the source of all explanations. This had to be the case since all the variables (money, prices, output, etc.) moved in the same direction. Only changes in demand could produce this. And yet, there is a difficulty here: while this holds for a view of the nominal cycle, the whole direction of the work was cast in real terms, i.e., it was business activity and what business was doing that was of interest.

The basis of the theory in GRS lies in the long gestation period for fixed investment and the secular growth of demand. At the start of an upswing there is excess capacity. Hence (and also because a sustained rise in profits is awaited) there is a long delay before investment rises. But the catching up of demand with capacity is going on all the time. Profits start to recover, supported by the rise in exports. The latter characterized all the major upswings, but is clearly not part of the theory of the cycle.

At length, investment starts to take place. Additions to capacity are by their nature in large units, and there is a long gestation period. As all firms operate under a similar stimulus, all firms respond, taking no account of each other's actions. There is thus excess capacity, which slows investment in the *next* recovery. But that is not what brings the recession. The turning point depends not on a fall of profits resulting from the introduction of new equipment, but "on the consequences for costs of relatively full employment. . . ." (1953, 557).

Note this is not a multiplier/accelerator theory, for there need not be (although there can be) a fluctuation in final demand. Money does enter, but only through the observation that interest rates generally rose in booms.

One of the reviewers, R. C. O. Matthews (1954), raised some objections to this theory, but these objections did not hint at the developments to come. Rather they were concerned with the behavior of individual time series relative to the cycle as a whole. Of most general interest are his comments on speculation. Many of the booms were characterized by "manias" (1954, 106). Such "manias" only took hold when trade was prosperous, and the collapse of speculative bubbles then started the downturn. And as "any purely speculative movement is a highly unstable phenomenon" (p. 101), even a modest rise in interest rates would be sufficient to prick the bubble and end the boom.

Gayer, Rostow, and Schwartz place great importance on exports as starting booms. There was a strong upward trend to these (due to the expansion of world population and rising real incomes, together with a secular fall in Britain's export prices).[6] Matthews (1954) expressed some reservations about this, but concluded that the data did not permit a clear-cut conclusion. In summary, then, GRS had an accelerator-based theory of the cycle, with secular demand growth combining with investment's gestation period, the lumpiness of investment, and investors' lack of foresight, to produce a cycle.

Keynes was not solely responsible for the focus on the role of investment and saving in cyclical fluctuations. Indeed, there was a long history that embodied this approach, dating at least from 1900, and GRS can be said to have drawn at least implicitly on that. Expectations had also long played a part in business cycle theory, having been present in some form in the earliest theories. They are present in GRS in a stronger form, but it is fair to say that only after the 1950s and 1960s did they come to dominate.

The change to the kind of theory now in fashion has its origins in a suggestion by Hayek (1933) summarized in the following quotation:

> The incorporation of cyclical phenomena into the system of economic equilibrium theory, with which they are in apparent contradiction, remains the crucial problem of trade cycle theory. (p. 33n)

Robert Lucas ([1977] 1981) has sought to meet this challenge. In his 1977 paper, he set out some common characteristics of business cycles, and on the basis of these concluded that "business cycles are all alike." He then discussed modelling this regular pattern. Keynesian models of the cycle—the multiplier/accelerator is a good example—had, he argued, no role for money and had households, for arbitrary reasons, *choosing* "to supply labor at sharply irregular rates through time" (p. 218). This, as Lucas observes, is puzzling, for since the recurrent pattern of cycles allows rational forecasting, subjective probabilities can be identified with actual probabilities. Hence, quantity movements should be explained as "optimizing responses to movements in prices" (p. 222). Here Friedman and Schwartz come in. Secular movements in prices are due to secular movements in money. "This fact is as well established as any we know in aggregative economics. . . ." (p. 232). The evidence Lucas cites for this is Friedman and Schwartz (1963a).

Since money triggers price movements, money must be at the heart of the cycle. How, in view of the weak money-price link in the short run? *Because* of the weakness of that link; because the theory set out rests on the difficulty of telling relative from general price movements.

This line of attack is currently out of favor, not on theoretical grounds, but because of what is believed to be the implausible assumption that individuals cannot tell relative from absolute price changes, even a substantial time after they have occurred. McCallum (1986) notes that this assumption may be plausible for earlier periods, and suggests this contrast may help explain the fact that the amplitude of business cycles is smaller than it used to be. The problem with this interesting conjecture is that it may fit the United States, but certainly does not fit the experience of at least some other countries.

Business cycle research currently follows two main directions: real business cycles and sticky price business cycles. Real business cycle theories play down monetary influences. Money has no significance for real output and employment in the strong form of the theory. (There is also what may be called a "weak form," in which both money and technological shocks affect output.) This conclusion is reached partly by unhappiness with the Lucas theory, partly by evidence that seems to suggest no effect of money on output, and partly by the Nelson-Plosser (1982) argument that most fluctuations in aggregate variables are in the trend component, and that should be unaffected by monetary shocks. But, as McCallum (1986) says, the evidence is not persuasive. On statistical grounds McCallum rejects the Nelson-Plosser argument. Tests which claim to have ruled out any impact of money on output have ignored the money supply process. (They assume base control in a period of interest rate setting.) Hence the positive support for the real business cycle falls away and it is left depending on unhappiness with the Lucas-proposed alternative.

There is a clear link between the work of GRS and the most recent work on business cycles. GRS's study was of growth and fluctuations, and an implication was that there was great difficulty in separating trend and cycle. That difficulty was explicitly recognized in the 1950s and 1960s. Cyclical forces affect the trend, and the kind of trend that is eliminated affects the resulting fluctuations. As Robert Gordon put it, "it is better not to think of business cycles as fluctuating around any 'normal' level. . . . There is no justification for regarding the secular movements as a path of moving equilibrium, around which cyclical fluctuations take place" (1961, 256).

Nevertheless, despite this link we have come a long way from Gayer, Rostow, and Schwartz (and their reviewers and immediate successors). It should be observed, though, that in one respect they are well ahead of current developments. Real business cycle theories, driven by technological shocks, should surely have a close connection, as GRS posit, between growth and cycles. In fact real business cycle theories do not as yet do so; most business cycle models describe an economy with a stationary mean. But on the other hand, within these new models individuals cannot persist in their mistakes. The kind of repeated errors by businessmen that GRS relied on are not now allowed in formal models. Further, in many models, money has a dominant role, not the modest one they hinted it may have had at the upper turning point. It is also noteworthy that these advances in theory are advances in a special sense. We know more only in the sense that we know we know less than we once thought we did; there is no longer a widely accepted theory of the cycle around which historical research can be organized. Although Gayer, Rostow, and Schwartz did not point to this conclusion, it was led to by their demonstration of the repetitive nature of cycles.

Something that remains to be said, and has not to our knowledge been said before, is that this work deserves to stand as perhaps *the* pioneering work in British, and possibly any, econometric history. There used to be a sport of trying to identify the birth of the cliometric movement, and since much of the activity went on in the United States, Conrad and Meyer's *The Economics of Slavery in the Antebellum South* (1958) usually featured, while some British names such as Cairncross and Matthews sometimes got a mention. *Growth and Fluctuation* predates them all. It is the kind of blend of history, statistics, and economic analysis that is still aimed for by those who think of themselves as "new" economic historians. It gathers the essential data, subjects them to the most sophisticated statistical techniques available, and employs economic analysis in their interpretation. As Victor Morgan said at the time: "The present volumes certainly form one of the most solid and useful exercises in the interpretation of history by means of economic analysis that have yet appeared" (1954, 860).

2.2 Monetary Trends

Some thirty years after first working on British economic history, Anna Schwartz returned to the subject. The main product of this return was *Monetary Trends in the United States and the United Kingdom, 1875–1975* (1982), co-authored with Milton Friedman.[7] As the authors explain in their preface (pp. xxviii–xxix), a draft of the book was "submitted tentatively to an NBER reading committee" in 1966. This reading committee suggested broadening the coverage "to include the United Kingdom and perhaps other countries." Note that *Monetary Trends* was not published until 1982. Again to quote Friedman and Schwartz, "We understand how much of a start the earlier three volumes [i.e., *Monetary Statistics* (1970), *Monetary History* (1963b), and Phillip Cagan's *Determinants* (1965)] had given us for the United States analysis of this area. . . ." They express regret over the delay, and say that ". . . in retrospect we probably made a mistake in accepting the reading committee's suggestion."

That judgment is one with which it is hard to agree. *Monetary Trends* was received with considerable excitement in Britain, almost immediately manifested by a number of lengthy reviews, a conference at the Bank of England, and working papers prompted by some of these initial reactions. And perhaps most important of all, the volume raised a large number of questions about British monetary history.[8]

It is useful now to consider the questions raised in a little detail. To do so we examine first the reviews, and then the Bank of England conference and its aftermath.

2.2.1   The Reviews

In his review, David Laidler (1982) paid particular attention to the findings for the United Kingdom. He did, however, start with some perceptive remarks about the statistical method and the underlying model, remarks which are worth sketching here because they remind us of the so-called disequilibrium money tradition pioneered in this century by Clark Warburton (1950), in which Friedman and Schwartz can be interpreted as working. (We say "so-called" because a better name would focus on the distinction between short- and long-run equilibria, and would also avoid confusion with the buffer stock approach which has been called a disequilibrium money approach by Charles Goodhart. The above name does, however, seem to be the generally accepted one.) Laidler places the book in a long-established intellectual tradition. He remarks initially that *Monetary Trends* can be viewed as summing up the National Bureau's work on U.S. monetary history and opening up such work in the United Kingdom. It sums up work on the United States because many of the preliminary questions that should be answered before conclusions for that country are finally established were answered in one of the previous three volumes. It opens up work on the United Kingdom because of the ground it clears and because of the large number of subsequent questions it prompts. Before turning to these and to why they emerge, it is worth noting that Laidler, in commenting on the econometric techniques used, writes that "The econometrics *per se* never relies on anything more complex than least squares estimators. . . . The ratio of human intelligence to computer time that has gone into the production of this book is, that is to say, refreshingly high" (p. 251). This is important in that some of the initial discussions paid great attention to econometrics, and, as Laidler suggests might be the case, the outcome was far from being that a higher ratio of computer time to intelligence would unequivocally have been a good thing.

The book *is* about trends, and is to some degree concerned with establishing the long-run validity of the quantity theory's neutrality propositions. This theory contrasts with a view of the world where the demand for money is always unstable, disturbances principally originate on the real side of the economy, and the price level is either given exogenously or endogenously determined by a Phillips curve, and is, in any event, unimportant in producing equilibrium. This is in sharp contrast to the view that a major driving force in the economy is a gap between desired and actual real balances, and that this gap, although it may produce real effects, produces only transitory ones and permanently affects only the price level.

The analytical model of this book is not Keynesian—interest rates do not move to clear the money market—nor what has become known as new-classical (now a shorthand term for continuous market clearing). Rather it is one in which an excess supply of nominal (and initially real) money drives nominal income. We can for a time be off the long-run demand curve for real cash balances. Despite that, a money demand function can be estimated. The basic unit of observation in *Monetary Trends* is the cycle phase, and that is sufficiently long for transitory disturbances to work themselves out. (This is an important point, to which we turn below.) The demand for money function estimated on cycle-phase–by–cycle-phase data then shows striking stability and, indeed, a perhaps even more striking similarity between the United Kingdom and the United States.[9]

These results established, Friedman and Schwartz go on to report that they find no support for the existence of a Phillips curve or, indeed, in the United Kingdom *any* effect of money on real income. There we come to a finding that should surely generate further work. Their study demonstrates that money supply changes have little, if any, effect on real income over a cycle phase. This leaves open—or, perhaps, opens up—the question of what the effect may be within the cycle. Is there an effect? Is it stable? Or is it, perhaps, a product of particular money supply regimes where it is rational, albeit maybe ultimately wrong, to expect a stable, or at any rate a very sluggish, price level?[10]

Initial reaction to this result was not well-conceived. The result was thought to be surprising, apparently because many readers took it as saying something about what occurred *within* a cycle. In fact while, as remarked above, it does direct attention to what goes on within a cycle, it tells one about what happens *over* a cycle—quite a different matter. Viewed that way, the result should not have been a surprise. In his 1972 study, for example, Phillip Cagan found that income responded to monetary fluctuations and this offset the initial impact of money on nominal interest rates well within a cycle phase. To quote,

> The estimated pattern [of lag coefficients] indicates that monetary effects on aggregate expenditures are quite rapid. In table 7-3 the cumulative effect reaches unity six months after the initial change in monetary growth. Unity is the total long-run effect. There is overshooting, however, and the cumulative effect settles back close to unity by the eighteenth month. (pp. 110–11)

Despite this, Charles Goodhart was so surprised by the finding that he sought to replicate it over what he called the "raw" data—that is to say, the basic annual data—and found it confirmed. This *is* a striking finding. How can it be explained? It certainly requires explanation, for it is notably at variance with, for example, Attfield, Demery, and Duck's 1981 paper which found that over the years 1963–78, unanticipated money did affect output in the United Kingdom.

David Laidler, in his review of Friedman and Schwartz, advanced an explanation of the result which, although perhaps redundant to the cycle-phase finding, is certainly worth discussion when Goodhart's result is noted. His argument turned on the openness of the U.K. economy. Suppose that there is an increase in the nominal quantity of money. This rise in the money-income ratio would be expected to stimulate output. But it is prevented from doing so by a devaluation of sterling which, by the law of one price, quickly affects the U.K. price level and results in the *real* stock of money being, for all practical purposes, unaffected by the change in the nominal quantity. There would thus be a rise in the nominal quantity of money and in the price level, but no transitory rise in the real quantity of money and thus in output.

"A few observations like this could easily swamp a weak tendency for money and output to be positively correlated elsewhere in a time series. . . ." (1982, 253). This may explain the Goodhart finding, but it still leaves problems. It does not really fit the episode examined in Williamson and Wood (1976), in which it is reported that, in the particular episode studied, output growth and inflation were *both* produced by monetary expansion and preceded the ultimate devaluation. Nor does it accord with Attfield, Demery, and Duck (1981) where at any rate, unanticipated money seemed to affect output.

It is useful to turn next to the *Journal of Economic Literature* reviewers. Of the three 1982 *JEL* reviews, one (Mayer) focused on the United States, one (Hall) focused on what was not in the book, and one (Goodhart) was subtitled "A British View." It should be noted that the last was a British view written from the British central bank, for it places emphasis on institutional and operational matters which Friedman and Schwartz ignore. But it also dealt with, and raised, wider issues. Some of these overlap with those raised by Laidler (1982), but others, notably a stimulating discussion of the data, do not and are considered here first.

Friedman and Schwartz converted their data to cycle-phase averages. (This is turned to again below when we consider some econometric issues.) Goodhart (1982) suggests that although there are advantages from Friedman and Schwartz's point of view, the loss—such as the inability to use Granger-Sims techniques—outweighs the gain. This is more likely an example of the data being organized for the tests, for the method is well suited to a "disequilibrium money" approach (in the Warburton, rather than the Goodhart sense—see p. 88 above). Rather more important are the adjustments made to income and price data to take account of price controls. The importance of these lies in their novelty; no substantial study of the effect of price controls in the United Kingdom precedes Friedman and Schwartz's work. Here, however, they already have followers. Rockoff and Mills (1986) have carried out a comparative study of U.K. and U.S. wartime experience, while Capie and Wood (1988) and Capie, Pradhan, and Wood (1989) have written papers concerned with Second World War and 1960s price controls in the United Kingdom. (The 1988 study fully supports the findings of Friedman and Schwartz, but lays stress on factors additional to price controls, particularly the wartime rationing system, while the 1989 paper suggests controls to be somewhat less effective than Friedman and Schwartz find.)

Goodhart's (1982) comments on the money demand function—what interest rate or rates to use, and so forth—do not open up fresh territory, but in his examination of the money-output connection he draws attention to a whole range of issues. As noted earlier, Goodhart redid the statistical work on the money-output relationship. He did it on the "raw" data—i.e., the unsmoothed annual data—and found that the U.K. evidence is *"consistent* with the monetarist view" (p. 1546, Goodhart's italics). Now of course the result he finds has nothing to do with the "monetarist view." Insofar as such a thing can be identified, it relates to long-run results. If the long run turns out to be a year, then so be it, but it is no part of monetarism that it has to be. Nevertheless, reflecting on that finding, Goodhart raised some interesting questions.

In regressions with the rate of change of prices as the dependent variable, the main explanatory variables are contemporaneous money growth (lagged money for 1946–75) and the lagged dependent variable. But drawing from his experience in a central bank, and drawing also on some prior work of Friedman's, Goodhart suggests that interest rate setting induces procyclical money stock variation, so that *current* inflation affects *current* money growth (and current interest rates). There may, therefore, be simultaneity. Dropping current variables on these grounds then allows past output growth, as well as past money growth, to affect inflation. What are we to make of this?

Goodhart suggests that questions of endogeneity and simultaneity need to be considered, as they were for the United States in the prior volumes of this series. That recommendation is wise; some of the work is now being done, and more surely will be. But that is not all that can be said. If today's income growth causes today's money growth, then yesterday's income caused yesterday's money. Hence it may well be that the effect of yesterday's income on inflation is spurious, or rather, the result of it causing money growth. Thus inflation could well be purged of any causal impetus from output. In summary, what Charles Goodhart's arguments do is *not* refute the conclusions of Friedman and Schwartz on the impact of money on prices and output, but strengthen the case for a short-term analysis, and provide some initial hypotheses to be explored.

Goodhart also suggests that the exchange rate regime may be important; with a fixed exchange rate, money growth may respond to output growth. Goodhart says Friedman and Schwartz consider and reject this. Surely a misreading; they argue that regardless of the source of the money growth, the money growth will have subsequent effects. (This is stated particularly clearly in fn. 10, p. 319, and fn. 14, p. 325.)[11] But although a misreading, it is a potentially fruitful one, in that it directs attention to the various sources of money growth and prompts study of whether the source affects the *speed* of impact. (As Friedman 1979 suggested was possible.)

Goodhart also directs attention to the possibility that the United Kingdom has not experienced severe enough monetary fluctuations to show a "strong statistical relationship between money growth and output growth" (p. 1548).[12] He conjectures that this is due to the benevolent and efficient stabilization policy of the Bank of England. There is, however, another interpretation which he hints at, and comparison of the two is certainly worthy of serious study. The other interpretation is that this better monetary policy resulted from different institutional structures. This may be correct. The episode when money most clearly affected output in the United States was the Great Depression, when the Federal Reserve System failed to act as a lender of last resort. As

Anna Schwartz has pointed out, no such failure has occurred in the United Kingdom since 1866 (1986). The idea that large monetary fluctuations affect output while small ones do not—or, at any rate, not enough to show up in econometric results—seems to fit the facts. But if only large monetary changes affect output, why this is so is still an unanswered question.[13]

Turning next to interest rates, *Monetary Trends* contains (in addition to a masterly exposition of the interaction of money growth with interest rates), a reexamination of the Gibson paradox and a closely connected analysis of price expectations formation. As Goodhart (1982) points out, while Friedman and Schwartz provide most cogent explanations of why interest rates should not (until recently) have adapted to inflation—explanations based on the nature of the monetary standard and the temporary nature of most inflations—these explanations are better suited to explaining long rates than short rates. The behavior of short rates remains a puzzle.[14]

Before considering what *Monetary Trends* provoked at the Bank of England, two other reviews are worth noting as raising interesting points. As was observed by Friedman and Schwartz in their preface, the U.S. content of *Monetary Trends* was underpinned by an extensive body of analysis on numerous issues. One of these was the determination of the money stock. They had not carried out such a detailed preliminary study for the United Kingdom. This was taken up by Tim Congdon in a 1983 review in *The Banker* unprecedented in length for that magazine, an indication in itself of the importance attached to the book. The review is both puzzling and interesting. Its starting point is that Friedman and Schwartz "fail to recognize that the money supply is itself the result of an economic process" (p. 117). What Congdon means is that the institutional setting within which the money stock is determined differs between the United Kingdom and the United States, and that he thinks they should take account of this. His concern was not, however, with the main substance of the book, for he acknowledged that what he saw as an omission would not affect trends. Rather he argued that as the Bank of England set interest rates and supplied whatever money was demanded at that rate, Friedman and Schwartz's account of short-term money income relationships and short-run interest rate movements was likely to be wrong. Again, in a different form, a complaint which some other reviewers had made: that the book really was about trends, as its title implied.

Congdon (1983) is also to some degree misleading, for his description of the Bank's procedure is accurate only for a limited part of the period.[15] Nevertheless, he does direct attention to several important areas of research which can be built on the work in *Monetary Trends*. The first is one which has been, and is being, developed extensively by Anna Schwartz: the role of the lender of last resort, and how the central bank carries out this role. As she has described (1986), the Bank of England took on this task in the nineteenth century. After 1866, the British banking system was much more stable than the American, and there was in Britain no collapse in the money stock such as triggered the Great Depression. This demonstration that institutions do matter raises interesting and important questions. Why did the Bank of England take on the lender-of-last-resort role, and did its acceptance affect its day-to-day behavior in the money markets?

These questions have been examined in a recently completed Ph.D. thesis (Ogden 1988). The answer to the first question is not simple, for the process was gradual and seems to have been the result of numerous influences inside and outside the Bank, and of personality clashes and their resolutions; it was not a straightforward response to the recognition of a responsibility. The answer to the second question, as given by a close examination of the daily discount figures, is however a straightforward and unqualified negative.

On the question of central bank operating procedures, does it matter for the behavior of interest rates if central banks conduct monetary policy by interest rate setting? As Friedman and Schwartz have argued and demonstrated several times (in *Monetary Trends* and elsewhere), once money is in the economic system, it does its work, regardless of how it got there. It is hard to believe that this does not apply to long-term rates regardless of central bank operating procedures. But what of short-term rates? If a central bank sets a short-term rate and supplies whatever money is necessary to hold that rate, then that rate and other rates linked to it, will very likely respond differently from how they would have behaved had there been a similar amount of money supplied without pegging the rate. The short-run dynamics of short-term rates probably are affected by the central bank's money stock control procedure. Confirmation of this would be of interest in itself, and would also resolve some puzzles over the behavior of short-term rates in periods of high inflation, such as the First World War when, contrary to its pre-war procedure, the Bank did engage in interest rate stabilization.[16]

Finally, in examining issues prompted by reviews of *Monetary Trends*, we move to the stability of the money demand function Friedman and Schwartz estimate. This is considered more extensively below, but it should be remarked that in a brief review Michael Artis (1983, 461) described Friedman and Schwartz as "straining for effect" in finding a function which fitted the United Kingdom throughout their data period. He was not particularly surprised by stability of the function; he had (with Mervyn Lewis) found a function that was stable over long periods. But stability for *so* long seemed to him a puzzle. Indeed, and partly because of the role of dummies in the money demand function, there remained a suspicion that the interwar years were special and that "Keynes was generalizing from an idiosyncratic episode" (Friedman and Schwartz 1982, 622).[17] The results Friedman and Schwartz obtain for these years suggest that the intensive study of the interwar years which is now under way will not only help understanding of these years, but also help clarify whether the *General Theory* should be retitled—perhaps *A Special Theory . . .*[18]

2.2.2 The Bank of England Conference

Some institutional information is now in order. The Bank of England from time to time convenes a meeting of a "Panel of Academic Consultants." This panel comprises not an unchanging group but individuals invited to attend according to the subject being discussed. They meet, together with Bank of England and Treasury staff, to discuss two previously circulated papers on a theme chosen by the Bank. The Bank convened such a meeting to discuss *Monetary Trends,* and the two papers presented, along with a brief introduction by Robin Matthews, were published by the Bank of England in 1983.

In his introduction, Matthews made five points, all worth repeating—one because of the foresight it displayed, and the others because, extracted from the discussion, they reveal in their overlap with reviewers' remarks the homogeneity of the reactions the book provoked. Matthews drew attention to the publication delay which had made some of the results of the book confirmations rather than first demonstrations. Second, he remarked on the absence of institutional discussion (but did not, like some others, suggest why it might be important). He raised questions of causal direction in an open economy, thus agreeing with Friedman and Schwartz about the underpinning of the U.S. section. Like Artis (1983), he asked whether the observed money demand stability over such an extraordinary period was not perhaps more than was required. And, on the econometric results of one of the Bank papers, he (presciently as it turned out) hazarded the judgment that the final word was not yet in.

What did the papers have to add to that? The first paper to be discussed, and first in the Bank's publication, was by Arthur Brown (1983). All the other reactions to *Monetary Trends,* broadly speaking, accepted its main results and suggested developments that could be set against the background thus established. Brown attempted to reject these results. In doing so he paid perhaps a greater tribute to the work of Friedman and Schwartz than did any more well-disposed reviewer. For it is largely due to their work (and that of others prompted by them) that the view of the world which Brown attempts to defend seems "a bit obsolete," to borrow a phrase Laidler used in his review; and, it should be added, so far as guiding future research is concerned, guides it only to a dead end.

It is a view in which velocity is an irrelevance (p. 13–14), "cost push" is an important cause of inflation (p. 26), and the Phillips curve provides a permanent tradeoff and stable basis for policy (p. 24). British inflation is often imported (in contrast with Williamson and Wood 1976), and has little to do with money growth. There is well exemplified what has been called "adding up economics"—explaining a movement in some aggregate, e.g., national income, as due to its biggest or fastest moving component (house building, for example, p. 33, and again, p. 34, where long-term growth, which presumably has something to do with supply, "is attributable to the fact that growth depended on foreign demand"). There is even the traditional confusion between relative prices and the general price level: "All these outstanding price changes are associated with changes in foreign trade prices. . . ." (p. 35).

The conclusions of the paper are summarized as answers to a series of questions (pp. 40–43). There we find all the points noted above, together with the extraordinary statement that "Strict truth of a simple quantity theory implies that velocity is constant. . . ." Friedman and Schwartz have consigned to works on the history of thought many of the views set out by Arthur Brown. But with this statement, scope for fresh research emerges. How can a view, adamantly rejected by that distinguished quantity theorist Henry Thornton in 1802, persist in being repeated and believed over a century and a half later?

Finally, in work prompted by *Monetary Trends* we come to an econometric study. This was by David Hendry and Neil Ericsson (HE) (1983).[19] Their paper made two points: Friedman and Schwartz had used "old-fashioned" econometrics, and, when modern econometric techniques were applied to their data, a money demand function stable over their whole period cannot be found.[20] The first point is correct, but should certainly be viewed as a factual statement rather than a criticism. What surely needs to be considered is not the vintage of the techniques, but whether they are appropriate for the data and whether they give reliable results.

Setting these points aside, however, how did the econometric criticisms stand up? The answer has to be that the criticisms are not well directed. HE engaged in extensive data mining and, although claiming to reject the Friedman and Schwartz equation, in fact do not really do so. Rather, they reject an equation which omits a demographic variable and the own rate on money—which Friedman and Schwartz regard as important, and spend some pages discussing—and present an equation that uses different interest rates from those discussed and chosen with some care by Friedman and Schwartz. In other words, their assertions are not supported by their own finding.

Further, the HE claim that modern econometrics (i.e., theirs) rejected the findings of Friedman and Schwartz on the demand for money was quickly subject to a direct challenge in a paper by Sean Holly and Andrew Longbottom (1985). They wrote,

> In this paper we extend the work of HE on the demand for money and find that after all it is possible—using the methodology which HE employ—to observe a long run underlying demand for real money balances which does support the claims of Friedman and Schwartz. In particular we can find a long run demand for money relationship which is very similar to that which Friedman and Schwartz estimate using the methodology. (p. 1)

HE have not yet (1988) responded to this challenge. It is, however, notable that the methods of the HE paper are highly sensitive to minor changes in data (such as can occur, for example, when different authors have chosen different ways of linking two series to give a longer run of data), in data period, and in computing techniques. It may appear that not all advances in econometrics represent progress.

One aspect of the statistical methods used by Friedman and Schwartz has recently been discussed by Saleh Neftci (1986). His paper is a general examination of NBER business cycle methodology and the NBER practice of converting data to cycle-phase averages, which procedure Neftci regards as embodying the assumption that ". . . the state of the cycle is important even after account is taken of the relevant calendar time variables" (p. 11). If, he writes,

> a cyclical time unit can be consistently defined, . . . we can transform these time series using this newly defined time unit. This transformation of the series will eliminate some types of movements in macroeconomic data while highlighting any remaining periodicities, namely any "long cycles" and the trend component. One such procedure that uses a cyclical time unit is phase averaging (Friedman and Schwartz 1982 and HE 1984). (p. 39)

Is this phase-averaging technique appropriate, in the sense that applying it to the data gives information additional to that which can be obtained from the use of straightforward (calendar time) variables? Neftci shows that it does, under certain circumstances, given such information. He thus severely qualifies Hendry and Ericsson's strident rejection of the technique.[21] In particular, the technique not only eliminates serial correlation due to the business cycle and eliminates "measurement error" (these points are discussed by HE), it can help to capture long-run relationships. The particular long relationship that the procedure helps capture is a nondeterministic trend. Suppose, for example, we have a nondeterministic trend whose slope alternates between slow growth and fast growth, with uncertain length of each phase, then phase averaging would capture (approximately) the random movements in the trend. A crucial issue in future evaluation of the NBER procedure is thus the nature of the trend. On this point, evidence is starting to accumulate. Neftci reports some work which, tentatively, supports the nonlinear assumption (p. 45). And, addressing the question directly, Nelson and Plosser (1982) have claimed that trends are stochastic. But this work is still far from uncontroversial. Plainly, Robin Matthews's (1983) caution in summing up the import and the econometric work was well founded, and plainly, too, Friedman and Schwartz have managed to stimulate further work by econometricians as well as by monetary economists.

2.3 Conclusion

It is easy to say that Anna Schwartz, by her two, co-authored, massive volumes, and by her papers, has made a major contribution to the understanding of Britain's economic history. Summing up that contribution without injustice to part of it is harder. Nevertheless, three aspects of her work must be highlighted in conclusion.

The analytical framework now generally used is somewhat different from that in Gayer, Rostow, and Schwartz. But that volume remains unchallenged as a source of carefully constructed data for the years it covers, and its interpretations are derived with such care that, despite changing intellectual fashions, they too have to be taken very seriously by any current scholar of the period. The book's imprint on the study of eighteenth- and nineteenth-century Britain is indelible. *Monetary Trends* covers a different time period and uses a different intellectual framework, but this volume, too, will surely have an influence on all future work on British monetary history from 1870. By focusing on trends, it sets an agenda for future work—what goes on over shorter time spans—and provides a clearly delineated background to which, like studies of the period covered by Gayer, Rostow, and Schwartz, future studies must either conform or, if dissenting, do so explicitly and with caution.

But perhaps most important of all is the example provided by the method of Anna Schwartz's work. It is always clear, meticulously thorough, and in its conclusions carefully considered. Her work on British economic history is not only important to future scholars, it is an example to them.

Notes

1. The raw data are still extant, typewritten in 861 densely packed pages. It is a great pity that these pages are not in published form. They contain enormous detail but have been available only on microfilm, which is less than enticing. There must be a case for publishing these data, for to have monthly data for 1790–1850 on series such as exchange rates in six foreign centers, and the yield on consols, etc., would facilitate work in the area and stimulate further testing of hypotheses.

2. This was done by Mitchell (1913, 1927).

3. In this sense the "measurement without theory" attack on Burns and Mitchell was unfair since they never abjured theory. The Bureau had developed certain techniques in collation and measurement, and although the study by GRS was not a Bureau project, these techniques were drawn on heavily. It is interesting to note the early objectives of those who set up the Bureau, and this concentration on objective fact: "The Committee will concern itself wholly with matters of fact, and is being organized for no other obligation than to determine the facts and to publish its findings" (Fabricant 1984, 6).

4. A tribute to empirical work was paid by Robert Lucas in one of his theoretical papers on the subject. He wrote, "The features of economic time series [which he was about to describe] listed here are, curiously, both 'well known' and expensive to document in any careful and comprehensive way. A useful, substantively oriented introduction is given by Mitchell (1951), who summarizes mainly interwar U.S. experience. The basic technical reference for these methods is Burns and Mitchell (1946). U.S. monetary experience is best displayed in Friedman and Schwartz (1963). An invaluable source for earlier British series is Gayer, Rostow, and Schwartz (1953), esp. Vol. II. The phenomena documented in these sources are, of course, much more widely observed. Most can be inferred, though with some difficulty, from the estimated structure of modern econometric models. An important recent contribution is Sargent and Sims (1976), which summarizes postwar U.S. quarterly series in several suggestive ways, leading to a qualitative picture very close to that provided by Mitchell, but within an explicit stochastic framework, so that their results are replicatable and criticisable at a level at which Mitchell's are not" (Lucas 1981, 236, n. 4).

5. It is also worth remembering that Gayer was interested in monetary policy and had himself written a book in the 1930s on the subject of monetary stabilization. Apparently he never suggested that this should influence the work on the British economy.

6. Note the importance of *trend* factors in producing cycles—this looks forward to Nelson and Plosser (1982).

7. Anna Schwartz had given British academics two advance indications of what was in this volume. These were in her comment on a paper by Alan Budd et al. (1984), and in her Henry Thornton Lecture at the City University ([1980] 1988). The comments on Budd et al. set out the results on the U.K. and U.S. money demand functions that were reported in detail in *Monetary Trends,* and noted the lack of connection between money and output which was also set out in that volume. In her lecture, "A Century of British Market Interest Rates," she used the work in *Monetary Trends* to examine the impact of inflation on real and nominal interest rates. Did inflation, as Thornton conjectured, introduce a gap, equal to the inflation rate, between the real and nominal interest rates? She found that, over most of the century she looked at, support for

Thornton was not strong, but it became so toward the end of the period. She attributes the change to the increased price level variability, consequent upon the shift to a fiduciary standard, and the associated increased rewards to anticipating inflation.

8. Some indication of just how important this opening up of British monetary history was is that in our forthcoming books (Capie and Wood 1989 and 1990), we touch on a large number of previously explored topics in British monetary history, yet only some of these are on the list of subjects suggested for future study on the work of Friedman and Schwartz.

9. In abnormal times, such as the interwar years of depression and abnormal liquidity preference, dummies were necessary in the statistical work.

10. Friedman and Schwartz raise a topic of great importance for all future studies when they discuss expectations. As they point out, a forecasting procedure which turns out to be *systematically* wrong when viewed with hindsight may have been perfectly rational given the information available at the time.

11. It is worth pointing out that the results obtained in the article (cited on p. 325) are in fact due to chance. It was found that over the gold standard years in the United Kingdom, income Granger-caused money. That was, it was argued, to be expected, and some inferences were drawn from the confirmation. In fact the inferences hold, but the confirmation depended on the chance that there was no gold discovery sufficiently large to cause a gold inflow of such size as to offset in the estimates the effects of gold inflows resulting from income growth. Theory alone should have led one to the conclusion that in an open economy with a fixed exchange rate, the "causal" relationship (in the Granger sense) between money and prices would reveal nothing about causation, but would depend on the relative size and frequency of external and internal monetary shocks.

12. Goodhart at this point confuses Granger-Sims timing studies with studies of causality, an error he carefully avoids earlier.

13. This has bearing on whether rules should be contingent or noncontingent. The claims for contingent rules all rest on the assumption that *small* movements in money affect output. If that proves false, the grounds of debate are shifted rather dramatically. Bernanke's (1982) conjectures may be relevant here.

14. The puzzle may be solved by recent work, e.g., T. C. Mills (1985, 1987) and Mills and Stephenson (1986), which suggests the real rate (ex ante as well as ex post) may not be exactly constant. But such studies are as yet at a very preliminary stage.

15. See Wood (1983) for a discussion of this part of the period for which Congdon's description of Bank of England procedures is accurate. This part comprises the years from 1945 to about 1970, and also occasional episodes thereafter.

16. The behavior of the Bank in this period is described in Sayers (1976). In conjunction with Michael Bordo and Ehsan Choudhri, Anna Schwartz is currently engaged in an analytical and econometric study of the effect of interest rate setting on money stock control. A study of this question based on Canadian data has recently appeared.

17. Friedman and Schwartz, we should make clear, are referring to the experience of the United States only at this point.

18. Examples of such studies are cited in Broadberry (1985).

19. It should be remarked that their paper, which purported to be "An Econometric Appraisal of Monetary Trends," in fact dealt with only one chapter in a twelve-chapter volume.

20. There was also an important difference between the two pairs of authors on research method. HE placed complete reliance on formal econometric tests.

Economic analysis, in their implicit view of research, may suggest questions but is not qualified to comment on answers. Hypotheses stand or fall according to purely statistical criteria. Friedman and Schwartz, by contrast, explicitly regard formal statistical testing as a part—only a part—of evaluating a hypothesis. It is hard to believe that the Hendry-Ericsson approach, which essentially ignores the environment from which the data came and the reasons for examining them, is the best way to advance knowledge of the economy.

21. Neftci (1986, 41) very neatly summarizes their florid and rhetorical criticisms as follows: "For example, assume that the processes Y_t and X_t are related to each other through a relation:

$$Y_t = \Sigma\beta_s X_{t-s} + f(t) + \epsilon_t \qquad (10)$$

where $f(t)$ is (possibly) a nonlinear trend, and where ϵ_t is i.i.d.

Then, phase-averaging as described in (8) is like applying two complicated filters to Y_t and X_t. These filters will be nonlinear in the data, since the γ_k^i are selected after analyzing the observed time series Y_t and X_t and some observations are eliminated. Because of this nonlinear nature of the filter, it is generally not possible to quantify precisely the effects of phase-averaging. However, one can make the following comments:

1. The phase-averaging shown in (8) will lead to a loss of information about the system (10), since many data points would be eliminated.
2. If the original ϵ_t were white, ϵ_k^* may exhibit complicated heteroscedastic behavior.
3. More importantly, the selection of $|\gamma_x^i|$ after observing the realization of Y_t and X_t may in general introduce a correlation between X_t^* and ϵ_t^*—even where there was none originally, so that linear projections will give biased estimates of the $|\beta_s|$.
4. Because the filters applied to Y_t and X_t are different, $|\beta_s|$ would not be the same as $|\beta_s^*|$."

References

Artis, M. 1983. The review of *Monetary trends. Manchester School of Economic and Social Research* 53(4): 486–87.

Artis, M. J., and M. K. Lewis. 1984. How unstable is the demand for money in the United Kingdom? *Economica* 51: 473–76.

Attfield, C. L. F., D. Demery, and N. W. Duck. 1981. A quarterly model of unanticipated monetary growth output and the price level in the U.K., 1963–1978. *Journal of Monetary Economics* 8: 331–50.

Bernanke, B. 1982. Non monetary effects of the financial crisis in the propagation of the Great Depression. *The American Economic Review* (June): 257–76.

Broadberry, S. 1985. *The British economy between the wars: A macroeconomic survey.* Oxford: Basil Blackwell.

Brown, Arthur. 1983. Monetary trends in the United Kingdom. Bank of England, Panel of Academic Consultants Paper no. 22.

Budd, Alan, Sean Holly, Andrew Longbottom, and David Smith. 1984. Does monetarism fit the U.K. facts? In *Monetarism in the United Kingdom,* eds. B. Griffiths and G. E. Wood. London: Macmillan.

Burns, A. F., and W. C. Mitchell. 1946. *Measuring business cycles.* New York: NBER.

Cairncross, A. K. 1953. *Home and foreign investment.* Cambridge: Cambridge University Press.

———. 1954. Review of *The growth and fluctuation of the British economy. American Economic Review* 44: 156–59.

Cagan, P. 1965. *Determinants and effects of changes in the stock of money, 1875–1960.* New York: Columbia Univ. Press, for the NBER.

———. 1972. *The channels of monetary influences on interest rates.* New York: Columbia University Press.

Capie, F. H., and G. E. Wood, eds. 1986. *Financial crises and the world banking system.* London: Macmillan.

———. 1988. An anatomy of wartime inflation. In *The economic history of the Second World War,* eds. H. Rockoff and G. Mills. Cedar Rapids: University of Iowa Press.

———. 1989. *Monetary history of the U.K., 1870–1920.* St. Albans: Unwin Hyman.

———. 1990. *Monetary history of the U.K., 1921–1988.* St. Albans: Unwin Hyman. Forthcoming.

Capie, F. H., M. Pradhan, and G. E. Wood. 1989. Prices and price controls: Are price controls a policy instrument? In *Macroeconomic policy and economic interdependence,* eds. D. Hodgeman and G. E. Wood. London: Macmillan.

Congdon, T. 1983. Has Friedman got it wrong? Review of *Monetary Trends. The Banker* (July): 117–25.

Conrad, Alfred N., and John R. Meyer. 1958. The economics of slavery in the antebellum South. *Journal of Political Economy* 56, no. 2 (April): 95–130.

Fabricant, Solomon. 1984. *Toward a firmer basis of economic policy: The founding of the National Bureau of Economic Research.* Cambridge, Mass.: NBER.

Friedman, M. 1974. A theoretical framework for monetary analysis. In *Milton Friedman's monetary framework,* ed. Robert J. Gordon. Chicago: University of Chicago Press.

Friedman, M. and A. J. Schwartz. 1963a. Money and business cycles. *Review of Economics and Statistics* 45, no. 1, part 2 (February): 32–64.

———. 1963b. *A monetary history of the United States, 1867–1960.* Princeton, NJ: Princeton University Press.

———. 1970. *Monetary statistics of the United States.* New York: Columbia University Press.

———. 1982. *Monetary trends in the United States and the United Kingdom: Their relation to income, prices, and interest rates, 1867–1975.* Chicago: University of Chicago Press.

Gayer, A. D., W. W. Rostow, and Anna J. Schwartz. 1953. *The growth and fluctuation of the British economy 1790–1850: An historical, statistical, and theoretical study of Britain's economic development.* 2 vols. Oxford: Clarendon Press; 2d ed. 1975, Hertfordshire: Harvester Press.

Goodhart, C. A. E. 1982. *Monetary trends in the United States and the United Kingdom:* A British review. *Journal of Economic Literature* 20(4): 1540–51.

Gordon, Robert. 1961. *Business fluctuations.* New York: Harper & Row.

Haberler, Gottfried von. 1937. *Prosperity and depression.* Geneva: League of Nations.

Hall, Robert E. 1982. *Monetary trends in the United States and the United Kingdom:* A review from the perspective of new developments in monetary economics. *Journal of Economic Literature* 20(4): 1552–56.

Hawtrey, R. G. 1913. *Good and bad trade: An enquiry into the causes of trade fluctuations.* London: Longmans Green & Co.

Hayek, F. A. von. 1933. *Monetary theory and the trade cycle.* London: Jonathan Cape.

Hendry, David, and Neil Ericsson. 1983. Monetary trends in the United Kingdom. Bank of England, Panel of Academic Consultants Paper no. 22.

Hodgman, D., and G. E. Wood, eds. 1988. *Macroeconomic policy and economic interdependence.* London: Macmillan.

Holly, Sean, and Andrew Longbottom. 1985. Monetary trends in the U.K.: A reappraisal of the demand for money. London Business School EFU Discussion Paper no. 147.

Imlah, A. H. 1953. Gayer, Rostow, and Schwartz on the British Economy. *Journal of Economic History* 13: 270–73.

Juglar, Clement. 1889. *Des crises commerciales et de leur retour periodique.* Paris: Libraire Guillaumin.

Keynes, John Maynard. 1936. *The general theory of employment, interest, and money.* London: Macmillan.

Laidler, David. 1982. Friedman and Schwartz on monetary trends: A review article. *Journal of International Money and Finance* 1(3): 293–305.

Lucas, R. E. 1975. An equilibrium model of the business cycle. *Journal of Political Economy* 83: 1113–44.

———. 1977. Understanding business cycles. *Journal of Monetary Economics Supplement* 5: 7–29. Reprinted in Lucas 1981.

———. 1980. Two illustrations of the quantity theory of money. *American Economic Review* no. 70: 1005–14.

———. 1981. *Studies in business cycle theory.* Oxford: Basil Blackwell.

Matthews, R. C. O. 1954. Review of *Growth and fluctuation of the British economy. Oxford Economic Papers* vol. 6. Reprinted in *British economic fluctuations,* eds. D. Aldcroft and P. Fearon, 97–130. Condon: Macmillan.

———. 1959. *The trade cycle.* Cambridge: Cambridge University Press.

———. 1983. Introduction. Bank of England, Panel of Academic Consultants Paper no. 22.

Mayer, T. H. 1982. *Monetary trends in the United States and the United Kingdom:* A review article. *Journal of Economic Literature* 20(4): 1528–39.

McCallum, B. T. 1986. On "real" and "sticky price" theories of the business cycle. *Journal of Money, Credit and Banking* 18 (November): 397–414.

Mills, T. C. 1985. An empirical analysis of the U.K. Treasury bill market. *Applied Economics* 17(4): 689–704.

———. 1987. The behaviour of short-term interest rates in the U.K. *Applied Economics* 19(3): 331–41.

Mills, T. C., and Michael J. Stephenson. 1986. Modelling real returns on U.K. government stock. *Bulletin of Economic Research* 38(3): 237–56.

Mitchell, W. C. 1913. *Business cycles: Cycles of prosperity and depression.* Vol. 3. Memoirs of the University of California, Berkeley. Berkeley: Univ. of California Press.

———. 1927. *Business cycles: The problem and its setting.* Studies in Business Cycles no. 1. NBER.

———. 1951. *What happens during business cycles: A Progress Report.* Studies in Business Cycles no. 5. NBER.

Morgan, Victor E. 1954. Review of *The growth and fluctuation of the British economy. The Economic Journal* 63 (December): 858–60.

Neftci, Saleh. 1986. Is there a cyclical time unit? *Journal of Monetary Economics Supplement* 24: 11–48. Carnegie Rochester Conference Series.

Nelson, Charles, and Charles I. Plosser. 1982. Trends and random walks in macroeconomic time series: Some evidence and implications. *Journal of Monetary Economics* 10 (2): 139–62.

Ogden, E. 1988. *The Bank of England as lender of last resort*. Ph.D. diss. City University, London.

Phelps, Brown, E. H. 1954. Review of *The growth and fluctuation of the British economy*. *Economica* 64: 70–73.

Rockoff, H., and G. Mills. 1986. Price controls in the U.K. and U.S. In Rockoff and Mills 1988.

———. 1988. *The economic history of the Second World War*. Cedar Rapids: University of Iowa Press.

Sargent, T. J., and C. A. Sims. 1976. Business cycle modelling without pretending to have too much a priori economic theory. University of Michigan Working Paper (March).

Sayers, R. S. 1976. *The Bank of England, 1891–1944*. Cambridge: Cambridge University Press.

Schwartz, Anna J. 1984. Comment on "Does monetarism fit the U.K. facts?" by A. Budd et al. In *Monetarism in the U.K.*, eds. B. Griffiths and G. E. Wood. London: Macmillan.

———. 1986. Real and pseudo-financial crises. In F. H. Capie and G. E. Wood. *Financial crises and the world banking system*, eds. London: Macmillan.

———. 1988. A century of British market interest rates. Henry Thornton Lecture no. 2 (1980), City University, London. In *Monetary economics in the 1980s*, eds. F. H. Capie and G. E. Wood. London: Macmillan.

Thornton, Henry. [1802] 1939. *An enquiry into the nature and effects of the paper credit of Great Britain*. Reprint. London: Allen & Unwin.

Warburton, Clark. 1950. The monetary disequilibrium hypothesis. *The American Journal of Economics and Sociology* 10, no. 1 (October): 1–11.

Williamson, J., and G. E. Wood. 1976. The British inflation: Indigenous or imported? *American Economic Review* 66: 520–31.

Wood, G. E. 1983. The monetary policy decision process in the United Kingdom. In *The political economy of monetary policy: National and international aspects*, ed. Donald R. Hodgman. Proceedings of the Federal Reserve Bank of Boston Conference no. 26.

Zarnowitz, V. 1985. Recent work on business cycles in historical perspective: A review of theories and evidence. *Journal of Economic Literature* 23 (June): 523–80.

Comment   David Laidler

I very much enjoyed reading this paper, and was particularly pleased by the attention which Capie and Wood have paid to Anna Schwartz's earliest work on Britain, carried out with Gayer and Rostow. The very fact that this work, begun more than fifty years ago, still retains its

David Laidler is a professor of economics at the University of Western Ontario.

importance today speaks eloquently of the lasting value of the care and discipline which have always marked Anna's contributions to our subject. These qualities are all too rare, and the empirical basis of our economic knowledge would be a good deal stronger if more of us would follow the example Anna has set throughout her distinguished career.

Fortunately for my ability to function as a discussant, my pleasure in reading this paper did not arise from finding myself in complete agreement with it. My dissent is more from particular details of the argument though, than from its broad outlines. I share Capie and Wood's (and Anna's) views on the importance of monetary factors in the business cycle, on the basic soundness of the framework for analyzing them that the quantity theory tradition provides, and on the necessity for continuously and carefully testing theoretical arguments against empirical evidence. Even so, two aspects in particular of Capie and Wood's analysis seem to me to require a little more thought before their conclusions are accepted. I do not completely share their views on the historical development of business cycle theory, or on the way in which inflationary impulses are transmitted between countries under fixed exchange rates.

Business Cycle Theory

Economists in the 1920s and 1930s would have agreed with Capie and Wood that in their era, "a monetary theory of the cycle was . . . a prominent explanation" (p. 83). However, they would not have thought that they were thereby endorsing the view that fluctuations in the money supply are the key causative factor driving cyclical fluctuations. Most economists of the interwar years believed that systematic cyclical fluctuations could occur only in an economy whose activities were coordinated by monetary exchange. That is the sense in which they believed the cycle to be a monetary phenomenon. Comparatively few, however, attributed more than a permissive (or at most exacerbative) role to monetary variables in the propagation of cyclical impulses, whose origins lay outside of the monetary sector. To give some examples: Knut Wicksell, as an empirical matter, believed that cumulative processes of the type he analyzed (and which he himself did not systematically treat as cyclical phenomena) were more likely to be set in motion by exogenous increases in the "natural" interest rate than by any change in the money rate initiated by the banking system; this view was shared by virtually all those—Hayek and the Austrians, as much as the Stockholm school— who were later to produce self-consciously Wicksellian theories of the cycle; Keynes's stress in the *General Theory* on fluctuations in "animal spirits" as a source of economic disturbance reflects a longstanding consensus of Cambridge economists on this matter; and so on.[1]

If one seeks a pre-Keynesian prototype for the cycle theory that Anna Schwartz and Milton Friedman have done so much to establish, one must look not to the general body of European business cycle theory, nor even to the work of Mitchell and Burns—though the influence of their empirical methods is clearly crucial—but to the work of Irving Fisher. His discussion of "transition periods" in chapter 4 of *The Purchasing Power of Money* (1911) deals with a cyclical process set in motion by shocks to the quantity of money, and kept in motion by other monetary factors, namely the influence of inflation expectations on nominal interest rates and their interaction with profit expectations. This work represents a line in the development of business cycle theory quite distinct from that which Capie and Wood rightly identify as running from the work of Hayek ([1929] 1932) to that of Robert E. Lucas (1977). As an admirer of Friedman and Schwartz's analysis, I wish that Capie and Wood had been more critical of this latter approach, whose fundamentally Walrasian character seems to me to render it quite incompatible with work in the Fisher-Friedman-Schwartz tradition. One or two issues bear a little thinking about before the superiority of New-Classical cycle theory is accepted.

If "money matters" at all, it surely matters for mitigating the consequences of unforeseen market events. That is one reason agents hold money as a "temporary abode of purchasing power." But causation runs two ways here. We hold money because we are ignorant, but we remain more ignorant than we need to be because our money holdings protect us from the worst consequences of that ignorance. If this conjecture has any empirical content, it implies that the last thing a monetary theory of the cycle should do is assume that all agents within the economy make full use of all the information available to the economist looking into it from the outside. Moreover, historians, of all people, should be aware that the time during which individual business executives are in a position to make important decisions seldom spans more than a couple of cycles. That is hardly long enough for them to learn from their own mistakes; and are institutional memories so well designed in the business world that we can rely on the executives having learned from the mistakes of their predecessors?

Why then should a money-using economy, inhabited by mortal men and women who face significant marginal costs of acquiring and processing information, move over real time "as if" it was populated by immortals to whom most relevant information is a free good, as is the computing power needed optimally to extract from noisy signals estimates of those few data that are missing? Why should the repetition by one generation of the errors of its predecessors not be an important source of the continuity of cyclical phenomena? The superior compatibility of New-Classical business cycle theory with the historical record needs to be demonstrated before we conclude that the theory of Friedman and Schwartz has been superseded. Its premises should be treated as testable hypotheses, not undeniable axioms.

The Supply and Demand for Money

Capie and Wood correctly identify as the central characteristic of Friedman and Schwartz's monetary model the hypothesis that there can arise a discrepancy between the quantity of money in circulation and the amount that the nonbank public is willing to hold, given what we would nowadays call its "long-run" demand for money. This hypothesis is incompatible with New-Classical theory, where flexible prices prevent such a discrepancy ever occurring, and with Keynesian analysis, where interest rate movements similarly keep the supply and demand for money in perpetual equilibrium. The consequences of such a discrepancy for expenditure flows of all sorts are the driving force in models of the cycle deriving from the quantity theory tradition. Clark Warburton's work is surely important here, as Capie and Wood note, but one does not have to work too hard to extract a similar story from *The Purchasing Power of Money,* or from some of Alfred Marshall's writings. This is not surprising because what are nowadays called "disequilibrium money" or "buffer-stock" effects reflect very much the same class of phenomena as that which a traditional quantity theorist might have labelled "cash balance mechanics."

There is, of course, more to Friedman and Schwartz's version of cash balance mechanics than the proposition that there often exists a state of affairs which can be characterized by the following inequality: $Ms \neq Md$. Capie and Wood correctly differentiate Friedman and Schwartz's product from Charles Goodhart's "buffer-stock" analysis, even though he too attaches great importance to this same inequality between the supply and demand for money.[2] Goodhart locates the source of most (or at least many) disturbances on the right-hand side of this inequality, and treats induced fluctuations in the supply of money as being crucial to absorbing their consequences. For Friedman and Schwartz the predominant causes of such inequalities are fluctuations in the supply of money, and their predominant consequences are fluctuations in the arguments of the demand function, namely interest rates, real income, and prices. Now in most cases I would take the Friedman-Schwartz view of these matters, but there is, as Capie and Wood note, one case where I do not, and that concerns the international transmission of price level shocks.

My disagreement here is important for the following reasons. In their work with cycle-phase data on the United Kingdom, Friedman and

Schwartz were able to find plenty of evidence linking money and prices, but none suggesting a chain of causation going from money through real output and employment to money, wages, and prices. Goodhart (1982a) repeated their work, using annual data, with similarly negative results. Taken at face value this would suggest that reducing (increasing) money growth in the United Kingdom leads to lower (higher) inflation with no effects on output and employment that endure long enough to show up in annual data. I simply do not believe that the recession of the early 1980s was independent of the anti-inflationary stance of Mrs. Thatcher's monetary policy; that the real aspects of the Heath-Barber boom of the early 1970s were independent of the inflationary money growth that their policies engendered; and so on. But if I do not believe these things, I have to explain why the mechanisms at work during these episodes do not appear to be generally present in United Kingdom data. That is why I find attractive the hypothesis that, on some occasions at least, inflationary impulses originating abroad, or arising from devaluations, might have disturbed domestic prices before they caused the money supply to vary, thus producing simultaneous contractions of real variables. It is also why I regret Capie and Wood's rejection of this hypothesis largely on the basis of a priori argument supported by some evidence drawn from but one episode.[3]

There is nothing theoretically novel about the mechanisms involved here. Thus Fisher (1911, 90) noted "When a single small country is under consideration, it is . . . preferable to say that the quantity of money in that country is determined by the universal price level, rather than to say that its level of prices is determined by the quantity of money within its borders."[4] Wicksell ([1905] 1935), in discussing the effects of gold inflows on domestic prices under the gold standard, suggested that ". . . this increase [in commodity prices] may even precede the arrival of the gold. . . ." (p. 197). Moreover, the effects in question do not have to be always at work to influence the results of applying regression analysis to a run of data. They only need to have been important from time to time. Nor do they have to work through commodity arbitrage. A transmission of foreign price or exchange rate shocks through domestic inflation expectations will also suffice. Nor do such shocks have to impinge on the long-run inflation rate to interfere with underlying empirical regularities. A disturbance in the inflation rate for a year or two while a new international structure of relative price levels is established could be enough to upset things. Moreover, my conjecture is supported by a certain amount of empirical evidence generated ten years or so ago by the Manchester Inflation Research Programme which Michael Parkin and I supervised.[5] I would not claim that this evidence is in any way definitive, but surely it should be followed up before the effects it seems to reveal are dismissed as irrelevant.

Thus, as their work on the monetary history of the United Kingdom progresses, I hope that Capie and Wood will keep an open mind about this question and will investigate the possibility that, when it comes to the international transmission of inflationary impulses, or the response of domestic variables to exchange rate changes, more than the price-specie-flow mechanism has sometimes been at work in generating their data. Obviously it requires the techniques of the historian, rather than the econometrician, to look into the possibly infrequent operations of other mechanisms, but no one is better able to employ those techniques in analyzing the United Kingdom experience than are Capie and Wood. Nor could there be a better tribute to Anna Schwartz than that they should follow up her pioneering research on such issues with the same care and discipline which she has always brought to such work.

Notes

1. Wicksell's views on the actual sources of price level movements are set out in *Interest and Prices* ([1898] 1936, ch. 11) where he argues that ". . . changes in the *natural rate of interest on capital* are . . . the essential cause of such movements" (p. 167, Wicksell's italics). His paper, "The Enigma of Business Cycles" (1907), which is included in the 1965 reprint of *Interest and Prices*, shows that he did not regard his cumulative process analysis as being of central importance to understanding the cycle. For an account of Austrian and later Swedish views on these matters, see Laidler (1987). Patinkin (1976) and Eshag (1963) are accessible sources of information on the development of Cambridge thought.

2. Goodhart's analysis is set out in (1982b). Other discussions of "buffer-stock" effects are to be found in Jonson (1976) and Laidler (1984).

3. I refer here to the evidence generated by Williamson and Wood (1976) on the 1967 devaluation, cited by Capie and Wood.

4. The discussion in which this passage occurs is not, however, entirely consistent with certain later passages in the *Purchasing Power of Money* that deal with inter-regional links: e.g., "The price level outside of New York City . . . affects the price level in New York City only via changes in the money in New York City. Within New York City it is the money which influences the price level, and not the price level which influences the money" (p. 172).

5. Here I would cite Cross and Laidler (1976) who showed, with evidence drawn from no fewer than nineteen fixed exchange rate open economies, that domestic inflation expectations seemed to be directly influenced by the behavior of world prices, that the influences in question were more important the more open the economy, and that exchange rate changes seemed to profoundly disturb the mechanisms at work here; and Carlson and Parkin (1975) whose analysis revealed an apparently important effect of the 1967 devaluation on British inflation expectations, and hence casts doubt on the conclusions drawn by Capie and Wood from the Williamson and Wood (1976) study about the irrelevance of such a phenomenon.

References

Carlson, J. A., and J. M. Parkin. 1975. Consumers' price expectations. *Economica* NS 42 (May): 123–38.

Cross, R. G., and D. Laidler. 1976. Inflation, excess demand and expectations in fixed exchange rate open economies: Some preliminary results. In *Inflation in the world economy*, eds. J. M. Parkin and G. Zis. Manchester: University of Manchester Press.

Eshag, E. 1963. *From Marshall to Keynes: An essay on the monetary theory of the Cambridge school*. Oxford: Blackwell.

Fisher, I. 1911. *The purchasing power of money*. New York: Macmillan.

Goodhart, C. A. E. 1982a. *Monetary trends in the United States and the United Kingdom:* A British review. *Journal of Economic Literature* 20 (December): 1540–41.

———. Disequilibrium money—A note. Bank of England. Mimeo.

Hayek, F. A. von. [1929] 1932. *Monetary theory and the trade cycle*. Trans. N. Kaldor and H. Croome. London: Routledge and Kegan Paul.

Jonson, P. D. 1976. Money, prices and output: An integrative essay. *Kredit und Kapital* 4: 499–518.

Keynes, J. M. 1936. *The general theory of employment, interest, and money*. London: Macmillan.

Laidler, D. 1984. The buffer stock notion in monetary economics. *Conference Papers* supplement to the *Economic Journal* 94 (March): 17–34.

———. 1987. The Austrians and the Stockholm school: Two failures in the development of modern macroeconomics? University of Western Ontario. Mimeo.

Lucas, R. E., Jr. 1977. Understanding business cycles. In *Stabilization of the domestic and international economy*, eds. K. Brunner and A. H. Meltzer. Carnegie Rochester Conference Series, vol. 5. Amsterdam: North Holland.

Patinkin, D. 1976. *Keynes' monetary thought: A study of its development*. Durham, N.C.: Duke University Press.

Wicksell, K. 1898. *Interest and prices*. Trans. R. F. Kahn, for the Royal Economic Society, 1936. Reprint. New York: Augustus Kelley, 1965.

———. 1905. *Lectures on political economy*. Vol. 2. Trans. E. Claassen, 1935. London: Routledge and Kegan Paul.

Williamson, J., and G. E. Wood. 1976. The British inflation: Indigenous or imported? *American Economic Review* 66 (September): 520–31.

General Discussion

Rostow recalled his collaboration, which began 48 years ago, with Anna Schwartz and Arthur Gayer on the study of the British economy from 1790 to 1850, evoking the enthusiasm of the participants in the project. He then responded to the point raised by Capie and Wood that the Gayer-Rostow-Schwartz (GRS) book did not pay sufficient attention to the monetary dimensions of the economy. According to him, the authors tried in the historical sections of the book on the financial system to weave in qualitative evidence with the limited data series they had available to them. He stressed two key differences between GRS and the modern mainstream monetarist perspective.

First, that GRS viewed the monetary sector as part of an endless, interactive process with real factors. In the historical part of the study they tried to capture how money interacted with all the other forces determining output, employment, prices, and real wages.

Second, that one consequence of regarding money and real factors as interacting endlessly and dynamically through time is that the distinction between the short period and the long period falls away. The long period becomes the accumulation of what happens in the short period. Trends—which are by no means linear in history, as Simon Kuznets and Arthur Burns demonstrated—become an ex post view of what, in fact, happened through historical time.

Rostow views Friedman and Schwartz's A Monetary History as really a study of how, in four respects, the authors judged money to be significant in the evolution of the American economy from 1867 on: in wars; in gold and its influence on prices; in the mechanism of cyclical downturns and deep depressions; and then, specifically, in determining the depth of the Great Depression after 1929. GRS were asking a different question: what happened to output, employment, prices, and real wages, and why?

Rostow expressed great admiration for Anna Schwartz's scientific contribution despite occasional differences with her conclusions.

DARBY, in response to Laidler's comment on the Capie-Wood paper, referred to his International Transmission of Inflation study with Lothian, Gandolfi, Schwartz, and Stockman which found evidence that the price-specie-flow mechanism, rather than price arbitrage, was the dominant channel of international transmission.

SCHWARTZ made the distinction between transmission under fixed exchange rates—the focus of the Darby et al. study—and flexible exchange rates.

LAIDLER pointed out that taking into account expectations—which is not quite the same thing as arbitrage—is important not so much for the international transmission of inflation per se, but for the issue of what different channels of transmission do to the relative timing of output, employment, and inflation changes in an open economy. He felt that the effects of a fairly weak expectations shock on the timing of changes in a few key wages and a few crucial nominal prices, in a particular cyclical upswing, could change the timing of aggregate variables relative to what is normal. In turn, this could create problems for the goodness of fit of regressions fitted to data taken from a number of cycles. He felt that evidence on the timing of cyclical variables in the domestic economy could reveal if there was a subordinate role for this mechanism.

Wood responded to Laidler's point on whether or not commodity arbitrage could conceal the short-term impact of nominal money on real income. He argued that Laidler's suggestion that a devaluation or an exchange rate change in a country like the United Kingdom could lead to prices rising so rapidly that money did not have time to grow in real terms before prices rose, might be an explanation for what Friedman and Schwartz found in *Monetary Trends* over cycle-phase averages and what Goodhart found with annual data.

Wood mentioned further that the period covered in *Monetary Trends* encompasses more than one exchange rate regime: the gold standard, the interwar years, then Bretton Woods. That again should surely complicate the story Laidler tells.

Finally, he made the point, based on studies by Lipsey and Kravis, that price arbitrage is very strong in commodity markets but becomes progressively weaker in semifinished goods and manufactured goods markets. Thus, though commodity arbitrage may be important, it is not sufficiently important to provide the explanation of why fluctuations in the nominal quantity of money did not affect output, even transitorally, in the United Kingdom.

Laidler doubted that money does not have transitory effects on output in the United Kingdom, citing evidence from particular cycles when the authorities slammed on the monetary brakes, slowing down both real output and the inflation rate. On some occasions monetary contraction showed up in the behavior of the money supply; on others, because the economy was on a fixed exchange rate, in the behavior of domestic credit.

As evidence that a currency devaluation changes something in the timing of relations between inflation and unemployment, he described some of the research he and his colleagues at Manchester did in the 1970s. Initially they could not get anything to fit until they dropped the years following devaluations. Doing this, they found that traditional expectations-augmented Phillips curves, that initially performed quite poorly, improved considerably.

Meltzer raised two issues concerning the monetary theory of the 1920s. The first issue was that the Cambridge school, including Marshall, Pigou, and Keynes, were all believers in a cycle driven by waves of optimism and pessimism, rather than a monetary theory of cycles. Second, he argued that proponents of a monetary theory of cycles, as discussed by Haberler, had a totally different idea of the source of the cycle than the modern view. For many of them it was overinvestment or overconsumption, fed by something in the internal dynamics of the system, not a monetary impulse. The idea of a monetary impulse can be found mainly with Irving Fisher who emphasized gold flows. According to Meltzer, Fisher's approach was an exception. The dominant theory of the business cycle at that time starts with a real shock to consumption or investment. The banking system then furthers the expansion of output produced by the real shock.

ROSTOW described the doctrinal underpinnings of the Gayer study. It was based on a mixture of the Marshall-Pigou approach and the Continental approach with emphasis on waves of optimism and pessimism.

MELTZER amplified on his distinction between monetary and real theories of the cycle. He views Hawtrey as having a real theory in which inventories change, and the banking system finances the opportunity for firms to rebuild their inventories. By contrast, he views Wicksell, in his 1907 *Economic Journal* article, as a proponent of a monetary theory of the cycle. For Wicksell, the initiating impulse was a reduction in bank rate simultaneously by all the central banks of the world.

LAIDLER disagreed with Meltzer's interpretation of Hawtrey and Wicksell's views. Hawtrey's notion of the unspent margin was not too dissimilar to an excess supply of cash balances, granting however that one source of this discrepancy was the real side. According to him, a reading of Wicksell's *Interest and Prices* posits fluctuations in what we would call the marginal efficiency of capital as driving the economy, with the banking system moving slowly to react to such shocks. In his opinion, Irving Fisher was the father of the monetary impulse view of the cycle.

O'DRISCOLL made the point that business cycle theorists of the 1920s were more interested in analyzing the cyclical process and less interested in the issue of proximate causation.

McCALLUM argued that pre-Keynesian cyclical theory should not be regarded as the same as what is now called real business cycle theory. An important part of Marshall's argument was that nominal wages would not adjust to shocks, so that with an unchanged stock of money, cyclical influences would come about because of changes in real wages. These changes resulted because nominal prices adjusted more rapidly than nominal wages. Thus his theory was one that mixed real shocks with a Keynesian view of the workings of the system. According to McCallum, Keynes's theory was very much a spelling out of the mechanism that was implicit in Marshall's 1887 analysis.

M. FRIEDMAN argued that all the above-mentioned predecessors had elements of a monetary theory since almost all emphasized the extent of the strain on the banking system. At the same time, none of them had a purely monetary theory. Rather they viewed the cycle as the result of waves of optimism (Pigou), of bursts of innovation (Schumpeter), or of action of the real forces that led to a reduction in real wages. But then in all of these cases—and this is where he believed Hawtrey fits in—they all spelled out the ways in which the banking system gets overtight and finally brings the boom to an end.

Rostow expanded on Marshall's theory of the cycle. Marshall's theory was based on his observation of the cycle which peaked in 1873 and on Mill's theory of the cycle, which in turn was based on the cycle that peaked in 1825. Both episodes were characterized by a rise in money market interest rates before the cyclical peak, suggesting to Rostow that the rise in interest rates and pressure in the money markets was a key part of the background to the crisis. Rostow then described other cycles characterized by a shock to the rate of return over cost (marginal efficiency of capital), in turn precipitating a financial crisis that occurred after the upper turning point. Thus, he argued, a sharp distinction needs to be made between the role of the monetary system in helping set the framework for the crisis—along with an increase in wages, raw material prices, and other costs—and uncertainties about the future profitability of the leading sectors during the boom.

Laidler and Wood, in response to a question posed by Milton Friedman, cited instances where Irving Fisher's work was influential in the development of the Cambridge approach.

Hetzel raised the question of whether the quantity theory tradition of Irving Fisher had much influence on the treatment of the business cycle in the United States in the 1920s.

M. Friedman replied that Fisher's influence was dominant and that Wesley Mitchell paid a great deal of attention to monetary influences on the cycle in his 1913 book.

Laidler pointed out that the Austrian economists—Hayek, Mises, and Robbins—as well as Wicksell and Robertson, referred to themselves as quantity theorists, but that was only with respect to their treatment of the relationship between the quantity of money and the price level. According to him, they did not propound a monetary theory of the cycle.

Bordo discussed the relationship between Clark Warburton's theory of monetary disequilibrium and its historical antecedents. Aside from Irving Fisher, the American proponents of the monetary theory of the cycle are not well known today.

Schwartz emphasized that many of these monetary theories basically were theories about the way the interest rate operated, and not about what happened to the quantity of money.

II   Monetarist Perspectives

3 Money-Income Causality— A Critical Review of the Literature Since *A Monetary History*

Phillip Cagan

3.1 Turns in Monetary Research

In the past three decades monetary research established a greater understanding and recognition of the role of money—a noteworthy achievement to which Anna Schwartz has been a major contributor. Earlier, in the 1930s, 1940s, and 1950s, the role of money had slipped far down the list of variables considered important in economic analysis and business commentary. Then in the 1960s, opinion began to turn. With Friedman and Schwartz's *A Monetary History of the United States, 1867–1960* (1963) leading the way, an outpouring of studies put new life into the traditional view of money as paramount. With the turn of opinion and the experience of the inflationary 1970s, few today any longer doubt the primary importance of money. Monetary economics continues to thrive on controversy, to be sure, but the difference is unmistakable: Now econometric models of the economy accord a central role to monetary variables, and business commentaries, far from ignoring monetary policy, focus on it. And the earlier barren disputes between Keynesians and quantity theorists graduated into more fruitful discussions about the proper conduct of monetary policy.

Lately, however, monetary research has turned again, and new studies claim that money has little or no effect on output and other real variables. What appeared so natural a marriage between monetarism and the theory of a stable competitive economy has produced a rather unnatural offspring—instantaneous price adjustments and rational expectations. This new view reaffirms the traditional monetary effects on

Phillip Cagan is a professor of economics at Columbia University.
The author thanks Bruce Lehmann for comments on an earlier draft and Kenneth Couch and Keun Lee for computational assistance.

117

prices but goes on to claim that changes in money affect *only* prices and perhaps only if the changes are exogenous. Other changes in money that may appear to influence real variables are dismissed as endogenous changes with no independent effects on the economy. In this view fluctuations in business activity are a real phenomenon with no monetary roots.

It is doubtful that anyone, even the practitioners of these models, firmly believes that the business cycle can be described as predominantly a real phenomenon. The supporting evidence is highly selective and limited. A less radical version of the new view admits that market prices may adjust sluggishly to monetary changes, so that *un*anticipated changes in money assumed to be exogenous do affect real variables. To what extent are monetary changes unanticipated as well as exogenous? The question is under debate. If most cyclical fluctuations in money are unanticipated and, even when endogenous, still affect prices and output, the new and older views would be compatible. But the two views interpret what is unanticipated differently. In the older view, long-run changes in monetary growth are absorbed by the price level, but all the short-run and cyclical changes play central roles in the business cycle; in modern jargon, these cyclical changes would all be unanticipated. The new view assumes, to the contrary, that the only unanticipated changes are very short movements, usually just isolated blips in the money series, and that all movements beyond one period are anticipated and immediately absorbed by prices. (Models with staggered wage contracts are an exception.) Although the length of a period in these models is usually unspecified, empirical work takes it to be one month or quarter. Nothing in the theory requires a period to be one month or quarter. But, unless one period covers the length of a business cycle, the new view and the older view clearly part company.

Much of the long-established evidence on the role of money comes from broad historical analyses. A broad historical analysis goes beyond a narrow dependence on time-series regressions. It draws on a wide-ranging examination of the institutional environment and economic events in a series of historical episodes. Statistical tests, including regression analysis, of these episodes may be run and prove useful, but they would be supplementary. Historical analysis relies on scholarship—a word on the way to losing its meaning in economics. It contrasts with the now common practice of gathering a handful of time series from a data bank and running them through a regression meat grinder.

The radical version of the new view in which money is endogenous and has no effects on the real economy is based on time-series regressions, and in particular on vector autoregressions, or VAR for short. This view and its evidence have made few converts. The Federal Reserve examines business conditions and decides policy, while the market watches anxiously in the firm belief that open market operations do something of utmost importance to the real side of the economy. If we accept the bulk of historical evidence as confirming important monetary effects on the real economy, contrary findings cannot be fully valid. And, if such contrary evidence is not valid, what kind of evidence in monetary research is acceptable and convincing? I want to address this wider issue about the validity of evidence from time-series regressions.

3.2 Endogeneity of the Money Supply

Central to most criticisms of evidence on monetary effects is the possible endogeneity of money. The empirical evidence that money, prices, and activity are related, now widely accepted, raises the question of the direction of influence. *A Monetary History* gives it major attention. Economic activity as well as policy decisions and institutional developments obviously affect monetary growth and fluctuations. The fact that money is significantly influenced by economic variables, however, does not itself imply the unimportance of monetary effects or justify downgrading their role. Friedman and Schwartz argued that the Fed could have prevented the decline in money in 1929–33 but failed to act. Stable monetary growth in that period would have changed the outcome of the business contraction. Even if the actual behavior of the money supply can be viewed as endogenous, it was possible for the Fed to have acted to stem the decline in money and to have alleviated the depression in output. There is an important difference between being endogenous with no independent effect and a mutual dependence in which policy can, when exercised, play a role.[1] Although those who deny monetary effects on output are surely not ignorant of this point, they continue to pay no attention to it. Regression methods foster this oversight because of their weak ability to disentangle a two-way dependence.

The issue of endogeneity has a long history in monetary controversies. It appeared in early banking theory as the commercial loan theory of credit or real bills doctrine (as named by Mints 1945), which held that if banks lent only short term to finance inventories on the way to market, the resulting quantity of bank deposits would be just right to produce a stable value of money. The attraction of the gold standard was that it produced an endogenous money supply that maintained a stable value of money in terms of gold. Much of the debate between monetarists and Keynesians turns on the endogeneity of money (Foster 1986). Thus critics of *A Monetary History* relied on endogeneity to counter the claim that money lies behind most fluctuations in activity.

Two initial prominent examples of this counterargument came in 1970 from Kaldor and Tobin.

Kaldor focused on the 1929–33 decline in the U.S. money stock, which he attributed to an independent shift towards the use of currency, because of increased payments for goods relative to assets and for labor relative to capital costs. This supposedly led to a large increase in the currency-deposit ratio which reduced the money supply. The only evidence Kaldor presented to support this explanation of the shift to currency was that the currency ratio did not return after the banking panic all the way to the low level of 1929. However, the continued high level of the currency ratio in the 1940s and 1950s can be attributed to other developments which I investigated in my work on the money supply (Cagan 1958, 1965). Kaldor might have argued with more force that the 1929–33 decline in the money stock did indeed reflect the banking panic, which in turn was produced by the contraction in business activity. If such an argument were valid, he could reach his conclusion that the money-income association simply showed the effect of income on money. A critical step in this endogeneity argument, however, requires evidence that the banking panic can be explained by the business contraction rather than other largely independent developments. Kaldor disregards all the studies of the genesis and role of banking panics in U.S. history. Business contractions do not fully explain panics. It follows that income did not cause money in these episodes, and the association reflects the reverse channel of influence.

There are two additional objections to Kaldor's type of endogeneity argument. First is the point made above: The fact that money may be endogenous does not prove or even imply that it has no reverse effect on activity. The money-income association reflects a changeable, two-way dependence. The importance of a two-way dependence is that money need not always be entirely endogenous. Policy actions can break the prevailing endogeneity, whereupon the existence of monetary effects means that they can be altered by policy to influence economic activity. Even if money were in some sense completely endogenous in 1929–33, therefore, the Fed's failure to stem the decline in money had devastating consequences for the economy.

The second point is that a two-way dependence cannot be confirmed by one observation. All we can confirm is a comovement, with indications of channels of influence possibly in both directions. Whether one or the other direction of influence dominates is never clear-cut in a single case. Friedman and Schwartz were well aware of this ambiguity, and devoted A *Monetary History* to analysis of a century of many different episodes. I also addressed the ambiguity in my book on the money supply (Cagan 1965). The comovements in money and business activity have persisted through a variety of cyclical episodes. In particular, the comovements appear as well in a group of severe cycles, some with and some without banking panics. The 1929–33 episode had a banking panic, which might appear to imply a one-way channel of influence running from a severe business contraction to panic to monetary decline. The evidence against that interpretation comes from the variety of monetary episodes. In 1914, for example, we had a banking panic but, thanks to a 1908 law authorizing the emergency issue of national bank notes, no large decline in the money stock and no severe contraction in activity ensued. Thus a single channel of influence of activity on money does not explain all the cyclical comovements in money and business. While the explanations for fluctuations in money vary, a persistent association between money and business remains: when money declines sharply, business activity also declines sharply, and not otherwise. How Kaldor and other critics could fail to grapple with this kind of evidence I can only ascribe to impatience to make an argument without examining the full range of historical evidence and without searching for interpretations that fit all of it.[2]

Tobin presented a theoretical model to demonstrate that the observed lead of monetary growth ahead of fluctuations in income does not prove causality. The model assumes that money is supplied endogenously at all times in response to changes in the demand for money.[3] Although money has no effect on income in the model, cycles in money turn out to lead those in income. This lead reverses the implication of standard models of money demand in which income affects the demand contemporaneously or with a lag and so moves ahead of cycles in a passive money supply. The reversed timing in Tobin's model occurs because of the peculiar nature of his money demand, as Friedman (1970) pointed out in his reply. Tobin's money demand, which follows convention in depending on transactions proxied by income and on financial wealth, unconventionally declines in business expansions because the usual increases in transactions demand are dominated by declines in wealth demand. Thus the wealth demand for money behaves countercyclically. How can that be? Tobin assumes, first, that in business expansions the increase in income raises tax revenues and reduces the government budget deficit and, second, that the issue of government bonds to finance the deficit falls off faster than corporate bonds are increased to finance more investment. During an expansion, therefore, the decline in the wealth demand for money produces a decline in the passive money supply ahead of income and gives the misleading appearance of causing a subsequent downturn in income—and conversely for cyclical contractions.

The timing in this model rests on fragile assumptions, however. If the government budget deficit is small, as it was for most of our history, a demand for money dependent on total financial wealth would not produce a lead over income, even for the special case here in which the supply is entirely passive to the demand.

Tobin goes on to point out, as had Walters (1967) earlier, that if money demand depends only on permanent income, exogenous changes in the money supply will produce large immediate changes in current income, because such changes are required to change permanent income sufficiently to bring money demand into equilibrium with the new supply. Such a relationship produces leads in money ahead of income that are short relative to the leads in Tobin's preceding model in which money does not affect income. Hence the preceding no-effect model is more consistent with the evidence of a long lead than is the permanent income model, contradicting a causal implication of leads. But this hardly proves that money cannot affect income. It need only imply that, given the observed long lead of money over income, the demand for money is not determined exclusively by permanent income. The demand is very likely subject to other influences and to adjustment lags that attenuate the large immediate effect on current income. A quarter century of research on the demand for money equation confirms the role of other influences and of lags in addition to the role of permanent income.

Although Tobin's model does not illuminate the actual relation between money and income, his argument succeeded in fostering skepticism of timing leads in economic variables as evidence of a direction of influence. Skepticism certainly has its place in empirical work, but timing leads deserve a word in their defense. Granted that leads are not by themselves conclusive evidence of directions of influence, as Kaldor and Tobin maintain, dismissing leads as irrelevant goes too far when our knowledge of the economic system points to the relationship suggested by an observed lead. The everyday world of business forecasting shows little skepticism of leads and for good reason. If a lead is moderately long, it is most likely not affected by feedback and therefore is suggestive of a causal relation. Most economic as well as physical effects travel forward in time.

There are some dangers of misinterpreting the appearance of a lead, to be sure. Rates of change shift the appearance of a timing sequence, as illustrated by a sine curve in which its rate of change both leads and lags its level. Nevertheless, misleading relationships involving rates of change can be uncovered by careful examination of the data. Another problem much discussed in recent literature involves expectations. The public may anticipate future changes in a variable and affect other variables ahead of the anticipated change. Thus asset prices may change before the economic events responsible for the change occur. But even in financial markets, which are most affected by expectations, such leads are surely not very long, given the sorry state of forecasting. The implication of rational expectations that observed leads may be misleading does not appear applicable to the nonfinancial sectors of the economy. A skepticism of leads based on rational expectations should not be carried too far.

3.3   Time-Series Regressions and Endogeneity

When empirical research became subservient to time-series regressions, largely since World War II, endogeneity of the variables on the right side of regressions was not thought to be a problem. Either causal sequencing was assumed by lagging the right-hand variables, or the use of annual data supposedly diminished any short-term feedback from the dependent variable. Time-series regressions came to be accepted as evidence of real-world relationships. (I take up the questionable validity of this acceptance below.)

The early study by Friedman and Meiselman (1963) called attention to the empirical importance of monetary effects on income by showing that money outperformed the driving variable of the Keynesian theory, autonomous investment. In extensions of their approach, the St. Louis equation confirmed the importance of money and the unimportance of fiscal variables (Andersen and Jordan 1968, Carlson 1986). Although fiscal variables sometimes rose above the floor of statistical insignificance, they never attained the importance they were supposed to have in the prevailing Keynesian theory. After a string of forecasting successes in the late 1960s, however, the St. Louis equation faltered in the 1970s and fell from favor. The inflationary 1970s nevertheless dramatically certified the importance of money for inflation and by implication also for output fluctuations.

The rational expectations developments in theory that rose to prominence in the late 1970s introduced new views of monetary effects. The new versions of the money-income regressions separated money into its anticipated and unanticipated components. Since the anticipated component is predictable, it must be endogenous to the economic system. This emphasis on anticipations presumes that the predictable, endogenous component of monetary growth is sizable and important.

Initial studies found that only unanticipated changes in money affect output, because prices fully absorb the anticipated changes. But then more sophisticated statistical tests reported that both components of monetary changes affect output. Apparently, empirical differences between the effects of anticipated and unanticipated monetary growth cannot be reliably established.[4]

These studies raise a question about the meaning and measurement of anticipated monetary growth. Clearly, after prices fully adjust to an increase in monetary growth, the temporary stimulation to output that occurred during the adjustment disappears. The only question concerns how rapidly the economy adjusts. If the measure of anticipated monetary growth implies a faster adjustment than in fact occurs, the analysis will show an effect of the anticipated growth on output. But there will be some measure of anticipated monetary growth consistent with the actual pace of price adjustment so that only the residual unanticipated growth correlates with output. Controversy arises here because the new view of expectations implies much faster adjustments than most studies can verify. No doubt anticipated money has little effect on output in data measuring cycle averages, but the more recent studies show that it has such effects in quarterly and even annual data. The existence of monetary effects is not at issue here. The only issue, to describe it in the new terminology, concerns how rapidly economic behavior becomes "rational." Since behavior is "rational" for cycle averages, the issue is whether it should be labeled "irrational" for shorter time spans, thereby suggesting some kind of failure of market adjustments. I might note that, if the stochastic component of economic variables can be characterized by permanent and transitory random shocks, rational economic behavior will respond to the expected values of the permanent component by filtering out the transitory component via an "adaptive expectations" adjustment which can take some time (Brunner, Cukierman, and Meltzer 1980).

Although motivated to examine the difference between anticipated and unanticipated monetary growth, these studies can also be interpreted as introducing a procedure—formalized later in "causality" tests—to remove endogenous changes in monetary growth that reflect predictable influences on the money supply. The residual changes in money, assumed to be "unanticipated," thus show an effect on output free of spurious correlation. Since the anticipated component of monetary growth is by derivation endogenous, the finding of later studies (see note 4) that it has equal effects on output can be faulted for depending on a variable that lacks exogeneity. Indeed, if an important component of money is anticipated, its endogeneity calls into question all regression studies that claim to find monetary effects.[5]

The old argument that correlation does not imply causation, which received little attention while econometric research focused on developing more sophisticated techniques, has now become a major issue. Consider the standard St. Louis equation, which regresses changes in nominal GNP on concurrent and past changes in money and government expenditures. These variables are assumed to represent unidirectional effects on GNP. That assumption can be questioned by the likely feedback from GNP to the concurrent change in money. In an attempt to avoid this feedback, the concurrent monetary variable can be omitted from the regression, with the purpose of isolating the effect of monetary changes that precede the change in GNP and likely have the major impact. Unfortunately, this does not necessarily eliminate the possibility of any feedback.

Feedback produced by expectations is one kind frequently discussed that may reach beyond concurrent movements. Thus policy may produce monetary changes in anticipation of future changes in GNP. Such feedback could, in principle, account for an observed correlation between GNP and earlier monetary changes. Nevertheless, this possibility seems far-fetched. Policy is generally not based on forecasts more than a quarter or two ahead. Even if this could be done accurately, the resulting relationship would not ordinarily produce a *positive* correlation with GNP, since policy is as often used to try to offset anticipated movements in aggregate demand as to reinforce them. To explain a positive feedback we must assume a channel working through the currency and reserve ratios, but it is hard to see why expectations should move these ratios ahead of developments in the economy. Feedback through expectations beyond the concurrent period, therefore, can surely be largely ignored, and in practice they usually are.

However, a potentially serious form of feedback can result from normal serial correlation in the money and GNP series. Suppose GNP affects money concurrently. The serial correlation in GNP will then transmit its concurrent feedback to monetary changes earlier and later in time. The resulting correlation with earlier monetary changes will give the appearance of their causal influence on GNP even if no such influence actually exists. To take a simple extreme example, suppose economic activity generated a concurrent cyclical fluctuation in the currency ratio and thence in the money supply. There is indeed evidence of such an effect (Cagan 1965). Cyclical fluctuations implant serial correlation in economic data. The fluctuations in economic activity will correlate with past changes in money, contaminating the evidence of the St. Louis equation. The correlation will, of course, also appear between activity and future changes in money, giving the impression that money is endogenous to past changes in activity as well.

The possible presence of this form of feedback still leaves open whether it can account for the association between money and income. When Friedman and Schwartz and I discussed this question of the direction of influence, we concluded that the money-income association could be explained only in part by the effect of activity on money, because the sources and nature of this effect varied considerably over time and could not account for the consistency of the observed association. The historical evidence indicated that only a strong monetary effect could account for such a consistent association over a long history of cycles.

Such historical analysis of the evidence has not satisfied a preference for formal statistical testing, however, and regressions have become the accepted form of empirical analysis. The new "causality" tests emphasize the point that the existence of serial correlation and feedback compromise evidence based solely on conventional time-series regressions.

3.4 Testing for Causality

I see the motivation for the revolution in method introduced by Granger (1969) and Sims (1972) as residing in the feedback problem. To ascertain the effect of a variable that is partially endogenous, their causality tests remove the serial correlation in a pair of variables and then look for any remaining correlation between them. This "whitening" of the data eliminates the appearance of feedback that is carried by serial correlation backwards and forwards in the data. The basic idea is that only a cross correlation that survives the extraction of serial correlation in the individual series provides evidence of a direction of influence that can be identified by statistical means.

Much has been written in criticism of these tests because of the initial claim that they identified causal influences. Philosophical critics objected to the derivation of something so basic as a "cause" from unstructured statistical relationships (Zellner 1979). So at best the tests can claim only to look for exogeneity and temporal sequences. Econometric critics pointed to the problem of expectations and technical difficulties of prewhitening (Feige and Pearce 1979). As general propositions, the criticisms carry weight, but in application to the money-income relationship, we have specific knowledge to make judgments about expectations. Expectations are simply too weak and inaccurate to account for strong correlations over more than a short time horizon. As for the philosophical question of causality, economists do traditionally reach tentative conclusions from statistical time sequences about directions of influence when our theory gives a sound basis for expecting such influences.

The difficulties of prewhitening are another matter. Similar to the studies of unanticipated money, the tests of causality at first found an effect of money on output as well as prices. However, many subsequent studies reported mixed or negative results, particularly for foreign countries, apparently owing to differences in the method of removing serial correlation from the variables.[6] Although these studies are not all equal in technical sophistication and quality of scholarship, it is still not a simple matter for readers to determine the degree of validity of a particular study, much less a group of studies covering different countries and periods. Despite the number of clear indications of monetary effects the totality of this literature leaves the evidence subject to considerable doubt. As concluded by Feige and Pearce (1979, 532),

Since a variety of prefilters can be used to attain the objective of whitening regression residuals, we are left with the uncomfortable conclusion that an essentially arbitrary choice left to the discretion of individual researchers can significantly affect the nature of the economic conclusions derived from the test procedures.

3.5 The VAR Statistical Method

These causality tests disregard the possible influence of other variables on the two under examination—a major deficiency. This led Sims (1980b) to expand the number of variables included by means of a VAR method. To examine monetary effects, the VAR groups money with a set of other relevant variables, usually output, prices, interest rates, and sometimes bank credit, and regresses each one on lagged values of themselves and each other. The estimated coefficients of these regressions show the effects of the lagged values of the variables on each other, after the correlation between the lagged values of all the right-hand variables has been removed. In practice this method avoids the need for prewhitening the data because it effectively removes the serial correlation in each variable as well as the cross correlation of the right-hand variables with concurrent and past values of each other. What remains are statistically exogenous movements in the right-hand variables, attributable to events from outside the system of variables being examined. Only if these exogenous movements in money then correlate with subsequent movements in output, in which correlations of output with past values of itself and the variables other than money have also been removed, does uncontaminated evidence of a monetary effect exist.

In view of the problem of disentangling multiple influences, VAR is a legitimate and welcome attempt to deal with spurious correlation. It can help to confirm effects that are obscured by relationships among endogenous variables. Let us leave aside the various econometric objections (Leamer 1985, Cooley and LeRoy 1985). I want to raise objections of a practical nature that have received less attention. I have no quarrel with the purpose and the method, but rather take exception to the interpretation of the results. The VAR seems to me to be hopelessly unreliable and low in power to detect monetary effects of the kind we are looking for and believe, from other kinds of evidence, to exist.

A VAR test can answer two questions. First, how much effect does an exogenous disturbance in one of the variables of the system have on output? An unfortunate ambiguity arises here if concurrent disturbances in the different variables are correlated. In the absence of a theoretical structure, a sequential ordering of concurrent correlated disturbances must be imposed arbitrarily. If we are willing to treat all of the concurrent disturbances in money as exogenous, the VAR can answer an important second question about the effect of monetary changes. This is given by the statistical significance of the lagged monetary variables in a regression of output on the lagged values of money and the other variables of the system.

In the widely noted article by Sims (1980b), money affected output in the VAR system but, in the post–World War II period, not after an interest rate was included. The interest rate in that period accounted for most of the effect on output previously attributed to money. In other studies a credit variable equals and sometimes surpasses the effect on output and prices of money. The findings of these studies are not all in mutual agreement, but the overall implication is that money responds endogenously to other economic variables and that its observed simple correlation with output and perhaps also prices may reflect a spurious correlation produced by other economic influences.[7]

3.6   Interpretation of an Interest-Rate Effect

Sims (1980b) explained the result that an interest rate knocks out the significant effect of money by extending the theory that business recessions reflect exogenous declines in the marginal product of investment: Businesses anticipate this decline in investment opportunities, which leads to a reduction in investment expenditures and eventually in output. In the meantime, before the anticipated decline in the marginal product of investment actually occurs, the decline in investment reduces the prices of new capital goods and *increases* the yield on existing capital as measured by the ratio of its still intact returns to its lower market prices. Interest rates follow this rise in capital yields. Such a rise in interest rates would, as Sims suggests, correlate negatively with the subsequent decline in output. But one wonders how much a three-month interest rate would be affected by the yield on existing capital goods. Would not the assumed decline in borrowing more likely succeed in lowering short-term interest rates?

The sequence of effects outlined by Sims puts an unbelievable weight on the ability of investors to foresee future changes in the marginal product of investment. To avoid this, alternative theories are available to account for an association between interest rates and future output. A rise in interest rates is widely thought to work to depress output. If money is not to play an active role, however, we must assume that the money supply adjusts passively to induced changes in its demand. In Sims's VAR results, money declines as interest rates rise, which he attributes to a passive response of supply to a decline in the demand for money balances induced by the rise in interest rates and fall in output. This reasoning attributes movements along the supply curve improperly to movements along the demand curve. The subsequent fall in output could reduce monetary growth, but the earlier rise in interest rates would ordinarily increase monetary growth as banks expand to take advantage of higher rates and as the Fed partially accommodates the expansion. In any event, what then becomes of the decline in monetary growth that Friedman and Schwartz found to lead business downturns? Apparently the VAR relates the monetary decline to the concurrent rise in interest rates. To attribute that relation to a passive response of the money supply to a decline in its demand seems to me shaky. The widely accepted explanation of a *negative* relation between interest rates and money goes the other way, such that the monetary change induces the change in interest rates.

Sims does consider a possible monetary interpretation of his results, whereby interest rates reflect but precede exogenous changes in money. He conjectures that this might happen if policy changes in the monetary base have delayed effects on the money stock but affect interest rates immediately. Yet he rejects this alternative hypothesis, because the interest rate continues to dominate in his VARs even after the monetary base is substituted for the money supply.

Sims overlooked the alternative explanation subsequently pointed out by McCallum (1983). If the Fed targets interest rates, money becomes endogenous to the interest-rate target. Nevertheless, it is monetary policy, setting interest rates in response to market developments, that determines the outcome.

The historical importance of interest-rate targeting certainly raises doubts about a business cycle theory based on exogenous shocks to interest rates. But McCallum's point, while important, may not provide a full explanation. Interest-rate targets have not always determined monetary policy, particularly beyond very short-run horizons, so that many longer-run fluctuations in money have other explanations. No doubt many of these monetary fluctuations are also related through policy decisions and banking responses to market developments. Nevertheless, to attribute all or most monetary fluctuations to interest rates conflicts with other evidence. In the straightforward NBER analysis of cyclical turning points, monetary growth displays long and variable leads, while short-term interest rates have little or no leads on a positive basis over business cycle peaks (Cagan 1966). This apparent inconsistency with the VAR results calls for further study.[8]

3.7   The VAR in Practice

With the VAR results we have arrived at the anomalous situation in which the latest econometric techniques frequently find that money does not affect activity, and perhaps not prices either, even though such effects are confidently expected in financial markets, by the monetary authorities themselves, and indeed by most economists. What is going on here? This is not a case of research ignoring some of the messy but unimportant details of reality. These results conflict with the major effects of money as widely perceived. A conflict between research results and widely perceived reality has never stopped economists, to be sure, but it should give pause for second thoughts.

The VAR literature is growing apace, and perhaps some plausible and generally accepted interpretation of these anomalous results will soon emerge. Much leeway exists for tinkering with the form of the equations. Economic research often gives birth to conflicting results which subject a line of research to controversy. But usually controversies can be understood in terms of differing hypotheses about economic behavior. For example, when money stood near the bottom of the totem pole of relative importance, nonmonetary explanations of the business cycle invoked theories of an investment accelerator, or the "animal spirits" of businessmen, or shocks to the consumption function—all capable of empirical interpretation and examination. In most of the VAR results, by contrast, one struggles in vain to decipher what they imply about economic behavior, inasmuch as the VAR method cooks the data beyond recognition.

To illustrate the VAR method I regressed real GNP on lagged values of itself, the GNP deflator, the commercial paper rate, and money, from first-quarter 1951 to second-quarter 1987. The variables are log levels, and each right-hand series is represented by eight lag terms. This is one equation of a typical four-variable VAR system to test for monetary effects. With the commercial paper rate excluded to form a three-variable system, the money terms are collectively highly significant, but with the commercial paper rate included the money terms have a much lower, though still significant, level of .035. No detrending was applied. Sims (1980b) found money to be insignificant in the latter four-variable system with monthly data using industrial production for real GNP and twelve lag terms. Stock and Watson (1987) resurrected the significance of money for the same monthly system, but for a shorter period beginning with 1960 and after detrending the data. The major differences in results depending on the data series used and on the time period covered illustrates a certain lack of robustness of VAR.

Figure 3.1 shows the residual terms of my quarterly real GNP regression with the money terms first included and then excluded. As shown by the amplitude of the residuals, the predicted values of both regressions lie mostly within 1 percent of the level of real GNP. The two residual series differ by only a small fraction of the amplitude of business cycle fluctuations. From the point of view of predicting GNP, the

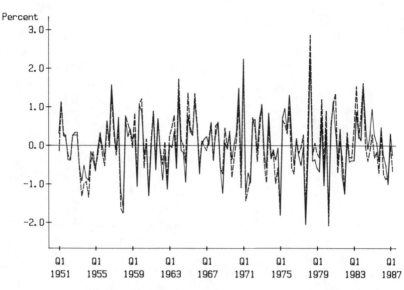

Fig. 3.1   Residual terms from regressions of real GNP on lagged values of real GNP, GNP deflator, commercial paper rate, and with M1 included (solid) and excluded (dotted), quarterly, 1951–1987 Q2. *Note:* Residuals from regressions described in fn. 9.

economic as opposed to statistical significance of including money here hardly pays its way.

What does the contribution of the money terms, buried in these computations, look like? Figure 3.2 gives their picture. It is based on the principle that the partial correlation of a dependent on an independent variable in a multiple regression is equivalent to the simple correlation between the residuals of the two variables from regressions on the other independent variables. Thus, in this case, the eight lagged monetary variables are regressed in turn on the other independent variables (including the other seven monetary variables, which excludes the one as dependent variable), and the residuals of these regressions are cumulated in a sum for each date which is weighted by the regression coefficients of the monetary terms in the full four-variable regression. The correlation of this series in figure 3.2 with the residuals of the regression excluding the money series (the dotted series in figure 3.1) is equivalent to a test of the combined significance of the eight money terms.[9]

Figure 3.2 shows the contribution of the monetary terms to real GNP in the VAR regression, as just described, and figure 3.3 shows the quarterly rates of actual monetary growth and the tendency of their fluctuations to lead business turns. The VAR by comparison attenuates

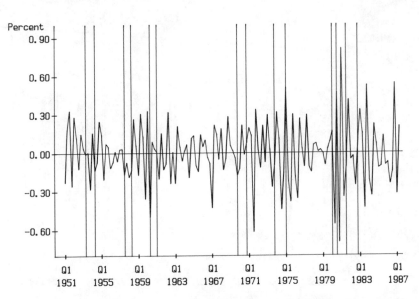

Fig. 3.2   Contribution of monetary terms to real GNP in a four-variable VAR system, quarterly, 1951–1987 Q2. *Note:* Shorter periods between vertical lines represent NBER business recessions. Weighted sum of residuals derived as explained in fn. 9.

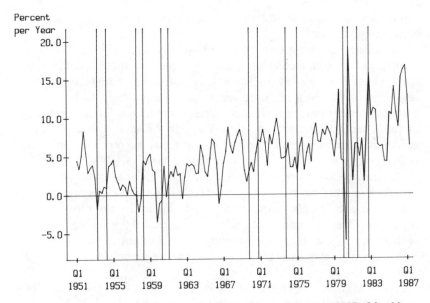

Fig. 3.3   Monetary growth (M1), quarterly, 1951–1987 Q2. *Note:* Shorter periods between vertical lines represent NBER business recessions.

and largely eliminates the cyclical fluctuations in monetary growth (and in real GNP as well) before testing for their correlation. Note the relatively small amplitude of fluctuation of the monetary contribution in figure 3.2. (The comparison of amplitudes between figures 3.2 and 3.3 is admittedly made difficult by the difference in units. Figure 3.2 shows quarterly deviations on the order of one-third of a percent, largely offsetting over each of several quarters. Figure 3.3 shows annual rates of change, with cyclical fluctuations on the order of roughly 4 percentage points, that is, 4 percent in a year.) Thus VAR looks to the noncyclical, very short-run movements in economic variables to identify their cross effects. This critically limits the evidence and poses serious problems for identifying monetary effects.

3.8   Deficiencies of the VAR Method

VAR originated as a welcome response to the largely neglected problem of spurious correlation among economic variables. But are its results trustworthy? Its application to money points up three problems that the generally voiced econometric criticisms gloss over. These are the linearity of regressions, the complex interaction between money and interest rates, and the elimination of most of the cyclical fluctuations in money. The first two are not problems confined to VARs, as will be noted.

Linearity governs all regression analyses and may often be a reasonable approximation to a moderately nonlinear reality. But for monetary effects it is not reasonable and cannot be made so by transformations to logarithms or to first differences. The limitations of linearity apply to St. Louis–type equations as well as VARs. Monetary episodes vary substantially in timing and cannot all be represented by the same values of parameters and fixed lag patterns. This seems clear from historical analysis.[10] Perhaps the variability in the timing of monetary effects can be represented by a complex dynamic system, but certainly not by a three- or four-variable VAR or by any system of equations we are now capable of specifying. Moreover, the timing varies from stage to stage of business cycles, so regressions fit to subperiods covering a few cycles do not avoid the problem. Thus a fixed lag pattern estimates a varying lag pattern as an average, which reduces the estimated correlation between money and the variables it affects. The extent of the reduction could be substantial, possibly to the point of not showing a significant effect. Money illustrates the theoretical point that a linear *in*dependence does not rule out a nonlinear dependence of some kind. (See Snowder 1984.)

Consider the variation in the lag of monetary effects in recent cyclical downturns. In 1966 and 1969 monetary growth (M1) peaked about a half year before business activity did. The monetary peak preceded the business peak at the end of 1973 by about a year and preceded the sharp decline in output in October 1974 by almost two years (though the peak in output came earlier and was followed by a plateau). By comparison, the lag in monetary effect was just a few months at the early 1980 business peak precipitated by the imposition of credit controls, and again just a few months at the mid-1981 business peak which appeared short because the escalation of inflation had earlier reduced monetary growth in real terms. One average lag pattern does not capture the variety of these episodes. The variations in monetary relationships reflect their complexity and not changes in "monetary regimes," as that term has recently been used.

As a second problem with VARs that include an interest rate, the varying interaction between money and interest rates can hide monetary effects. Interest rates can at times influence monetary growth positively because of a response by bank lending and monetary policy, and at other times a tight or easy monetary policy affects interest rates negatively. These interactions make both money and interest rates partly endogenous. In addition, the cyclical pattern of interest rates conforms to business activity, so that the rise of rates in expansions correlates negatively with the subsequent decline in activity. If the movements in interest rates that are exogenous to monetary growth have a more systematic cyclical pattern than do the movements in monetary growth that are exogenous to interest rates, the VAR will show a closer correlation between interest rates and business activity than between money and activity. Yet this finding would give the wrong impression of the monetary process at work. And there would be no way to determine the true relationship by linear regression methods.

As a specific example take the 1969 episode. The Fed reduced monetary growth drastically beginning in April.[11] In due course a credit crunch developed in September producing sharp increases in interest rates, and business turned down in December. Given a fairly consistent relation between interest rates and business activity and the timing variability of monetary effects, the VAR analysis will find support for the role of interest rates in the 1969 episode and downplay the decline in monetary growth. But that misrepresents the paramount role of monetary policy in this episode.

A third problem with VARs is that the particular technique for dealing with spurious correlation eliminates important monetary changes. By removing all serial and cross correlations from economic series, VAR reduces them to exogenous movements and looks for correlation between these movements in each pair of series. But these exogenous movements are little more than isolated blips in the series, which in monetary growth have little effect on GNP. The financial system filters out the effect of monetary blips. Only changes in monetary growth that are maintained for an extended period of time affect business activity. These extended changes in monetary growth, however, exhibit serial correlation and, despite their variable lags in affecting output and prices, tend to be correlated with cyclical movements in other economic variables. The VAR accordingly eliminates the correlated movements in money as endogenous to the economic system. Thus does this technique give new meaning to the old cliché of "throwing the baby out with the bath water." Only the monetary changes that have little effect on GNP survive elimination in the VAR process.

Will money be more prone to the emasculation of the VAR process than other economic variables? It is likely to be. The interrelationships of the financial system produce comovements in money and interest rates and other credit variables that appear to be more systematic than the varying effects of money on business activity. The latter effects will therefore have low power in VAR tests.

3.9 General Observations about VAR and Time-Series Regressions

Despite the above objections to VAR, the problem it addresses of endogeneity and spurious correlation cannot be waved aside. Indeed, the VAR methodology derives from the accepted treatment of endogenous independent variables in conventional time-series regressions. The conventional treatment of endogeneity in economic models has essentially assumed it away. In econometric estimation the lagging of independent variables supposedly makes them exogenous. As the VAR method indicates, this is not valid. Instrumental variables, widely used to avoid spurious correlation with the residual error term, are generally not exogenous to the system; they may reduce some spurious correlation but do not eliminate it. In reality nearly all the important effects in the economy reflect movements in variables that are basically endogenous to the system. Even monetary and fiscal policy, which are typically treated as exogenous, basically are not.[12] Their endogeneity is sometimes handled by introducing reaction functions, based on a quadratic tradeoff between desired levels of inflation, unemployment, interest rates, and exchange rates. These functions have not worked. It is not possible to describe macroeconomic behavior solely in terms of exogenous variables. The economy is essentially a closed system. No doubt the weather is exogenous, but that is no help where agriculture plays a minor role. Even the sudden increase in oil prices by OPEC in 1973 and 1979 was not entirely exogenous and, in any event, cannot by itself fully explain the subsequent economic developments. Long-run movements reflecting resource and productivity growth can perhaps be treated as largely exogenous, but not their cyclical movements. Since regressions require exogenous independent variables, ordinary time-series regressions cannot provide valid evidence of economic effects.

As a specific example, endogeneity problems plague estimation of the money demand equation. In different studies of the standard equation a variety of specifications and explanatory variables are found to be significant. Not all of them are likely to be. Some of them are proxies for others, which means that the basic relationship cannot be identified precisely. Interest rates and real income are treated as exogenous, which supposes that changes in the money supply do not affect real income or interest rates. While possibly valid for the long run, these assumptions cannot claim validity for the short run. Some studies (Goldfeld 1973, Artis and Lewis 1976) claim comparable results whether the money demand equation treats the interest rate as a dependent or independent variable. The former is questionable, however, because real money balances have only a short-run influence on interest rates, quite different from the long-run relation, and because real income remaining on the right-hand side cannot be treated as independent of interest rates or real money balances. Furthermore, a study by Mehra (1978a) found that the interest rate and income are not exogenous to money when all are measured in nominal terms, yet the popular Koyck-lag adjustment, which gives better results when money balances are measured in nominal rather than real terms (Liang 1984, Fair 1987, but see Goldfeld and Sichel 1987), thus suffers from lack of exogeneity. Finally, when joint estimation of a supply equation takes account of the effect of interest rates on money supply as well as demand, the interest rate is either treated as an exogenous variable or is assumed to be determined by the demand and supply of money (Teigen 1964, Brunner and Meltzer 1964, Gibson 1972), ignoring the effect of investment demand. The VAR method tells us that these estimation procedures are invalid and the results highly questionable.

To be sure, any sweeping rejection of regression analysis needs qualification. While cross-section data also suffer from spurious correlations, these are often amenable to treatment. Time-series regressions sometimes give acceptable estimates of the parameters when the precise specification of an equation and the exogeneity of the independent variables can be taken for granted, as in some micro industry studies. Where interrelationships play out in a short time horizon and feedback is minimal, regressions can identify influences. Thus some work on asset price movements and relationships appear legitimate. And strict random walk hypotheses can be tested by time-series regressions.

In general, however, time-series regressions sit on a shaky foundation. Explanatory variables are employed that do not meet the statistical criterion of exogeneity. The well-known prevalence of correlation among virtually all economic variables and the ease of finding statistical significance in almost any specification of economic equations raise warning flags. It is increasingly difficult to take the myriad runs of computer printouts seriously, except as simple descriptions of the data. Can anyone have confidence in regression methods when numerous studies of the same relationships for the same period give contradictory results? Time-series regression studies give no sign of the scientific ideal of converging toward the truth. If the call to take the "con" out of econometrics (Leamer 1983) led to a new practice of checking the robustness of regression equations to changes in specification, the result would be that few time-series regressions would stand up to a wide-ranging sensitivity analysis. Other variables can invariably be found to reduce any given partial correlation. Understandably, analyses showing lack of robustness heretofore have not appeared in articles offered to journals or accepted for publication. (See the proposal by Feige 1975.) The VAR method calls our attention to the deficiency of present practices.

The existence of endogeneity and its corollary of multicollinearity and spurious correlation has long been recognized as a problem for economics as a nonexperimental science. The early warning of Yule (1926)—"Why do we sometimes get nonsense correlations?"—has long been simply ignored, though the problem is receiving increasing attention (Granger and Newbold 1974, Leamer 1983, Lovell 1983, Los 1986). The VAR methodology tells us to dismiss any apparent effects of variables that cannot be certified as exogenous. Its solution is to isolate exogenous "shocks" to the variables. VAR depends on the exogenous movements being sufficiently strong and numerous to show up after their extraction from the original data. It can identify a relationship among economic variables if some indication of it remains after the systematic movements in the time series are removed.

But, while the VAR method can help to confirm economic effects, its results, when often negative, are not conclusive. Money has difficulty passing VAR tests, yet by all other indications it plays an important role in business fluctuations. If the movements in money identified as endogenous by VAR and extracted from the data series were instead eliminated by monetary policy, would the economy be the same? Hardly anyone thinks so. Since regression analysis cannot evaluate the effect of these monetary changes, it fails in its principal purpose.

Although skepticism of time-series regressions has become widespread, the practical consequences are widely resisted. The purpose and limitations of the VAR method argue for less dependence on macroeconomic regression fitting of all kinds, but too much capital has been invested in econometric time-series techniques for this to happen, at least very soon. As practiced today, empirical macroeconomics could not survive without them.

Yet empirical research need not be so dependent on time-series regressions. It can proceed as it did before the computer made multiple regressions so cheap and plentiful. Economic research can reemphasize the kind of careful historical analysis that we honor Anna Schwartz for at this conference. In such research the mutual relationship among variables can be studied, and the subtle differences among historical episodes can provide clues to the channels of influence at work. The pseudo-precision of regression analysis once seemed to promise statistical tests of monetary effects, but now this appears to have been an illusion. In contrast to the questionable, conflicting, and obscure results of time-series regressions, general historical analysis presents understandable evidence and, though lacking the finality of formal statistical testing, usually converges to a consensus on the facts and often also on an interpretation of the facts. I see an indication here and there in the journals of a return to empirical studies where regressions may supplement but do not dominate a broad analysis. Anna Schwartz's monetary research (1987) will not, it may be hoped, be the last of a fine tradition of scholarship.

Notes

1. Suppose monetary changes are induced by the variable Z, so monetary effects on GNP are attributable to Z. The question is, if the effect of Z on money could be altered, would Z still have the same effect on GNP? If monetary effects exist, the answer is no, despite the fact that money is otherwise endogenous when determined by Z.

2. Kaldor carried his argument of an endogenous money supply to the amazing conclusion that money has no effect on anything, apparently including prices. He does accord a minor role to "liquidity," as described in the Radcliffe Report (1959), but not to any ordinary concept of money. In his model of the economy the price level appears to be tied to labor costs without a monetary anchor. For a similar view see Davidson and Weintraub (1973). Fortunately, that point of view no longer has much of a following.

On the importance of the range of evidence in *A Monetary History*, see Hirsch and de Marchi (1986).

3. Buiter (1984), in support of Tobin's argument, notes that endogeneity of the money supply hides its effects in the data. He concludes that changes in policy regimes are needed to validate monetary effects. Cottrell (1986) defends Kaldor with an argument also based on the endogeneity of money.

4. The emphasis on unanticipated monetary growth began with studies by Barro (1977, 1978, 1981) and Barro and Rush (1980) of U.S. data. Dutkowsky and Atesoglu (1986) verified that the model held up in postsample forecasts to

1984. Confirmatory support that only *un*anticipated changes in money affected output was provided by Leiderman (1980) for the United States, Wogin (1980) and Darrat (1985a) for Canada, Attfield, Demery, and Duck (1981a, 1981b) and Bellante, Morrell, and Zardkoohi (1982) for the United Kingdom, Darrat (1985b) for West Germany, Blejer and Fernandez (1980) for Mexico, and Attfield and Duck (1983) for a cross section of eleven countries. Kormendi and Meguire (1984) found that monetary shocks affected output in forty-seven countries while the effects faded with time, which by suggesting no effect in the long run was consistent with the Barro thesis of the neutrality of anticipated monetary changes. Similarly, Haraf (1978) found that monetary surprises affected inventories and orders before aggregate output, but appeared to have no long-term effect. Brocato (1985) verified the U.S. output effects of unanticipated money, though he ignored the anticipated component. Grossman (1979) concluded that only unanticipated changes in policy affected U.S. output, on the assumption that policy determined aggregate demand as proxied by nominal GNP. Enders and Falk (1984) found that only unanticipated money affected output for an individual industry, U.S. pork production.

Many other studies cast doubt on these results, however. Barro (1979b) could not confirm his U.S. results for three foreign countries: for Mexico, anticipated money affected output, and for Brazil and Colombia, all monetary effects were weak, though the inability to fit adequate money supply functions precluded clear conclusions. Anticipated money dominated the effect on output in Japan (Pigott 1978). Small (1979) revised Barro's measurement of unanticipated money for the United States and found its effect to be no greater than that for anticipated money, though in reply, Barro (1979a) defended his results. Froyen (1979) and Sheffrin (1979) also reported that anticipated money affected U.S. output. Darby (1983) found an extremely weak effect of unanticipated money on output for seven foreign countries and only a small effect for the United States post–World War II. In a study of the pre–World War I U.S. data under the gold standard (Rush 1985), neither monetary component affected output. Kimbrough and Koray (1984) got mixed results for Canada and negative results for the United States on output effects of unanticipated money; in addition, they could not reject an effect of anticipated money for either country. Similarly, in Darrat (1985c) deflated aggregate money dominated unanticipated money in unemployment effects for three European countries. Demery, Duck, and Musgrave (1984) could find only qualified support for unanticipated money effects on real variables for West Germany. Korteweg (1978) showed that anticipated money growth correlated with inflation in the Netherlands, but could find no effect of money on output at all. Boschen and Grossman (1982) and Boschen (1985) reported no differences in output effects of observed and unobserved money, which contradicts the supposed importance of anticipations.

Another series of studies revised Barro's estimation procedure and found the same effect for anticipated and unanticipated money. These studies of U.S. data were Cuddington (1980), Makin (1982), Gordon (1982), Mishkin (1982a, 1982b, 1983), Driscoll et al. (1983a), Merrick (1983), Carns and Lombra (1983), Sheehey (1984), Sheehan (1985), and Cecchetti (1986). Cecchetti (1987) also reported similar results for eight foreign countries, as did Darrat (1985e) for Italy, and Hoffman and Schlagenhauf (1982) for the United States and five foreign countries except for Canada, where anticipated money did *not* affect output. But Askari (1986) found that output was affected for Canada using a more complicated statistical test. In a trivariate autoregression of U.S. real GNP, prices, and money, McGee and Stasiak (1985) found that anticipated money affected real GNP in the short run, though not the long run. For post–

World War II U.K. data, Garner (1982) and Driscoll et al. (1983b) found that anticipated money affected output in the short run, as did Demery (1984) when allowance was made for expected changes in velocity; Driscoll, Mullineux, and Sen (1985) rejected the neutrality (that is, no effect on output) of anticipated money and rational expectations in a joint test; and Bean (1984) rejected neutrality for anticipated M1 but not £M3.

To avoid the endogeneity of anticipated money, Rush (1986) showed that only shocks to the monetary base affected unemployment in the United States from 1920 to 1983 (except for the 1930s), and the estimated effect of the anticipated base had the wrong sign and presumably had no real effects.

5. Nor is the interpretation of *un*anticipated money free of ambiguity. Pesaran (1982) points out that, if the money supply were determined passively by interest-rate targeting, the correlation of the derived unanticipated monetary growth with output could be interpreted as consistent with Keynesian types of nonmonetary effects on output. I find this Keynesian interpretation doubtful because the Barro (1977) money supply equation implies a negative effect of government expenditures on output. Nevertheless, possible spurious correlation opens up these results to alternative interpretations. Rush (1985) interpreted the lack of correlation between U.S. money and output in pre–World War I in his study as due to the endogeneity of money.

6. In addition to Sims's study (1972), evidence of a monetary effect was also found for the United States by Neftci and Sargent (1978), Brillembourg and Khan (1979), and Hafer (1981). Two-way effects between money and income were reported by Hsiao (1979b) in one test and only a weak relationship in a second test, and by Thornton and Batten (1985), who also found a short-run one-way effect of the monetary base, as did Mehra (1978). Paulter and Rivard (1979), however, found one-way effects of all the monetary aggregates but no effect of the base. Ciccolo (1978) reported a monetary effect for the U.S. interwar period and a weak two-way effect for the post–World War II period. For other countries: Huffman and Lothian (1980) found mixed results for the United Kingdom—two-sided effects for post–World War II (as did Mixon, Pratt, and Wallace 1980), a weak monetary effect for 1870–1914, and a strong monetary effect for 1837–70; Hsiao (1979a), supported by Osborn (1984), found two-way effects for Canada, as did Komura (1982) for Japan, Layton (1985) for Australia, and Wachter (1979) for money and prices in Chile; and unidirectional monetary effects were reported by Sharpe and Miller (1975) and Jones (1985) for Canada, von Hagen (1984) for West Germany, and by Darrat (1985d, 1986) on prices for three major OPEC, and three North African, countries.

Decidedly mixed results subject to the prefiltering method or the test used were reported by Sargent (1976), Schwert (1979), and Kang (1985) for the United States, and Kamath (1985) for India. Falls and Hill (1985) found for the United States that money "caused" prices but not output for 1972–79, and the reverse of those effects for 1979–83, apparently owing to the change in policy regime. Christiano and Ljungqvist (1988) claim that insignificant monetary effects for the United States reflect an inappropriate first-differencing of the data.

Negative results of causality tests for money were reported by Barth and Bennett (1974) for Canada, qualified by Auerbach and Rutner (1978); Feige and Pearce (1979) and Geweke (1986) for the United States; Pierce (1977) for monetary effects on U.S. retail sales; Williams, Goodhart, and Gowland (1976) for U.K. output in post–World War II, though they did find a monetary effect on prices; Mills and Wood (1978) for the U.K. gold-standard period (1870–1914); Van Hoa (1981) and Weissenberger and Thomas (1983) for West Germany; and Parikh (1984) for Indonesia. Although money and prices appear to be causally independent in post–World War II Spain, C. and F. Hernández-Iglesias (1981) argue that bidirectional causality is difficult to detect without large changes as in hyperinflation.

7. An early VAR study by Sargent and Sims (1977) found that money affected unemployment in the short run, and Sims (1980a) confirmed this result for GNP in the United States but not in West Germany, where the effect was weak and in the long run nonexistent. For pre–World War I, Dwyer (1985) found a monetary effect on prices in the United States but none in the United Kingdom. Eichengreen (1983) subdivided the U.K. pre–World War I period and found effects of the monetary base after 1870 but not before. For both the United States and United Kingdom pre–World War I, Huffman and Lothian (1984) found evidence of monetary effects on real income, but also cross-country feedback on money consistent with the specie-flow mechanism. Their VAR included an interest rate, as did a trivariate test showing monetary effects on income and an interest rate for India (Laumas and Porter-Hudak 1986).

However, monetary effects often disappear when an interest rate is included and partially do so when a debt variable is included. Sims (1980b) found no effect in the United States for post–World War II data with an interest rate, nor did Hsiao (1982) for Canada. U.K. postwar output depended on monetary policy when proxied by M1 and an interest rate, but not when proxied by M1 and M3 without the interest rate (Bean 1984). For post–World War II U.S. data, Myatt (1986) reported that money does not affect prices, and Fackler (1985) that neither money nor a debt variable affects quarterly real GNP or prices, though possibly money and debt do so indirectly through the interest rate. Litterman and Weiss (1985) reported that a measure of the real interest rate is the exogenous source of changes in money, prices, and output. Eichenbaum and Singleton (1986) showed that these results could be sensitive to statistical technique: A monetary effect on real GNP was significant when they removed a linear trend from the data, but was not significant when they used first differencing. In a more elaborate model adjusted for trend, Bernanke (1986) found a significant monetary effect, as did Stock and Watson (1987) using the same data series as Sims (1980b). It is difficult to diagnose how differences in statistical procedure affect all these results.

Friedman (1983a, 1983b) initiated the VAR study of credit or debt and monetary effects. He reported that money and debt shared comparable effects on real income. McMillin and Fackler (1984) tested a range of financial aggregates including money and found that all except bank credit affected income, though there was feedback from income particularly to money. No consensus has emerged about debt. Porter and Offenbacher (1983) found the effects of money to be somewhat stronger than those of debt, but found the results to be sensitive to the measurement and ordering of the variables. King (1986) also found money stronger than a bank loans variable and the results sensitive to ordering. Bernanke (1986) used a structural model to order the variables and found bank loans and money to be of equal importance. In Granger-causality tests (Hafer 1985), both M1 and debt affected GNP, but debt made no marginal contribution after the monetary effects, and the feedback of GNP was greater on debt than on money. (In related earlier studies of policy indicators, debt and money had comparable effects [Davis 1979] and debt effects on GNP that were independent of M1 largely reflected the liquid asset component and, in the 1970s, largely M2 [Cagan 1982]).

8. A problem also arises with VAR results attributing a major exogenous influence to bank credit. Bernanke (1986) argues that shocks to the supply of

bank credit affect the amount rationed to bank-tied borrowers, who reduce spending and contract aggregate demand. If banks are unable to lend to their borrowers, however, a given total supply of credit will reach other borrowers in the economy. If the total supply declines, one reason could be a reduction in monetary growth. If the VAR removes correlated movements in money and credit, it eliminates important monetary effects on aggregate demand from consideration.

The emphasis on rationed bank credit resurrects a largely forgotten controversy of the 1950s (see Bach and Huizenga 1961).

9. The VAR test determines the level of significance of the monetary variables in the OLS regression

$$(1) \quad \log O_t = \text{const.} + \Sigma a_i \log O_{t-i} + \Sigma b_i \log M_{t-i}$$
$$+ \Sigma c_i \log P_{t-i} + \Sigma d_i \log R_{t-i} + \varepsilon_t$$

where O is real GNP, M money stock (M1 version), P GNP price deflator, R commercial paper rate, and ε the residual error; $a, \ldots, d$ are regression coefficients, and the summation Σ runs from $i = 1$ to 8 (eight lagged quarters).

The two series in figure 3.1 are the residual values of the regression with the money terms excluded (solid) and included (dotted).

The money series in figure 3.2 was derived as follows. Each lagged value of money in the above regression was regressed on the other independent variables. That is, eight regressions were run, one for each of the lagged log $M(k)$, $k = 1, \ldots, 8$, in (1). Each of these series was regressed on

$$(2) \quad \text{const.} + \Sigma f_i \log O_{t-i} + \Sigma g_i \log P_{t-i} + \Sigma h_i \log R_{t-i}$$
$$+ \Sigma j_i \log M_{t-i} + \mu_i(k)$$

where f,g,h,j are regression coefficients and the summation Σ runs from 1 to 8 quarters, except for the monetary lags which omit the lag term that corresponds to the dependent variable in each regression.

Figure 3.2 shows the sum for each quarter t of $\Sigma \hat{b}_k \mu_t(k)$ for $k = 1, \ldots, 8$ where $\hat{b}_k$ is the estimated coefficients of b_i in (1). The simple correlation of this series with the residuals from regression (1) with the money terms excluded (the dotted series in figure 3.1) is equivalent to an F-test that all $b_i = 0$ in (1).

10. The literature lacks a consensus on the length of monetary lags but indicates considerable evidence of their variability. See Rosenbaum (1985).

11. This was clearly an exogenous decision of the authorities to combat inflation, not a passive response of the money supply to a decline in interest rates or economic activity. See my discussion in Cagan (1979, esp. pp. 113–18).

12. Goldfeld and Blinder (1972) claim that treating endogenous policy variables as exogenous produces little bias in estimates of relevant economic parameters. But see Crotty (1973) and Sims (1982). It would be useful to put this claim to a general test, because I find it highly questionable as a general proposition.

References

Andersen, Leonall, and Jerry Jordan. 1968. Monetary and fiscal actions: A test of their relative importance in economic stabilization. *Federal Reserve Bank of St. Louis Review* 50 (November): 11–24.

Artis, M. J., and M. K. Lewis. 1976. The demand for money in the United Kingdom: 1963–1973. *The Manchester School of Economic and Social Studies* 64 (June): 147–81.

Askari, Mostafa. 1986. A non-nested test of the new classical neutrality proposition for Canada. *Applied Economics* 18 (December): 1349–57.

Attfield, Clifford L. F., and Nigel W. Duck. 1983. The influence of unanticipated money growth on real output: Some cross-country estimates. *Journal of Money, Credit and Banking* 15 (November): 442–54.

Attfield, Clifford L. F., D. Demery, and N. W. Duck, 1981a. Unanticipated monetary growth, output and the price level: U.K. 1946–77. *European Economic Review* 16 (June/July): 367–85.

———. 1981b. A quarterly model of unanticipated monetary growth, output and the price level in the U.K. 1963–1978. *Journal of Monetary Economics* 8 (November): 331–50.

Auerbach, Robert D., and Jack L. Rutner. 1978. A causality test of Canadian money and income: A comment on Barth and Bennett. *Canadian Journal of Economics* 11 (August): 583–94.

Bach, George L., and C. J. Huizenga. 1961. The differential effects of tight money. *American Economic Review* 51 (March): 52–80.

Barro, Robert J. 1977. Unanticipated money growth and unemployment in the United States. *American Economic Review* 67 (March): 101–15.

———. 1978. Unanticipated money, output and the price level. *Journal of Political Economy* 86 (August): 549–80.

———. 1979a. Reply [to Small]. *American Economic Review* 69 (December): 1004–9.

———. 1979b. Money and output in Mexico, Colombia, and Brazil. In *Short-term macroeconomic policy in Latin America*, eds. J. Behrman and J. A. Hanson, 177–200. Cambridge, Mass.: Ballinger.

———. 1981. Unanticipated money growth and economic activity in the United States. In *Money, expectations, and business cycles: Essays in macroeconomics*, R. J. Barro, ch. 5, 137–69. New York: Academic Press.

Barro, Robert J., and Mark Rush. 1980. Unanticipated money and economic activity. In *Rational expectations and economic policy*, ed. S. Fischer, 23–48. Chicago: University of Chicago Press.

Barth, James R., and James T. Bennett. 1974. The role of money in the Canadian economy: An empirical test. *Canadian Journal of Economics* 7 (May): 306–11.

Bean, Charles R. 1984. A little bit more evidence on the natural rate hypothesis from the U.K. *European Economic Review* 25 (August): 279–92.

Bellante, Don, Stephen O. Morrell, and Asghar Zardkoohi. 1982. Unanticipated money growth, unemployment, output and the price level in the United Kingdom: 1946–1977. *Southern Economic Journal* 49 (July): 62–76.

Bernanke, Ben S. 1986. Alternative explanations of the money-income correlation. In *Real business cycles, real exchange rates and actual policies*, eds. K. Brunner and A. Meltzer, 49–99. Carnegie-Rochester Conference Series on Public Policy 25. Amsterdam: North Holland.

Blejer, Mario I., and Roque B. Fernandez. 1980. The effects of unanticipated money growth on prices and on output and its composition in a fixed-exchange-rate open economy. *Canadian Journal of Economics* 13 (February): 82–95.

Boschen, John F. 1985. Employment and output effects of observed and unobserved monetary growth. *Journal of Money, Credit and Banking* 17 (May): 153–63.

Boschen, John F., and Herschel I. Grossman. 1982. Tests of equilibrium macroeconomics using contemporaneous monetary data. *Journal of Monetary Economics* 10 (November): 309–33.

Brillembourg, Arturo, and Mohsin S. Khan. 1979. The relationship between money, income, and prices: Has money mattered historically? *Journal of Money, Credit and Banking* 11 (August): 358–65.

Brocato, Joe. 1985. Persistence under alternative forms of the Lucas supply function: Implications for the Lucas-Sargent price confusion hypothesis and Barro-type money models. *Quarterly Review of Economics and Business* 25 (Spring): 28–39.

Brunner, Karl, and Allan H. Meltzer. 1964. Some further investigations of demand and supply functions for money. *Journal of Finance* 19 (May): 240–83.

Brunner, Karl, Alex Cukierman, and Allan H. Meltzer. 1980. Stagflation, persistent unemployment and the permanence of economic shocks. *Journal of Monetary Economics* 6 (October): 467–92.

Buiter, Willem H. 1984. Granger-causality and policy effectiveness. *Economica* 51 (May): 151–62.

Cagan, Phillip. 1958. The demand for currency relative to the total money supply. *Journal of Political Economy* 66 (August): 303–28.

———. 1965. *Determinants and effects of changes in the money stock, 1875–1960.* New York: Columbia University Press.

———. 1966. Changes in the cyclical behavior of interest rates. *Review of Economics and Statistics* 48 (August): 219–50.

———. 1979. *Persistent inflation.* New York: Columbia University Press.

———. 1982. The choice among monetary aggregates as targets and guides for monetary policy. *Journal of Money, Credit and Banking* 14, part 2 (November): 661–86.

Carlson, Keith M. 1986. A monetarist model for economic stabilization: Review and update. *Federal Reserve Bank of St. Louis Review* 68 (October): 18–28.

Carns, Frederick, and Raymond Lombra. 1983. Rational expectations and short-run neutrality: A reexamination of the role of anticipated money growth. *Review of Economics and Statistics* 45 (November): 639–43.

Cecchetti, Stephen G. 1986. Testing short-run neutrality. *Journal of Monetary Economics* 17 (May): 409–23.

———. 1987. Testing short-run neutrality: International evidence. *Review of Economics and Statistics* 69 (February): 135–39.

Cheng, Hsiao. 1979a. Autoregressive modeling of Canadian money and income data. *Journal of the American Statistical Association* 74 (September): 553–60.

———. 1979b. Causality tests in econometrics. *Journal of Economic Dynamics and Control* 1 (November): 321–46.

Christiano, Lawrence J., and Lars Ljungqvist. 1988. Money does Granger-cause output in the bivariate output-money relation. *Journal of Monetary Economics* 22 (September): 217–35.

Ciccolo, John H., Jr. 1978. Money, equity values, and income: Tests for exogeneity. *Journal of Money, Credit and Banking* 10 (February): 46–64.
Cooley, Thomas F., and Stephen F. LeRoy. 1985. Atheoretical macroeconomics: A critique. *Journal of Monetary Economics* 16 (November): 283–
308.
Cottrell, Allin. 1986. The endogeneity of money and money-income causality.
Scottish Journal of Political Economy 33 (February): 2–27.
Crotty, James R. 1973. Specification error in macro-econometric models: The
influence of policy goals. *American Economic Review* 63 (December): 1025–
30, and Comment by Stephen Goldfeld with Reply by Crotty, *AER* 66 (September 1976): 662–67.
Cuddington, John T. 1980. Simultaneous-equations tests of the natural rate and
other classical hypotheses. *Journal of Political Economy* 88 (June): 539–49.
Darby, Michael R. 1983. Actual versus unanticipated changes in aggregate
demand variables: A sensitivity analysis of the real-income equation. In *The
international transmission of inflation*, eds. Michael Darby et al., ch. 9, 273–
88. Chicago: University of Chicago Press.
Darrat, Ali F. 1985a. Does anticipated monetary policy matter? The Canadian
evidence. *Atlantic Economic Journal* 13 (March): 19–26.
———. 1985b. Anticipated versus unanticipated monetary policy and real output in West Germany. *American Economist* 29 (Spring): 73–77.
———. 1985c. The monetarist versus the new classical economics and the
money unemployment linkage: Some European evidence. *Quarterly Journal
of Business and Economics* 24 (Summer): 78–91.
———. 1985d. The monetary explanation of inflation: The experience of three
major OPEC economies. *Journal of Economics and Business* 37 (August):
209–21.
———. 1985e. Anticipated money and real output in Italy: Some tests of a
rational expectations approach. *Journal of Post Keynesian Economics* 8
(Fall): 81–90.
———. 1986. Money, inflation, and causality in the North African countries:
An empirical investigation. *Journal of Macroeconomics* 8 (Winter): 87–103.
Davidson, Paul, and Sidney Weintraub. 1973. Money as cause and effect. *Eco-
nomic Journal* 83 (December): 1117–32.
Davis, Richard G. 1979. Broad credit measures as targets for monetary policy.
Federal Reserve Bank of New York Quarterly Review 4 (Summer): 13–22.
Demery, David. 1984. Aggregate demand, rational expectations and real output:
Some new evidence for the U.K., 1963.2–1982.2. *Economic Journal* 94
(December): 847–62.
Demery, David, Nigel W. Duck, and Simon W. Musgrave. 1984. Unanticipated
money growth, output and unemployment in West Germany, 1964–1981.
Weltwirtschaftliches Archiv 120, no. 2: 244–55.
Driscoll, M. J., J. L. Ford, A. W. Mullineux, and S. Sen. 1983a. Testing of the
rational expectations and structural neutrality hypotheses. *Journal of Mac-
roeconomics* 5 (Summer): 353–60.
———. 1983b. Money, output, rational expectations and neutrality: Some econometric results for the U.K. *Economica* 50 (August): 259–68.
Driscoll, M. J., A. W. Mullineux, and S. Sen. 1985. Testing the rational expectations and structural neutrality hypotheses: Some further results for the
U.K. *Empirical Economics* 10, no. 1: 51–58.
Dutkowsky, Donald H., and H. Sonmez Atesoglu. 1986. Unanticipated money
growth and unemployment: Post-sample forecasts. *Southern Economic Journal* 53 (October): 413–21.

Dwyer, Gerald P., Jr. 1985. Money, income, and prices in the United Kingdom: 1870–1913. *Economic Inquiry* 23 (July): 415–35.

Eichenbaum, Martin, and Kenneth J. Singleton. 1986. Do equilibrium real business cycle theories explain postwar U.S. business cycles? In *NBER macroeconomics annual 1986,* ed. S. Fischer, 91–139. Cambridge, Mass.: The MIT Press.

Eichengreen, Barry J. 1983. The causes of British business cycles, 1833–1913. *Journal of European Economic History* 12 (Spring): 145–61.

Enders, Walter, and Barry Falk. 1984. A microeconomic test of money neutrality. *Review of Economics and Statistics* 66 (November): 666–69.

Fackler, James S. 1985. An empirical analysis of the markets for goods, money, and credit. *Journal of Money, Credit and Banking* 17 (February): 28–42.

Fair, Ray C. 1987. International evidence on the demand for money. *Review of Economics and Statistics* 69 (August): 473–80.

Falls, Gregory A., and James Richard Hill. 1985. Monetary policy and causality. *Atlantic Economic Journal* 13 (December): 10–18.

Feige, Edgar L. 1975. The consequences of journal editorial policies and a suggestion for revision. *Journal of Political Economy* 83 (December): 1291–95.

Feige, Edgar L., and Douglas K. Pearce. 1979. The casual causal relationships between money and income: Some caveats for time series analysis. *Review of Economics and Statistics* 61 (November): 521–33.

Foster, Gladys Parker. 1986. The endogeneity of money and Keynes's general theory. *Journal of Economic Issues* 20 (December): 953–68.

Friedman, Benjamin M. 1983a. The roles of money and credit in macroeconomic analysis. In *Macroeconomics, prices, and quantities,* ed. J. Tobin, 161–89. Washington, D.C.: The Brookings Institution.

———. 1983b. Monetary policy with a credit aggregate target. In *Money, monetary policy and financial institutions,* eds. K. Brunner and A. H. Meltzer, 115–47. Carnegie-Rochester Conference Series on Public Policy 18. Amsterdam: North-Holland.

Friedman, Milton. 1970. Comment on Tobin. *Quarterly Journal of Economics* 84 (May): 318–27.

Friedman, Milton, and David Meiselman. 1963. The relative stability of monetary velocity and the investment multiplier in the United States, 1897–1958. In Commission on Money and Credit, *Stabilization policies.* Englewood Cliffs, N.J.: Prentice-Hall.

Friedman, Milton, and Anna J. Schwartz. 1963. *A monetary history of the United States, 1867–1960.* Princeton, N.J.: Princeton University Press.

Froyen, Richard. 1979. Systematic monetary policy and short-run real income determination. *Journal of Economics and Business* 32 (Fall): 14–22.

Garner, C. Alan. 1982. Test of monetary neutrality for the United Kingdom. *Quarterly Review of Economics and Business* 22 (Autumn): 81–95.

Geweke, John. 1986. The superneutrality of money in the United States: An interpretation of the evidence. *Econometrica* 54 (January): 1–21.

Gibson, William E. 1972. Demand and supply functions for money in the United States: Theory and measurement. *Econometrica* 40 (March): 361–70.

Goldfeld, Stephen M. 1973. The demand for money revisited. *Brookings Papers on Economic Activity* 3: 577–646.

Goldfeld, Stephen M., and Alan Blinder. 1972. Some implications of endogenous stabilization policy. *Brookings Papers on Economic Activity* 3: 585–640.

Goldfeld, Stephen M., and Daniel E. Sichel. 1987. Money demand: The effects of inflation and alternative adjustment mechanisms. *Review of Economics and Statistics* 69 (August): 511–15.

Gordon, Robert J. 1982. Price inertia and policy ineffectiveness in the United States, 1890–1980. *Journal of Political Economy* 90 (December): 1087–1117.

Granger, Clive W. J. 1969. Investigating causal relations by econometric models and cross spectral methods. *Econometrica* 37 (July): 424–38.

Granger, Clive W. J., and Paul Newbold. 1974. Spurious regressions in econometrics. *Journal of Econometrics* 2 (July): 111–20.

Grossman, Jacob. 1979. Nominal demand policy and short-run fluctuations in unemployment and prices in the United States. *Journal of Political Economy* 87, part 1 (October): 1063–85.

Hafer, R. W. 1981. Selecting a monetary indicator: A test of the new monetary aggregates. *Federal Reserve Bank of St. Louis Review* 63 (February): 12–18.

———. 1985. Choosing between M1 and debt as an intermediate target for monetary policy. In *Understanding monetary regimes,* eds. K. Brunner and A. Meltzer, 89–132. Carnegie-Rochester Conference Series on Public Policy 22. Amsterdam: North-Holland.

Haraf, William S. 1978. Inventories, orders and the persistent effects of monetary shocks. In Federal Reserve Bank of San Francisco, *West Coast Academic/Federal Reserve Economic Research Seminar,* 63–80.

Hernández-Iglesias, C., and F. Hernández-Iglesias. 1981. Causality and the independence phenomenon. *Journal of Econometrics* 15 (February): 247–63.

Hirsch, Abraham, and Neil de Marchi. 1986. Making a case when theory is unfalsifiable. *Economics and Philosophy* 2 (April): 1–21.

Hoffman, Dennis L., and Don E. Schlagenhauf, 1982. An econometric investigation of the monetary neutrality and rationality propositions from an international perspective. *Review of Economics and Statistics* 64 (November): 562–71.

Hsiao, Cheng. 1979a. Autoregresive modeling of Canadian money and income data. *Journal of the American Statistical Association* 74 (September): 553–60.

———. 1979b. Causality tests in econometrics. *Journal of Economic Dynamics and Control* 1 (November): 321–46.

———. 1982. Time series modelling and causal ordering of Canadian money, income and interest rates. In *Time series analysis: Theory and practice 1,* ed. O. D. Anderson, 671–99. Amsterdam: North-Holland.

Huffman, Wallace E., and James R. Lothian. 1980. Money in the United Kingdom, 1833–80. *Journal of Money, Credit and Banking* 12, part 1 (May): 155–74.

———. 1984. The gold standard and the transmission of business cycles, 1833–1932. In *A retrospective on the gold standard, 1821–1931,* eds. M. D. Bordo and A. J. Schwartz, 455–507. Chicago: University of Chicago Press.

Jones, J. D. 1985. Money, economic activity, and causality (A look at the empirical evidence for Canada, 1957–1983). *Economia Internazionale* 38 (March): 167–78.

Kaldor, Nicholas. 1970. The new monetarism. *Lloyds Bank Review* no. 97 (July): 1–18.

Kamath, Shyam. 1985. Monetary aggregates, income and causality in a developing economy. *Journal of Economic Studies* 12, no. 3: 36–53.

Kang, Heejoon. 1985. The effects of detrending in Granger-causality tests. *Journal of Business and Economic Statistics* 3 (October): 344–49.

Kimbrough, Kent P., and Faik Koray. 1984. Money, output, and the trade balance: Theory and evidence. *Canadian Journal of Economics* 17 (August): 508–22.

King, Stephen R. 1986. Monetary transmission: Through bank loans or bank liabilities? *Journal of Money, Credit and Banking* 18 (August): 290–303.

Komura, Chikara. 1982. Money, income, and causality: The Japanese Case. *Southern Economic Journal* 49 (July): 19–34.

Kormendi, Roger C., and Philip G. Meguire. 1984. Cross-regime evidence of macroeconomic rationality. *Journal of Political Economy* 92 (October): 875–908.

Korteweg, Pieter. 1978. The economics of inflation and output fluctuations in the Netherlands, 1954–1975: A test of some implications of the dominant impulse-cum-rational expectations hypothesis. In *The problem of inflation,* eds. K. Brunner and A. H. Meltzer, 17–79. Carnegie-Rochester Conference Series on Public Policy 8. Amsterdam: North-Holland.

Laumas, Prem S., and Susan Porter-Hudak. 1986. Monetization, economic development and the exogeneity of money. *Journal of Development Economics* 21 (April): 25–34.

Layton, Allan P. 1985. A causal caveat in the Australian money/income relation. *Applied Economics* 17 (April): 263–69.

Leamer, Edward E. 1983. Let's take the con out of econometrics. *American Economic Review* 73 (March): 31–43.

———. 1985. Vector autoregressions for causal influence. In *Understanding monetary regimes,* eds. K. Brunner and A. Meltzer, 255–303. Carnegie-Rochester Conference Series on Public Policy 22. Amsterdam: North-Holland.

Leiderman, Leonardo. 1980. Macroeconometric testing of the rational expectations and structural neutrality hypotheses for the United States. *Journal of Monetary Economics* 6 (January): 69–82.

Liang, Ming-Yih. 1984. Real *versus* nominal specification of the demand for money function. *Economic Inquiry* 22 (July): 404–13.

Litterman, Robert B., and Laurence Weiss. 1985. Money, real interest rates, and output: A reinterpretation of postwar U.S. data. *Econometrica* 53 (January): 129–56.

Los, Cornelis A. 1986. The ghost in the box: Comment on "What will take the con out of econometrics." Federal Reserve Bank of New York Research Paper No. 8601 (March).

Lovell, Michael C. 1983. Data Mining. *Review of Economics and Statics* 65 (February): 1–12.

Makin, John H. 1982. Anticipated money, inflation and uncertainty and real economic activity. *Review of Economics and Statistics* 64 (February): 126–34.

McCallum, Bennett. 1983. A reconsideration of Sims' evidence concerning monetarism. *Economics Letters* 13, nos. 2–3: 167–71.

McGee, Robert T., and Richard T. Stasiak. 1985. Does anticipated monetary policy matter? *Journal of Money, Credit and Banking* 17 (February): 16–27.

McMillin, W. Douglas, and James S. Fackler. 1984. Monetary vs. credit aggregates: An evaluation of monetary policy targets. *Southern Economic Journal* 50 (January): 711–23.

Mehra, Yash P. 1978a. Is money exogenous in money-demand equations? *Journal of Political Economy* 86, part 1 (April): 211–28.

————. 1978b. An empirical note on some monetarist propositions. *Southern Economic Journal* 45 (July): 154–67.

Merrick, John J., Jr. 1983. Financial market efficiency, the decomposition of "anticipated" versus "unanticipated" money growth, and further tests of the relation between money and real output. *Journal of Money, Credit and Banking* 15 (May): 222–32.

Mills, Terry C., and Geoffrey E. Wood. 1978. Money-income relationships and the exchange rate regime. *Federal Reserve Bank of St. Louis Review* 60 (August): 22–27.

Mints, Lloyd W. 1945. *A history of banking theory.* Chicago: University of Chicago Press.

Mishkin, Frederic S. 1982a. Does anticipated monetary policy matter? An econometric investigation. *Journal of Political Economy* 90 (February): 22–51.

————. 1982b. Does anticipated aggregate demand policy matter? Further econometric tests. *American Economic Review* 72 (September): 788–802.

————. 1983. *A rational expectations approach to macroeconometrics: Testing policy ineffectiveness and efficient-markets models.* Chicago: University of Chicago Press.

Mixon, J. Wilson, Jr., Leila J. Pratt, and Myles S. Wallace. 1980. Money-income causality in the U.K.: Fixed and flexible exchange rates. *Southern Economic Journal* 47 (July): 201–9.

Myatt, Anthony. 1986. Money supply endogeneity: An empirical test for the United States, 1954–84. *Journal of Economic Issues* 20 (March): 133–44.

Neftci, Salih, and Thomas J. Sargent. 1978. A little bit of evidence on the natural rate hypothesis from the U.S. *Journal of Monetary Economics* 4 (April): 315–19.

Osborn, Denise R. 1984. Causality testing and its implications for dynamic econometric models. *Economic Journal* 94 (Conference Papers Supplement): 82–96.

Parikh, Ashok. 1984. Causality between money and prices in Indonesia. *Empirical Economics* 9, no. 4: 217–32.

Paulter, Paul A., and Richard J. Rivard. 1979. Choosing a monetary aggregate: Causal relationship as a criterion. *Review of Business and Economic Research* 15 (Fall): 1–18.

Pesaran, M. H. 1982. A critique of the proposed tests of the natural rate-rational expectations hypothesis. *Economic Journal* 92 (September): 529–54.

Pierce, David A. 1977. Relationships—and the lack thereof—between economic time series, with special reference to money and interest rates. *Journal of the American Statistical Association* 72 (March): 11–22.

Pigott, Charles. 1978. Rational expectations and counter-cyclical monetary policy: The Japanese experience. *Federal Reserve Bank of San Francisco Economic Review* (Summer): 6–22.

Porter, Richard D., and Edward K. Offenbacher. 1983. Empirical comparisons of credit and monetary aggregates using vector autoregressive methods. *Federal Reserve Bank of Richmond Economic Review* 69 (November/December): 16–29.

Radcliffe Committee on the Working of the Monetary System. 1959. *Report.* Cmnd 827. London: H.M.S.O.

Rosenbaum, Mary S. 1985. Lags in the effect of monetary policy. *Federal Reserve Bank of Atlanta Economic Review* (November): 20–33.

Rush, Mark. 1985. Unexpected monetary disturbances during the gold standard era. *Journal of Monetary Economics* 15 (May): 309–21.

————. 1986. Unexpected money and unemployment. *Journal of Money, Credit and Banking* 18 (August): 259–74.

Sargent, Thomas J. 1976. A classical macroeconomic model for the United States. *Journal of Political Economy* 84 (April): 207–37.

Sargent, Thomas J., and Christopher A. Sims. 1977. Business cycle modeling without pretending to have too much *a priori* economic theory. In Federal Reserve Bank of Minneapolis, *New methods in business cycle research: Proceedings from a conference*, 45–109.

Schwartz, Anna J. 1987. *Money in historical perspective.* Chicago: University of Chicago Press.

Schwert, G. William. 1979. Test of causality: The message in the innovations. In *Three aspects of policy and policymaking*, eds. K. Brunner and A. H. Meltzer, 55–96. Carnegie-Rochester Conference Series on Public Policy 10. Amsterdam: North-Holland.

Sharpe, Barry C., and Michael B. Miller. 1975. The role of money in the Canadian economy. *Canadian Journal of Economics* 8 (May): 289–90.

Sheehan, Richard G. 1985. Money, anticipated changes, and policy effectiveness. *American Economic Review* 75 (June): 524–29.

Sheehey, Edmund J. 1984. The neutrality of money in the short run: Some tests. *Journal of Money, Credit and Banking* 16 (May): 237–40.

Sheffrin, Steven M. 1979. Unanticipated money growth and output fluctuations. *Economic Inquiry* 17 (January): 1–13.

Sims, Christopher A. 1972. Money, income, and causality. *American Economic Review* 62 (September): 540–52.

————. 1980a. Macroeconomics and reality. *Econometrica* 48 (January): 1–48.

————. 1980b. Comparison of interwar and postwar business cycles: Monetarism reconsidered. *American Economic Review* 70 (May): 250–57.

————. 1982. Policy analysis with econometric models. *Brookings Papers on Economic Activity* 1: 107–52.

Small, David H. 1979. Unanticipated money growth and unemployment in the United States: Comment. *American Economic Review* 69 (December): 996–1003.

Snowder, Dennis J. 1984. Rational expectations, nonlinearities, and the effectiveness of monetary policy. *Oxford Economic Papers* 36 (June): 177–99.

Stock, James H., and Mark W. Watson. 1987. Interpreting the evidence on money-income causality. National Bureau of Economic Research Working Paper no. 2228 (April).

Teigen, Ronald L. 1964. Demand and supply functions for money in the United States: Some structural estimates. *Econometrica* 32 (October): 476–509.

Thornton, Daniel L., and Dallas S. Batten. 1985. Lag-length selection and tests of Granger causality between money and income. *Journal of Money, Credit and Banking* 17 (May): 164–78.

Tobin, James. 1970. Money and income: Post hoc ergo propter hoc? *Quarterly Journal of Economics* 84 (May): 301–17.

Van Hoa, Tran. 1981. Causality and wage price inflation in West Germany, 1964–1979. *Weltwirtschaftliches Archiv* 117, no. 1: 110–24.

von Hagen, Jürgen. 1984. The causal role of money in West Germany—Some contradicting comments and evidence. *Weltwirtschaftliches Archiv* 120, no. 3: 558–71.

Wachter, Susan M. 1979. Structuralism vs. monetarism: Inflation in Chile. In *Short-term macroeconomic policy in Latin America*, eds. J. Behrman and J. A. Hanson, Cambridge, Mass.: Ballinger.

Walters, Alan A. 1967. The demand for money—The dynamic properties of the multiplier. *Journal of Political Economy* 75 (June): 293–98.

Weissenberger, Edgar, and J. J. Thomas. 1983. The causal role of money in West Germany. *Weltwirtschaftliches Archiv* 119, no. 1: 64–83.

Williams, David, C. A. E. Goodhart, and D. H. Gowland. 1976. Money, income, and causality: The U.K. experience. *American Economic Review* 66 (June): 417–23.

Wogin, Gillian. 1980. Unemployment and monetary policy under rational expectations. *Journal of Monetary Economics* 6 (January): 59–68.

Yule, G. Udney. 1926. Why do we sometimes get nonsense-correlations between times series?—A study in sampling and the nature of time-series. *Journal of the Royal Statistical Society* N.S., 89, part 1 (January): 1–64.

Zellner, Arnold. 1979. Causality and econometrics. In *Three aspects of policy and policymaking*, eds. K. Brunner and A. Meltzer, 9–54. Carnegie-Rochester Conference Series on Public Policy 10. Amsterdam: North-Holland.

Comment   Robert H. Rasche

Another paper presented at this conference proclaimed that the "dark age of vector autoregressions" has dawned (Bordo 1987). Cagan's paper assumes the role of the Center for Disease Control or the Surgeon General. It warns there is a pernicious, communicable, even fatal threat to our profession at large during these dark days, and that RATS (*R*egression *A*nalysis of *T*ime *S*eries) spread this plague!!

Phil Cagan's review of the literature of the past two decades on money-income causality is critical, exhaustive, thoughtful, and thought-provoking. It is truly a tribute to Anna Schwartz and a masterful counterattack on the various accusations against a fundamental proposition of *A Monetary History,* namely, that there is "an influence from income to money over the business cycle, yet . . . the main influence both secularly and cyclically runs from money to income" (Bordo 1987, 5). However, the traditions and requirements for discussants set by our profession are not satisfied if I stop at this point. Moreover, as a practitioner of the time-series techniques that are the object of the Cagan counterattack, I am unwilling to run up the white flag and passively surrender.

Counterattack: Hypothesis

The fundamental approach of the paper is the juxtaposition of two competing hypotheses. Cagan's maintained hypothesis throughout his review of the money-causality literature is: "Are time-series

Robert H. Rasche is a professor of economics at Michigan State University, East Lansing, and a research associate of the National Bureau of Economic Research.

regression techniques capable of detecting and measuring the impact of exogenous monetary disturbances on real output when the available time series reflect monetary regimes that permit endogenous changes in the money stock?'' My reading is that Cagan uniformly rejects this hypothesis, but rejects in favor of what? The alternative hypothesis in his analysis is ''Are historical analyses capable of detecting and measuring the impact of exogenous monetary disturbances on real output when the historical monetary regimes have permitted endogenous changes in the money stock?'' The major conclusion of his review is not just the rejection of the hypothesis of the adequacy of time-series regression techniques. It is the rejection of that hypothesis and the *acceptance* of the alternative hypothesis of the adequacy of historical analyses *on the basis* of the demonstrated inadequacies of the time-series techniques.

My evidence for this characterization of Cagan's argument is as follows: First, that the question of the (partial) endogeneity of monetary disturbances is not at issue is found early in the paper: ''The empirical evidence that money, prices, and activity are related, now widely accepted, raises the question of the direction of influence. *A Monetary History* gives it major attention.''

Second, there is the rejection of the hypothesis of the adequacy of time-series regression techniques: ''Regression methods foster this oversight because of their weak ability to disentangle a two-way dependence''; ''The new 'causality' tests emphasize the point that the existence of serial correlation and feedback compromise evidence based solely on conventional time-series regressions''; ''The VAR seems to me to be hopelessly unreliable and low in power to detect monetary effects of the kind we are looking for and believe, from other evidence, to exist''; and ''Since regression analysis cannot evaluate the effect of these monetary changes, it fails in its principal purpose.''

Third, the acceptance of the alternative hypothesis of the adequacy of historical analyses: ''In such [historical] research the mutual relationship among variables can be studied, and the subtle differences among historical episodes can provide clues to the channels of influence at work''; and ''. . . general historical analysis presents understandable evidence and . . . usually converges to a consensus on the facts and often also on an interpretation of the facts.''

Repulse: Weaknesses of the Attack on Time-Series Analysis

In my view, there are two problems that invalidate Cagan's conclusion. The first is that even if we accept the evidence presented as a conclusive demonstration that time-series regression techniques are inadequate for the task at hand, it does not follow that historical analyses are adequate. It is quite possible that both research strategies are "unreliable and low in power to detect monetary effects of the kind we are looking for," as it is also possible that both approaches can reliably detect such monetary effects given the way that central banks have operated historically. Cagan asserts (or assumes) that his rejection of time-series regression analysis validates the historical approach. There is no evidence in his review of the reliability or power of the historical analysis approach.

The second problem is there are occasions when there is a circularity in the argument against time-series regression techniques. In several places in the review, it is asserted that time-series analysis fails because it does not support known propositions. A closer examination reveals that the known propositions are the conclusions of previous historical research. Thus, the conclusion that the time-series techniques are inadequate is sometimes conditional upon the adequacy of the historical research approach. Should the technique or conclusions of the previous historical analysis be faulty, then the alleged failure of the time-series analysis may be no failure at all.

An example of this circularity of reasoning is the quotation above in which VAR analysis is dismissed because it does not detect "monetary effects . . . we believe, from other evidence, to exist." The only other evidence alluded to in the entire review is the conclusions of historical analyses. Later, the conditional nature of the rejection of time-series techniques is clear: "Linearity governs all regression analyses. . . . But for monetary effects it is not reasonable. . . . Monetary episodes vary substantially in timing and cannot all be represented by the same values of parameters and fixed lagged patterns. *This seems clear from historical analysis*" (emphasis added); and "Money has difficulty passing VAR tests, *yet by all other indications* it plays an important role in business fluctuations. . . . Since regression analysis cannot evaluate the effects of these monetary changes, it fails in its principal purpose" (emphasis added).

Regroup: Some Alternative Sources of Concern Regarding Specific Time-Series Techniques

Cagan specifically addresses four different types of time-series analysis: (1) the "Post Hoc Ergo Propter Hoc" criticism of timing analysis; (2) models that attempt to distinguish the effects of "anticipated" versus "unanticipated" monetary growth; (3) bivariate "causality" models; and (4) vector autoregresions (VAR). Extensive discussions of the first and third of these approaches appear in the existing literature and, for the most part, his review summarizes the existent criticisms of these time-series methods. Most of the new criticisms address the "anticipated" versus "unanticipated" money models and the VAR approach to time-series modeling. There are some interesting ideas in these two areas that deserve further elaboration.

The most important comment in Cagan's paper about the anticipated/unanticipated money literature is that "These studies raise a question about the meaning and measurement of anticipated monetary growth." The motivation for such models derives from a theoretical literature in which agents know the structure of the economy, possess information on the history of various "policy variables," and form expectations "rationally" based on this information set. Under these conditions, *and* if prices adjust to clear markets continually, then the conclusion follows that anticipated money growth, in the sense of the best forecast of money growth from the available information, does not affect real output.

A well-known class of models (Fischer 1977; Taylor 1979) relaxes only the assumption of market clearing and generates the result that both anticipated and unanticipated money growth have nonzero effects on real output. The different conclusion arises because in the latter models there is a difference between the best forecast of current money growth and the expectation of the inflation rate, given the available information set.

Relaxation of the assumptions on the information set in different ways would undoubtedly further muddy the waters. We need to remember that before the monumental work of *A Monetary History* and *Monetary Statistics,* data on the stock and growth rate of money in the United States were not available weekly from local newspapers (or even Federal Reserve statistical releases) at virtually no cost. *Banking and Monetary Statistics,* initially published in 1943, provides data only at semiannual intervals. As late as 1959, the "Details of Deposits and Currency" table in the *Federal Reserve Bulletin* provided data only on a last-Wednesday-of-the-month basis. As Friedman and Schwartz note in *Monetary Statistics:* "Comprehensive coverage of all banks at annual dates, did not become available until 1959, when the Federal Reserve System published its compilation of these reports in *All Bank Statistics,* and even this compilation goes back only to 1896" (1970, 212). The availability of information on economic statistics, which we so easily take for granted, is a recent phenomenon and one to which Anna Schwartz has made significant contributions.

None of this literature has progressed beyond the assumption of *known* reduced-form coefficients models. In reality, the best information that agents can possess is unbiased estimates of the true reduced-form coefficients that are subject to sampling error. Indeed, given the review that we have at hand, this is probably a heroic and inaccurate assumption about the true state of an agent's information set. Once stochastic coefficient reduced forms are part of the information set, then the meaning and measurement of anticipated money growth becomes considerably more complex. The effects of such models on the specification error of the available empirical studies of anticipated and unanticipated money growth remain undetermined.

The major thrust of Cagan's objection to VAR analysis is that the "VAR method cooks the data beyond recognition," and that monetary effects are not adequately represented by linearity (or log-linearity). The problem with this criticism is that it comes close to arguing that, in one way or another, monetary events are unique. If this is the case, then we will never untangle the interdependence of money and income, since as Cagan is aware, "a two-way dependence cannot be confirmed by one observation."

A more substantive criticism of commonly practiced VAR analysis is that it is incapable of answering the question of what effect money has on real output under the acknowledged nature of historical monetary policymaking. Given acceptance of a two-way dependence of money and income, the residuals or innovations studied in typical VAR analyses—which Cagan feels do not demonstrate the well-known effects of money on income—are just not the appropriate residuals. Sims (1980) clearly acknowledges that after construction of the moving average representation of a VAR system by the now conventional orthogonalization approach:

> The residuals whose effects are being tracked are the residuals from a system in which contemporaneous values of other variables enter the right-hand sides of the regressions with a triangular array of coefficients. (p. 21)

The structure of such a system is a Wold causal chain, not the structure of the economy that is of concern to Cagan or to *A Monetary History*. Given the restrictions that Sims imposes on the data, the moving average representations are not unique, i.e., the economic system of concern to Cagan is not identified. *The issue* in the interpretation of the VAR results is *identification*. It would appear that a skillful practitioner can use both historical analyses and time-series analyses to shed some light on the issue of a two-way dependence between money and income. To quote Sims (1980):

> We may sometimes be able to separate endogenous and exogenous components in policy variables by careful *historical analysis*, in effect using a type of instrumental variables procedure for estimating a structural relation between policy variables and the rest of the economy. (p. 12)

The message is that more information is available to analysts than that contained in economic time series. This additional information is important and can supplement time-series analysis in ways that overcome the inherent limitations of staring myopically at the time-series entrails. This message has a much higher marginal product than one that says we must abandon time-series analysis altogether and return to the fundamental scholarship of historical analysis. Certainly it is important to deplore the mechanical manipulation of economic time series, but it is also important to recognize that historical analyses and time-series analyses are not mutually exclusive, nor are they substitutes. Indeed, the highest quality "scholarship" in our profession combines the two approaches to produce lasting contributions to the advancement of our understanding. Anna Schwartz's contributions rank with the best in this latter tradition.

References

Bordo, Michael D. 1987. The contribution of *A monetary history of the United States, 1867–1960* to monetary history. Paper presented at the NBER Conference on Money in Historical Perspective (October). See also ch. 1 in this volume.

Fischer, Stanley. 1977. Long-term contracts, rational expectations and the optimal money supply rule. *Journal of Political Economy* 85 (February): 191–205.

Friedman, M., and A. J. Schwartz. 1963. *A monetary history of the United States, 1867–1960*. Princeton, NJ: Princeton University Press.

————. 1970. *Monetary statistics of the United States*. New York: Columbia University Press.

Sims, Christopher A. 1980. Macroeconomics and reality. *Econometrica* 48 (January): 1–47.

Taylor, John B. 1979. Staggered wage setting in a macro model. *American Economic Review* 69 (May): 108–13.

General Discussion

KOCHIN offered an alternative explanation for the dominance of interest rates in a VAR incorporating the money stock, an interest rate, and real output. He argued that, in an efficient market, interest rates absorb all the information available in the monetary series simply because interest rates are anticipating whatever information is available about future money. That information will be in the interest rate as it becomes available, which may be before it is incorporated in the money supply.

Thus, for example, if there is a projection in October 1989 of faster growth in the monetary base and higher inflation in the 1990s, and that information becomes available in October 1987, interest rates would go up during October 1987, even if the monetary base has not yet increased. So the rise in interest rates in 1987 will, according to the VAR analyst, cause the inflation of the 1990s.

POOLE, in a similar vein, pointed out that the interest rate, as a speculative price in the markets, filters out the noise in the money data. People in the markets are responding to the systematic part of the monetary influence, as well as other things. So it is not surprising that the interest rate drives out money.

CAGAN argued that the movements in interest rates are more systematically related to real GNP than is money. Otherwise they would both have an equal chance of playing that role.

McCALLUM reiterated his 1983 explanation for Sims's 1980 finding of little influence of monetary policy innovations in a VAR containing money, interest rates, and real output. He had argued that, if the monetary authorities are using the interest rates as an instrument, you would expect the interest rate to show up as a *better* indicator of monetary policy surprises than the money stock.

He raised an objection to Cagan's argument. Interest rate targets, Cagan stated, have not always ruled monetary policy, particularly beyond short horizons. According to McCallum, that statement seems to confuse the difference between an interest rate instrument and an interest rate target—a target being an objective of policy and an instrument being something to do with operating procedures. Interest rate instruments have been in effect throughout the postwar period, which is the period of concern here. Even during the 1979–82 regime, indirect interest rate instruments were used. Furthermore, his argument presumes that this obtains only at short-run horizons, that it is only over a period of a month or six weeks that these things are fixed and held rigid.

STOCKMAN warned against rejecting a statistical technique because the results are not all uniform. He pointed out that not all applications of the VAR approaches have treated data in exactly the same way. For example, there is a substantial difference in the results that people get if they take linear time trends out of the data rather than if they take growth rates. And that can be explained because taking the growth rates of a time series amounts to applying one filter to the data, while taking linear trends out is another filter altogether, and it makes sense that using different filters leads to different results. When we plot the squared gains from these filters, we find that taking the growth rate of a time series leaves more in at the higher frequencies while taking out linear time trends leaves less in at higher frequencies and more in at lower frequencies. The differences in the answers that economists obtain with different filters, therefore, gives us information that we could use for subsequent statistical analyses and for construction or evaluation of theories. If detrending versus taking growth rates makes a difference for the correlation of two economic variables, then we would like a theory that predicts this difference.

He then expanded on why using different filters may make a difference. He pointed out that if you plot the squared gain from these filters against frequency, you can compare the results of applying d-log filters to the data to taking out a linear time trend. In this kind of plot, the squared gain of a linear time trend is flat, except at a zero frequency. But the squared gain of the d-log filter rises, starting out lower at high frequencies and getting higher at low frequencies. The relationship between any two economic variables can differ across frequencies—there are high frequency relationships and low frequency relations. By using the d-log filter, one is looking mostly at the higher frequency relationships. By taking out a linear time trend and then looking at the detrended series, one is looking less at the higher frequency relations and more at the lower frequency relations than is the case with the d-log filter.

He argued that presumably economic theory should tell us something about whether there are some short-run relationships or long-run relationships between these variables. He described research he has done with Marianne Baxter where they found that the correlation between foreign and U.S. industrial production was about the same under pegged or floating exchange rates when they took linear time trends out of the data, while the correlations between growth rates of industrial production were lower under flexible exchange rates. That, he argued, suggests that short-run (high frequency) correlations are lower under flexible rates, while longer-run correlations are unaffected. And that might be explained by greater national monetary autonomy under floating rates, combined with a short-run, but not long-run, effect of money on industrial production.

McCallum made the point that the use of VARs is just a technique of *descriptive* statistics—that running a VAR is comparable to calculating the mean of a series of data, or calculating the standard deviation—it is just a slightly more complicated descriptive statistic. One is not going to get any understanding from any descriptive statistic unaided. It must be combined with some sort of understanding that relates the descriptive statistics to the characteristics of the system.

Brunner described a critique of Granger-causality tests in a paper by William Schwert published in the Carnegie-Rochester Conference Series (1979). Schwert argued that the tests are badly misnamed. They do not test causality but actually test incremental information. They simply reveal whether the addition of some variables raises our information level about the future value of the dependent variable. Brunner then gave an example to show that this is very different from a causality test. Suppose we construct a quantity theory world with specific stochastic processes controlling money, velocity, and output. The optimal forecast of inflation is determined by a distributed lag on past rates of inflation. Adding money to the regression yields nothing. All the relevant information is already contained in the past rates of inflation. But this does not mean that money has no causal effect. We know by construction that money substantially influences the ongoing inflation.

CAGAN reiterated the main point of his paper—that a lot of the theoretical objections to VARs did not focus on what the real problem was, namely, that VAR looks for a very rigid relationship between money and output that does not exist. By not finding that relationship, one should not jump to the conclusion that there was no effect.

In reply to Rasche, he accepted that there are a lot of problems with general historical analysis. You have to persuade by an accumulation of evidence, interpreting different episodes. This he believes is the best we can do. By contrast, econometrics provides formal statistical tests of these propositions. In his opinion, formal statistical tests where the t-statistic tells you yes or no is not sufficient to determine whether you have an effect. His paper is thus a protest against such use of econometrics.

III International Monetary Perspectives

4 Stability Under the Gold Standard in Practice

Allan H. Meltzer and Saranna Robinson

During her active career as a monetary economist and historian, Anna Schwartz returned to the history of monetary standards many times. In the famed *A Monetary History of the United States, 1867–1960* (Friedman and Schwartz 1963), in her work as executive director of the 1981–82 U.S. Gold Commission (Commission on the Role of Gold in the Domestic and International Monetary Systems 1982), in her introduction to the National Bureau volume *A Retrospective on the Classical Gold Standard, 1821–1931* (Bordo and Schwartz 1984), and in books and papers on British and U.S. monetary history before and after these volumes, she has both summarized past knowledge with careful attention to detail and added important pieces to our understanding of the way monetary systems work in practice.

One issue to which she and others have returned many times is the relative welfare gain or loss under alternative standards. Properly so; a main task of economic historians and empirical scientists is to test the predictions and implications of economic theory. Since theory does not give an unqualified prediction about the welfare benefits of different standards, evidence on the comparative performance under different standards is required to reach a judgment.

Measures of economic welfare or welfare loss usually include the growth rate of aggregate or per capita (or per family) consumption or output, the rates of actual and unanticipated inflation, and the risks or

Allan H. Meltzer is University Professor and John M. Olin Professor of Political Economy and Public Policy, Carnegie Mellon University. Saranna Robinson is a graduate student in the School of Urban and Public Affairs, Carnegie Mellon University.

The authors received helpful comments from Michael Bordo, Bennett McCallum, William Poole, Benjamin Friedman, and Anna Schwartz.

uncertainty that individuals bear. We use unanticipated variability of prices and output as measures of uncertainty and actual inflation as a measure of the deviation from the optimal rate of inflation. Eichengreen (1985, 6 and 9) includes the stability of real and nominal exchange rates under the gold standard as one of the benefits of the standard. While the evidence of greater real exchange rate stability under fixed exchange rates seems clear-cut, the welfare implications are less clear.[1] Given the same policy rules and policy actions, greater stability of real exchange rates under the gold standard may be achieved at the cost of greater variability in output or employment. This will be true if the alternative to exchange rate adjustment is adjustment of relative costs of production and relative prices when wages, costs of production, or some prices are slow to adjust. We, therefore, exclude exchange rate stability from the comparison and focus attention on the variability of unanticipated output, prices, inflation, and the growth rate of output.[2]

The following section discusses previous findings about the stability of prices and output and the rates of inflation and growth. We then consider the comparative experience of the seven countries in our sample under the classical gold standard. Bretton Woods, and the fluctuating exchange rate regime. Like most previous comparisons, our first comparisons are based on actual values or their rates of change. The variability of unanticipated changes in prices and output under the three regimes is a more relevant measure of variability and uncertainty. We obtain measures of uncertainty about the levels and growth rates of output and prices using a multistate Kalman filter based on the work of Bomhoff (1983) and Kool (1983). Subsequent sections describe our procedures, present some estimates of comparative uncertainty, and consider the relation between shocks in Britain and the United States under the gold standard. A conclusion completes the paper.

4.1 Previous Evidence

Bordo (1986) summarizes previous work on the stability of prices and output under the gold standard. For prices, there is strong evidence of reversion to a mean value. As is well known, the price level in most countries shows little trend under the gold standard if one chooses a period long enough for alternating periods of inflation and deflation to occur. This is true of the seven countries that we consider here; average rates of inflation under the classical gold standard range from 0.08 percent to 1.1 percent.[3]

While the long-term stability of the price level under the gold standard is often commented on favorably, it is not clear that ex post stability is desirable independently of the way in which it is achieved. Alternating periods of persistent inflation followed by persistent deflation do not have the same welfare implications as small, transitory fluctuations around a constant expected or average price level.[4] Long-term price stability achieved through canceling wartime inflations by severe postwar deflations imposes costs on consumers and producers, and particularly so, if the timing or magnitude of both the inflations and deflations is uncertain. A policy of maintaining expected stability of commodity prices, instead of stability of the nominal gold price, would have avoided postwar deflations by revaluing gold. In place of the long-term commitment to a fixed nominal exchange rate of domestic money for gold, countries could have made a commitment to a stable expected price level.

Cooper (1982) computed the rates of price change in four countries using the wholesale price index numbers available for the period. Cooper includes the years 1816 to 1913 but, for much of this period, major countries were not on the gold standard. We start the classical gold standard period in the 1870s when several countries chose to buy and sell gold at a fixed price, and we end the period in 1913, the last prewar year. Although many countries fixed their currencies to gold in the 1920s, the rules of the system differed and the commitment was weaker. Cooper's data for the years 1873–96 and 1896–1913 are shown in table 4.1.

The cumulative movement in each period is relatively large, although the average annual rate of change in the first two periods is 2 or 3 percent. For comparison, we have included the percentage change in consumer prices for the same four countries during 1957–70, approximately the years that the Bretton Woods system had convertible currencies. The comparison shows that while the average annual rates of change under the gold standard are similar (or lower) for some countries, they are higher for others.

The key difference between the price movements in the earlier and later periods is that there is no evidence of mean reversion in postwar data following Bretton Woods. Few would argue, however, that the deflations of 1920–21 or 1929–33, or the prior deflations in the nineteenth century that contributed to the reversions, reduced welfare less than the inflation of the 1970s.

Table 4.1   **Percentage Change of Price Indexes, Four Countries, 1873–1913 and 1957–70**

Years	United States	United Kingdom	Germany	France
1873–96	−53	−45	−40	−45
1896–1913	56	39	45	45
1957–70	38	55	36	88

Source: Cooper (1982, 9); *Economic Report of the President* (1971, 306).

A major, unresolved issue is the degree to which people could anticipate that inflation or deflation would occur. Bond yields are often taken as evidence of expected stability under the gold standard. Macaulay's series on railroad bond yields declines during the deflation of the 1870s and 1880s but continues to decline until 1899 or 1901, after gold, money, and prices had started to rise. The Macaulay yields are higher during the deflation of the 1870s than at the start of World War I, despite nearly twenty years of inflation. Although other factors may have been at work, the raw data give no support to the proposition that bond yields are a summary measure of anticipated price movements under the gold standard.

Rockoff (1984) presents some evidence suggesting that there was a basis for belief that prices would return to some mean value. His study considers the relation of gold mining and technological change in gold extraction to the relative price of gold. He concludes, tentatively, that many of the new gold discoveries and technical changes in methods of extraction were the result of an earlier rise in the relative price of gold. On his interpretation, long-term price movements for the period 1821 to 1914 appear to be the result of changes in demand along a relatively elastic long-run gold supply curve. Rockoff's evidence suggests a long-term, gradual reversion of commodity prices operating on the relative price of gold and the supply of gold.[5] This mechanism, relying on changes in the resources devoted to gold production and storage to maintain long-term price stability, is not clearly superior to other means of maintaining price stability. The fact that the mechanism operates with a lag of decades raises, again, the issue of whether it was anticipated in a sense relevant for people allocating wealth and choosing to consume or save at the time. Further, there is no reason to presume that people believed that reversion would occur. The rate at which mines would be discovered was highly uncertain. Countries could change the gold reserve ratio or leave the gold standard. Some countries did leave the standard, even in the 1870 to 1913 period that we study below.

Few studies of comparative variability are available. Bordo (1981) compared the standard deviation and coefficient of variation for the price level under the gold standard and after World War II. He found that these measures of price variability were higher under the gold standard for the United States but lower for the United Kingdom. Bordo does not separate postwar data into fixed and fluctuating rate periods.

Schwartz (1986) notes that the long-term price stability under the gold standard, which seems so apparent with hindsight, was not apparent to leading economists of the period. "What occasioned the criticism [of the gold standard] was precisely the long-term secular price movements—the rise in prices associated with the mid-nineteenth century gold discoveries and the decline in prices that began in the 1870s under an expanding international gold standard'' (p. 56). Jevons, Marshall, and Fisher (among others) not only criticized price instability under the gold standard, but proposed alternative standards to increase stability. At the minimum, this suggests that these economists did not regard the standard as an optimal arrangement to achieve stability of prices and output.

Schwartz's review of the pro and con arguments concludes that, while the classical gold standard did not achieve superior price stability, it may have produced greater long-term price predictability than achieved under alternative systems. To support this conclusion, she points to the prevalence of long-term contracts. It is not clear, however, that contracts are now significantly shorter and, if they are, whether the change reflects a change in opportunities or a change in long-term uncertainty. Klein (1976) reaches a conclusion similar to Schwartz's about predictability. The conclusion is based mainly on his finding, for the United States, that the serial correlation of price changes is substantially higher in the postwar years than under the gold standard. With increased serial correlation, people observing price changes can reliably extrapolate the direction of change given the knowledge of the serial correlation (and confidence that it will remain). Klein's measure of long-term price level predictability under the gold standard shows relatively little difference from the postwar period, however, while his measure of variability of prices shows a considerable decline in the postwar years. Further, we show in table 4.4 below that serial correlation of price changes in the United States under fluctuating rates is lower than under the gold standard.

The main argument for long-term predictability under the gold standard is that the commitment to the standard was credible, at least in those countries that maintained the standard at the same nominal price of gold whenever they were on the standard. The costs of long-term predictability, then, must include the costs of Britain's return to gold in 1821 and 1925 at the established parity. Our impression is that most of the literature regards this cost as higher than the benefit.

A major problem with the classical gold standard is that the system magnifies shocks to aggregate demand. An inflow of gold increases aggregate demand and supplies reserves that permit an expansion of loans and money. Monetary expansion augments the initial shock. Money growth rises in periods of economic expansion and falls in contraction. With slow adjustment of prices and costs of production, the effects of rising and falling growth rates of money is, first, an output and only later on prices and gold flows.

A second problem arises from gold holding. The right to own gold is a valuable right that may protect wealthowners from inflationary and confiscatory actions of government. Society bears a cost, however; when gold is held in place of capital, society's capital stock is lower, and per capita output is smaller. The fears that drive wealthowners to seek protection in gold holding are costly to society.

The principal virtue claimed for long-term price predictability is that knowledge that the price level will return to a mean value encourages long-term investment. The classical gold standard regime saw the expansion of railroads, steel mills, and other durable capital. The more inflationary postwar regime has also seen the building of durable capital, including steel mills, in Japan, Korea, Taiwan, Brazil, and elsewhere. Western Europe rebuilt its infrastructure. In the United States, durable capital took such forms as housing, office buildings, shopping centers, airline terminals, roads, bridges, and university buildings. While we do not dismiss arguments relating price predictability to investment in durable capital, we would like a clearer statement of the benefits of long-term price predictability and more evidence that the gold standard produced these benefits.

Bordo (1981) compared the growth rates and variability of output in the United Kingdom and the United States for 1870–1913 and 1946–79. He found that the average growth rate was higher, and the variability lower, in the later period for both countries. National Bureau data on business cycles expansions and contractions for the United States show that recessions were longer and expansions shorter under the gold standard than under the postwar regimes. Peacetime expansions and contractions from 1854 to 1919 are approximately equal: 24 and 22 months, respectively. From 1945 to 1982, peacetime expansions on average are three times the length of contractions: 34 and 11 months, respectively. The current expansion, beginning in 1982, will raise the average for postwar peacetime expansions by at least four months.

A commonly cited disadvantage of the gold standard and other fixed rate regimes is that the standard transmits shocks internationally. Easton (1984) computed the correlations between deviations from the trend of output in eight countries under the gold standard. He found moderate correlation of the deviations; some are negative, some positive. Correlations of 0.5 or 0.6 between Denmark and Norway or Sweden, and between Canada and the United States, suggest a high degree of transmission. There is, then, some evidence of the transmission of shocks across countries, as expected, but not all shocks are positive shocks to aggregate demand and output that produce positive correlation of shocks. Positive correlations may also result from transmission of negative shocks from one country to another. Further, Easton's method assumes that trends are constant. Below, we compute stochastic trends and deviations from such trends. We find very little evidence of positive correlation of shocks across countries under the gold standard.

Meltzer (1984) compared the variability of unanticipated shocks to prices and output in the United States under six monetary regimes from 1890 to 1980. He found that variability and uncertainty were greater under the two gold standard regimes, 1890–1914 and 1914–1931, than under the Bretton Woods or fluctuating rate regimes. The two gold standard regimes differ by the presence or absence of a central bank. Establishment of the Federal Reserve System in 1914 initially reduced the measures of uncertainty, but the decline did not persist. A larger and longer sustained decline in uncertainty occurred in the postwar period. The data suggest that, for the United States, uncertainty about the long-term price level and level of output was higher under the gold standard than under Bretton Woods or fluctuating rates.

The U.S. inflation rate has been higher on average in the postwar years than under the gold standard. People know this; they do not expect prices to be stable. The greater uncertainty found under the two gold standard regimes implies that the change in prices and output is predicted more accurately than under earlier regimes, although the expected price change is larger.

Figure 4.1, from the 1982 Report of the Gold Commission, shows the higher average rate of inflation and lower variability for the United

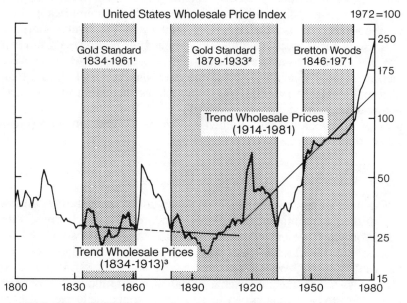

1/ Excludes 1838-1843 when specie payments were suspended.
2/ United States imposes gold export embargo from September 1917 to June 1919.
3/ Broken line indicates years excluded in computing trend.
Note: See Michael D. Bordo, Federal Reserve Bank of St. Louis <u>Review</u>, 63 (May 1981)

Fig. 4.1

States in the postwar period to 1980. From 1800 to about 1950, prices rose and fell without any obvious change in the (ex post) long-term trend. Variability around the trend is greater, and yearly changes are more erratic, until the middle 1950s.

Comparisons of the Bretton Woods and fluctuating exchange rate regimes in Meltzer (1984) shows no major difference in uncertainty about prices and output for the United States following the shift to fluctuating exchange rates. Meltzer (1988) finds that this conclusion does not hold generally. Germany and Japan reduced variability and uncertainty under the fluctuating exchange rate regime. Uncertainty increased in Britain. Several other countries show mixed results—a fall in the variability of unanticipated output and a rise in unanticipated price variability, or the reverse. Fluctuating exchange rates appear to permit countries to reduce variability and uncertainty, but countries may not adopt policies that achieve a gain in welfare.

The comparison for the gold standard with other regimes in Meltzer (1984) uses a Kalman filter to compute forecasts from quarterly data for the United States. Quarterly data may give excessive weight to short-term changes. Since the quarterly data for output and prices in earlier years were constructed by interpolation, they may introduce bias and error of interpretation. Further, U.S. experience under the gold standard may differ from the experience of other countries. Below, we reconsider the same issues using annual data for seven countries.

Any comparison between the gold standard and other standards must rely on data for the nineteenth century. Most data for that century were pieced together after the fact, so the data may be less accurate than data for the postwar period. We cannot check the extent to which the potential inaccuracy increases variability and forecasting errors in the indexes on which we rely. Below, we compare some series on prices for particular commodities to the indexes.

4.2 Inflation and Growth in Seven Countries

The data we analyze comes from seven countries that differ in size and in their commitment to the gold standard. These countries, with dates for which we have data, are shown in table 4.2. Also shown are the dates for the classical period, when many of the countries were on the gold standard. We refer to this period as the classical period to distinguish it from the gold exchange standard that followed World War I and the mixed standard before 1870. For comparison, we use data for the Bretton Woods system, 1950–72 for all countries, and for fluctuating exchange rates, 1973–85. Dating the end of Bretton Woods in 1972 instead of 1971 is arbitrary. In previous work using quarterly data there is little difference for main conclusions whether fluctuating rates

Table 4.2   **Dates Used in Data Analysis of the Gold Standard**

Country	Dates Used	Start of Classical Period
Denmark	1870–1913	1875
Germany	1875–1913	1875
Italy	1861–1913	1881[a]
Japan	1873–1913[b]	1898
Sweden	1861–1913	1873
U.K.	1870–1913	1870
U.S.	1889–1913	1889

[a]Italy was not on the gold standard during most of the classical period. 1881 is the start of stabilization. The lira was on gold from 1884 to 1894, and was inconvertible from 1894 to 1913.

[b]Output data starts in 1878. Japan was on a bimetallic standard from 1879 to 1897.

start in third quarter 1971 or first quarter 1973. Here, all data are annual. We start the fluctuating rate regime in 1973.

Growth rates of output and rates of inflation differed under the different regimes. We divided the classical period into two phases. The first, a period of deflation, ends in 1896; from 1897 to 1913 prices rose under the impact of new gold discoveries and new techniques for extracting gold.

Table 4.3 shows the experience of the seven countries in four periods. Real growth is highest in countries other than the United States under the Bretton Woods regime and, with the exception of Italy, lowest under fluctuating exchange rates. The fluctuating rate period includes the two oil shocks and the disinflation of the 1980s, so it is not clear that lower growth is a direct consequence of the fluctuating rate regime.

Several countries show faster growth in the inflationary phase of the classical period than in the deflationary phase. There is, however, little evidence of significant correlation across countries between the inflation rate and the rate of growth within a regime. Nor do we find a relation between inflation and growth in our data for individual countries.

The faster real growth under the Bretton Woods regime cannot be explained entirely as a recovery from wartime destruction. The same result is found if we start the regime in 1960. Several explanations of the growth have been proposed, including the built-in flexibility of a larger government, increased trade under GATT rules, and the development of the European Community, but little has been done to test these explanations. It is clear, however, from the comparative data that the welfare gain from rising living standards is highest in the years of the Bretton Woods regime.

If the welfare loss from inflation increases with the average rate of inflation (or deflation), the loss is greater in the postwar regimes than

Table 4.3   **Growth and Inflation Under Different Regimes (percent per annum[a])**

Country	From Start of Classical Period to 1896	1897–1913	1950–72	1973–85
	Real Growth			
Denmark	2.9	3.4	3.7	1.3
Germany	2.1	2.4	5.9	1.6
Italy	0.9	2.8	5.3	1.8
Japan	3.8[b]	3.9	7.5	3.4
Sweden	3.3	2.2	3.6	1.1
U.K.	1.9	1.8	2.6	1.2
U.S.	2.8	3.8	3.4	2.0
	Inflation			
Denmark	− 1.2	0.8	4.9	7.7
Germany	− 0.3	1.1	3.5	3.4
Italy	− 0.4	1.6	4.1	13.5
Japan	1.9[c]	2.3	5.1	3.3
Sweden	− 0.9	1.3	10.5	8.7
U.K.	− 0.4	0.9	3.1	10.5
U.S.	− 2.0	2.0	2.9	6.8

[a]Computed as $(\log X_{t+k} - \log X_t)/k$.
[b]1878–96 under a bimetallic standard.
[c]1873–96.

in the classical period. The average rate of inflation is highest under fluctuating rates. This is misleading. As is well known, adoption of fluctuating exchange rates came as a consequence of rising inflation under Bretton Woods. Although average rates of inflation are higher for four of the seven countries, all of the countries in our sample had reduced inflation by the 1980s. For most countries in our sample, inflation was below the average rate under Bretton Woods by 1986.

Short-term persistence of price movements was common under the gold standard, but short-term persistence is generally highest for the yearly rates of inflation under Bretton Woods. We use first-order serial correlation coefficients to measure persistence in actual price changes. Table 4.4 shows the correlations. Only Italy and Japan show any evidence of short-term reversion. For several countries, the degree of short-term persistence is not very different under the gold standard than under fluctuating rates. This is contrary to the inference of Klein (1976) who predicted increased serial correlation. Klein may have had a higher order correlation in mind. Our calculations (not shown) suggest that first-order serial correlation is typically highest of all.

Many of the claims about predictability and uncertainty under the gold standard and other regimes cannot be resolved with data on actual rates of change. To go beyond these comparisons, we require a pro-

Table 4.4 | First-Order Serial Correlation of Annual Price Changes

Country	Gold Standard	Bretton Woods	Fluctuating Rates
Denmark	0.38	0.42	0.60
Germany	0.14*	0.39	0.34*
Italy	−0.33	−0.09	−0.33
Japan	−0.15*	0.09*	0.38*
Sweden	0.31	0.52	0.34*
U.K.	0.32	0.49	0.34*
U.S.	0.21	0.60	0.18*

*Indicates autocorrelation not significant as measured by 2 standard deviations.

cedure that separates anticipated from unanticipated values. The following section describes the procedure we used.

4.3 Computing the Shocks

We chose the multistate Kalman filter (MSKF)[6] because it has several advantages over conventional forecasting techniques. Specifically, the MSKF: (1) recognizes and separates permanent and transient errors in the level of the series as well as permanent changes in the slope; (2) is sensitive to changes in level and scope and can alter its degree of sensitivity to compensate for changes in the series due to real changes in the economic system (such as a change in monetary regime) or changes in noise; and (3) produces a forecast of the series as well as a joint parameter distribution which allows us to obtain more information through a decomposition of the forecast errors into their subcomponents (Harrison and Stevens 1971).

To implement the MSKF, we used the following model:

$$(1) \qquad x_t = \bar{x}_t + \varepsilon_t \qquad \varepsilon_t \sim \eta(0, \sigma_\varepsilon^2),$$

$$(2) \qquad \bar{x}_t = \bar{x}_{t-1} + \overset{*}{x}_t + \gamma_t \qquad \gamma_t \sim \eta(0, \sigma_\gamma^2), \text{ and}$$

$$(3) \qquad \overset{*}{x}_t = \overset{*}{x}_{t-1} + \rho_t \qquad \rho_t \sim \eta(0, \sigma_\rho^2),$$

where x_t is the actual (log) level of the series to be forecast, $\bar{x}$ is the permanent level of the series, and $\overset{*}{x}$ is the permanent growth rate. The variables ε_t, γ_t, and ρ_t are, respectively, transitory shocks to the level of the series, permanent shocks to the level of the series (transitory shocks to the growth rate), and permanent shocks to the growth rate. These shocks are serially uncorrelated with zero means and variances shown in equations (1), (2), and (3). Combining equations (1) through (3) we have

$$(4) \qquad x_t = \overset{*}{x}_{t-1} + x_{t-1} + \varepsilon_t + \gamma_t + \rho_t.$$

In conventional forecasting systems, $\varepsilon_t + \gamma_t + \rho_t = e_t$, the forecast error. This breakdown of the forecast error provided by the MSKF is one of the advantages mentioned at the start of this section.

The basic model described in equations (1) through (3) is equivalent to Holt's (1957) system:

$$(5) \qquad\qquad e_t = x_t - (\bar{x}_{t-1} + \overset{*}{x}_{t-1}),$$

$$(6) \qquad\qquad E(\bar{x}_t) = \bar{x}_{t-1} + \overset{*}{x}_{t-1} + A_1 e_t, \text{ and}$$

$$(7) \qquad\qquad E(\overset{*}{x}_t) = \overset{*}{x}_{t-1} + A_2 e_t.$$

Holt's smoothing constants A_1 and A_2 are functions of the variance ratios $\sigma_\gamma^2/\sigma_\varepsilon^2$ and $\sigma_\rho^2/\sigma_\varepsilon^2$, respectively.

The basic model is also similar to the familiar ARIMA $(0,2,2)^7$ model shown in equation (8).

$$(8) \qquad\qquad \Delta^2 x_t = (1 - Q_1\beta - Q_2\beta^2)a_t \qquad a_t \sim \eta(0,\sigma_a^2).$$

The standard problem with the two more conventional forecasting systems is the choice of the parameters which determine system sensitivity (i.e., A_1 and A_2 in Holt and Q_1 and Q_2 in Box-Jenkins). The problem arises because of the inherent tradeoffs. A highly sensitive system responds quickly to real changes when they occur, but also overreacts to transient changes. On the other hand, a relatively insensitive system does not react to noise, but is also slow to react to real changes. The MSKF overcomes this problem.

In modeling economic time series, we can think of three basic states corresponding to the three errors, ε_t, γ_t, and ρ_t. In state 1 the series continues at some average level with occasional large transient changes in that level. This corresponds to large σ_ε^2 and small σ_γ^2 and σ_ρ^2. In state 2 the series stays at one level, experiences a permanent change in level, then continues fluctuating around the new level. In this case σ_γ^2 dominates σ_ε^2 and σ_ρ^2. In state 3 we have a permanent change in the growth rate, and σ_ρ^2 dominates. Figure 4.2, from Harrison and Stevens (1971), shows the three types of change.

Unless we are in the trivial case with $\sigma_\varepsilon^2 = \sigma_\gamma^2 = \sigma_\rho^2 = 0$, we can never know $\bar{x}_t$ and $\overset{*}{x}_t$ with certainty. Our knowledge about $\bar{x}_t$ and $\overset{*}{x}_t$ is given by a bivariate normal distribution. Successive observations of the series, x, modify this distribution. Let the joint posterior distribution of $(\bar{x}, \overset{*}{x})$ at time $t - 1$ be bivariate normal:

$$(9) \qquad\qquad (\bar{x}_{t-1}, \overset{*}{x}_{t-1}|x_{t-1}) \sim \eta\,(\phi_{t-1}),$$

where $\qquad \phi_{t-1} = \{E\bar{x}_{t-1}, E\overset{*}{x}_{t-1}, \sigma_{\bar{x}_{t-1}}^2, \sigma_{\overset{*}{x}{t-1}}^2, cov(\bar{x}_{t-1}, \overset{*}{x}_{t-1})\}.$

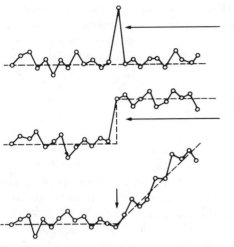

Transitory

Permanent change in level

Permanent change in growth rate

Fig. 4.2

The posterior distribution at time t is also bivariate normal:

(10) $$(\bar{x}_t, \overset{*}{x}_t | x_t) \sim \eta(\phi_t),$$

where $$\phi_t = B(\sigma_{t-1}; \sigma_\varepsilon^2, \sigma_\gamma^2, \sigma_\rho^2).$$

The B-function revises the posterior probability distribution at time t using Bayesian forecasts, the posterior distribution ϕ_{t-1}, and the generating variances. The relative importance given to recent and past observations in revising the probability weights depends on the past history of shocks. When a high probability is assigned to being in state 1 (transitory changes), observations in the distant past carry more weight. Forecasts are less sensitive to new information; the expected value of x_{t+1} is not much affected by the error in time t. The reason is that the error is expected to be mostly transitory. In the opposite case, when past history implies that permanent changes are relatively frequent, state 2 or state 3 is considered more likely, so more recent observations of x receive greater weights in determining forecasts. Each period, the weights on the various shocks—the probabilities assigned to each shock—are revised to make use of new information and to reflect the accuracy of the forecasting model in the recent past.

The program also revises the estimate of the conditional variance of the forecast error each period. The assumptions on which this computation depends are discussed in Kool (1983).

A possible disadvantage of the estimation procedure is that there is no allowance for mean reversion. As shown in equation (3), growth rates are pure random walks. However, if mean reversion is slow, errors from this source are largely offset by the revision of the weights each period. The random walk has the advantage of permitting the values currently expected for prices or output in the distant future to be computed from information available today. The forecast for k periods in the future, made at the beginning of time t, is

$$_tE(x_{t+k}) = \bar{x}_{t-1} + k\overset{*}{x}_{t-1}$$

Another disadvantage of the MSKF procedure is that forecasts are based on a single time series. Information in related series is ignored. In practice, we have used vector autoregressions (VARs) to relate forecast errors for prices and output to lagged values. In previous work (Meltzer 1985) the VARs have added only a relatively small amount of additional information. This suggests that the MSKF procedure is relatively efficient.

In practice the MSKF combines six filter models to analyze the data. The six models decompose the data into two groups, with ε_t, γ_t, and ρ_t errors in each group. The two groups separate normal errors and outliers, the latter consisting of 5 percent of the errors. Separating errors into normal and outlier values permits the program to give less weight to large, one-time changes.

Since the MSKF model is equivalent to an ARIMA model with adjustable coefficients, forecast errors are typically smaller for MSKF than for the ARIMA model. An additional advantage is that each forecast depends only on data for periods prior to the time the forecast is made. In practice, of course, the forecasting technique was not available for most of the period. We treat the forecasts and errors as an approximation to the information available to a relatively accurate forecaster at the time.

To evaluate the forecast accuracy of the MSKF, forecasts using several ARIMA models and a random walk[8] were generated for German prices and real output. The time periods are 1875–1913, 1950–72, and 1973–85, as in previous tables. Forecast errors are measured using both mean absolute percentage error (MAE) and root mean square error (RMSE). None of the alternative ARIMA models had MAE or RMSE values as low as the values for the random walk. Further, table 4.5 shows that, with minor exceptions, the MSKF performs as well or better than the random walk model under all monetary regimes and for both variables.

Comparison of the MSKF forecasts of prices and output to the means and standard deviations of actual price level and output series provides some additional information about the properties of the forecasts. These

Table 4.5   **Comparison of Forecast Accuracy for Germany**

Model	Real Output			Prices		
	GS	BW	FR	GS	BW	FR
Errors measured using MAE						
MSKF	0.11	0.49	0.16	0.12	0.76	0.96
Random walk	0.40	0.48	0.16	0.73	0.83	0.94
Errors measured using RMSE						
MSKF	0.01	0.07	0.03	0.01	0.03	0.04
Random walk	0.05	0.07	0.04	0.04	0.04	0.03

Notes:

$$\text{MAE}_t = \frac{X_t - F_t}{X_t} \times 100.$$

$\text{RMSE}_t = \sqrt{(X_t - F_t)^2}$ F_t = forecast of X_t.

GS = gold standard; BW = Bretton Woods; FR = fluctuating rates.

are shown in table 4.6. The distributions of the MSKF forecasts very closely approximate the distributions of the actual series being forecast. In virtually all cases the means and standard deviations of the forecast values are equal to or within a few one-hundredths of the actual values.

Data for the period before World War I and after World War II are treated separately in our analysis. Wartime and interwar data are omitted. The reasons are that data are not available for all countries during wartime, and interwar data for German prices are affected by the hyperinflation. This has a cost, however. The MSKF program uses some arbitrary values for the initial prior probabilities. Initial forecast values depend on these weights. In practice, this problem is reduced for several countries during the classical period by starting the analysis when the data series begin, but using only values for the classical period. Both sets of dates are shown in table 4.2 above.

We treat the annual data for 1950 to 1985 as one data set. An alternative procedure would analyze the two postwar regimes separately. It would remove the influence of the Bretton Woods period from the forecasts made during the early years of the fluctuating rate period. The shift in regime would be analyzed as a break in forecast patterns instead of a gradual transition with uncertainty about whether countries would return to a fixed rate regime. The tradeoff is that forecasts would depend considerably more on the arbitrary conditions assumed at the start of the new regime. This would have considerable impact in the fluctuating rate period which has only thirteen annual observations. The analysis, as performed, carries the probability weights from the Bretton Woods period into the start of the fluctuating rate period. The

Table 4.6   Descriptive Statistics: Actual Values and MSKF Forecasts

	Means			Standard Deviations		
	GS	BW	FR	GS	BW	FR
Real Output						
Denmark	7.41	9.41	10.01	0.24	0.31	0.06
	7.44	9.45	10.02	0.25	0.31	0.06
Germany	9.82	13.43	14.16	0.28	0.43	0.08
	9.82	13.50	14.18	0.29	0.41	0.08
Italy	4.29	11.91	12.66	0.18	0.38	0.08
	4.30	11.89	12.65	0.18	0.39	0.08
Japan	8.67	11.02	12.33	0.17	0.63	0.16
	8.67	11.10	12.38	0.19	0.66	0.16
Sweden	7.66	9.78	10.34	0.33	0.28	0.05
	7.68	9.82	10.36	0.33	0.28	0.05
U.K.	8.07	9.01	9.45	0.23	0.20	0.05
	8.09	9.04	9.46	0.24	0.20	0.05
U.S.	4.36	14.24	14.79	0.30	0.24	0.09
	4.40	14.27	14.81	0.30	0.24	0.09
Prices						
Denmark	3.98	6.02	7.30	0.08	0.31	0.34
	3.97	6.06	7.39	0.08	0.33	0.33
Germany	4.37	3.80	4.55	0.08	0.20	0.16
	4.37	3.83	4.60	0.08	0.21	0.14
Italy	3.02	2.88	4.43	0.08	0.26	0.60
	3.02	2.87	4.42	0.09	0.27	0.60
Japan	3.12	3.48	4.52	0.13	0.29	0.18
	3.09	3.53	4.56	0.12	0.28	0.15
Sweden	4.47	6.14	7.29	0.08	0.22	0.37
	4.48	6.18	7.38	0.10	0.27	0.37
U.K.	3.96	5.84	7.26	0.06	0.25	0.47
	3.96	5.88	7.38	0.06	0.26	0.46
U.S.	3.25	3.65	4.51	0.10	0.16	0.28
	3.26	3.67	4.58	0.12	0.18	0.27

Notes: For each country, first line is actual value, second line is MSKF forecast. GS = gold standard; BW = Bretton Woods; FR = fluctuating exchange rates.

weights are then revised as new information arrives. The procedure we adopted has greater intuitive appeal as a model of learning about the consequences of a change in regime than the use of arbitrarily chosen values for the underlying variances and prior probabilities.[9]

4.4   Forecast Errors in Different Regimes

No monetary system can insulate output and the price level totally from real shocks to the economy. Monetary regimes can affect the variability of output and prices, however, and the size or frequency of unanticipated disturbances. A welfare-maximizing monetary rule would reduce variability to the minimum inherent in nature and institutional arrangements. Since we do not know the welfare-maximizing monetary rule, we compare the *relative* performance under three monetary regimes: the gold standard, Bretton Woods, and fluctuating exchange rates.

Two measures of variability are available: the mean absolute error (MAE) of one-period-ahead forecasts and the root mean square error (RMSE). Since there are occasional large shocks or forecast errors, we rely on the MAE estimates for our comparisons to avoid excessive weight on large errors. This section compares the forecast errors for output and prices, computed using the MSKF program, for seven countries under the three regimes.

The estimates of ε, γ, and ρ permit computation of three measures of variability. The first, a measure of the variability of the level of the variable, is the sum of $\bar{\varepsilon} + \bar{\gamma} + \bar{\rho}$, where the bar indicates the MAE. This measure is more useful for prices than for output, since price stability increases welfare while stable output with rising population implies a decline in per capita output. The second measure, $\bar{\gamma} + \bar{\rho}$, omits the transitory error in the level of output; $\bar{\gamma}$ shows the variability of transitory changes in the growth rate of output and $\bar{\rho}$ shows the variability of permanent changes in the growth rate. Their sum gives the variability of the measured growth rate of output and the measured rate of price change. Third, we show $\bar{\rho}$, the mean change in the permanent growth rate of output and the maintained rate of inflation. $\bar{\rho}$ is a measure of uncertainty about sustained future growth and inflation.

Table 4.7 shows the data for the levels and growth rates of output. Several features deserve comment.

First, variability of output is usually higher under the gold standard then in the postwar regimes. The only exceptions are the United Kingdom and Italy under fluctuating rates.

Second, there is considerable similarity in the MAEs of different countries under the gold standard. Denmark, Germany, and Italy have about equal values, as does the United States when a few large values are omitted. This suggests that common shocks may have dominated under the gold standard. To test this proposition, we computed the correlation across countries for each output shock (ε, γ, ρ) separately. The number of statistically significant positive correlations is considerably higher under fluctuating rates and Bretton Woods than under the gold standard, so the hypothesis is rejected.[10]

Third, the United Kingdom and Japan have very different experiences under the three regimes. The United Kingdom has the lowest variability of any country under the gold standard and the second highest under fluctuating exchange rates. Japan suffered the greatest

Table 4.7   Mean Absolute Error Forecasts of Output and Growth
                   (in percentages)

Country	Classical Period			Bretton Woods			Fluctuating Rates		
	(1)	(2)	(3)	(1)	(2)	(3)	(1)	(2)	(3)
Denmark	3.1	2.7	1.6	2.6	2.2	1.2	2.5	2.2	1.2
Germany	3.0	2.2	0.6	2.6	2.3	1.3	2.2	2.0	1.3
Italy	3.1	2.3	0.9	1.9	1.5	0.8	5.0	4.7	2.8
Italy[a]							3.0	2.8	1.7
Japan[b]	14.1	12.3	8.0	2.6	2.1	1.2	1.6	1.4	0.9
Japan[c]	11.4	10.1	6.6						
Sweden	3.8	3.2	1.3	1.9	1.6	0.9	2.0	1.9	1.1
U.K.	2.1	1.5	0.6	1.9	1.5	0.8	2.6	2.3	1.3
U.S.	4.3	3.3	1.5	1.7	1.4	0.7	3.1	2.8	1.7
U.S.[d]	3.2	2.4	1.1						

Note: (1) = output; (2) = growth; (3) = sustained growth rate.
[a]Omits two largest errors, 1983 and 1984.
[b]Based on Okhana's estimates of national income. Classical period includes 1880–96 under bimetallism and 1897–1913 on gold.
[c]Omits four largest errors—1882, 1883, 1885, 1899—in classical period.
[d]Omits three largest errors—1893, 1895, 1908—in classical period.

variability under the gold standard and benefited from the lowest under fluctuating rates.

Fourth, the United States has the lowest variability under Bretton Woods, although the differences with Sweden, Italy, or the United Kingdom are not large. The relatively low variability for the United States under Bretton Woods and for the United Kingdom in the classical period suggests that countries at the center of the exchange rate system may benefit from lower output variability. This would occur if, on balance, other countries absorb output shocks received from the center. There is some evidence of this for the gold standard, but not for the Bretton Woods system. The correlations of shocks show seven (out of a possible twenty-one) negative values in the range -0.4 to -0.5 under the gold standard. Five of the seven involve the United Kingdom. Under Bretton Woods and fluctuating rates, all statistically significant correlations are positive.

Fifth, the results for the United States are qualitatively similar to those based on quarterly data in Meltzer (1984). Variability of output and growth is highest under the gold standard. In part, the greater variability reflects relatively large errors in years of recession—1893 and 1908—but the severity of recessions may reflect the operation of the gold standard. One difference from the quarterly data is that the variability of our measure of sustained growth, $\bar{\rho}$, is slightly lower under the gold standard than under fluctuating rates. This finding differs from the one based on quarterly data and suggests slightly greater stability of the anticipated long-term path of output relative to the fluctuating rate period.

Sixth, uncertainty does not increase uniformly under fluctuating exchange rates. Japan shows later variability on all measures, and variability in Germany and Denmark either declines or remains the same. The principal increases in uncertainty are in the United States, the United Kingdom, and Italy.

An alternative explanation of the higher variability experienced in some countries under the gold standard is that sectoral shifts in production have worked to make output less variable in recent years. The relative decline in agriculture and rise in manufacturing and services is often suggested as a principal reason for the change. This explanation fails to account for the experience of the United Kingdom, where variability is lower under the gold standard than under fluctuating rates, or of Germany, where the differences under the three standards are relatively small. Nevertheless, we tried to estimate the importance of change in output mix. To separate the effects of agriculture and manufacturing, we computed the variability of measures of industrial production under the gold standard for Germany and the United States. The MAEs for U.S. industrial production 1889–1913, comparable to columns (1) to (3) of table 4.7, are, respectively, 8.50, 6.54, and 2.70. For Germany, the computations are for 1875–1913, the same period used in table 4.7. The German values are 2.80, 2.24, and 1.00. The calculations for Germany do not differ importantly from the calculations for total output in table 4.7. For the United States all values are higher. Both calculations suffer from the fact that shocks to agriculture affect the demand for manufactures, the output of manufacturing industries, and the series on industrial production. Neither the data for Germany nor for the United States show evidence, however, that the use of total output or GDP biases our result against the gold standard.

Finally, to pursue the issue of the relative variability of agricultural and industrial output, we computed the same measures of variability for a major crop in the United States and Germany under the gold standard. We chose corn production for the United States and rye production for Germany. The numbers reported are the same calculations as columns (1) to (3) in table 4.7. The values for U.S. corn are 15.42, 10.24, and 3.26, respectively, and for German rye, 9.44, 7.15, and 3.40. Under relative variability, the ratios of U.S. corn to U.S. industrial production are 1.8, 1.6, and 1.2; the ratios of German rye to German industrial production are 3.4, 3.2, and 3.4.

These data suggest that variability in the production of agricultural products was larger than the variability of industrial production under the gold standard. For Germany, where variability of industrial production is lower than in the United States, relative variability for agricultural products is higher. Unlike the more ambiguous results for industrial production, the data on relative variability provide some evidence that the decline in the relative size of the agricultural sector may have contributed to the decline in variability over time. For Germany, the relative variability is large enough to reverse our previous conclusion. For the United States, this is not the case. Adjustment using the relative variability measure narrows the difference between the gold standard and the Bretton Woods, but does not change the ranking.

A problem with these results is that comparison of a single series on agricultural production to an index of industrial production may bias the result. This would occur if total agricultural production is less variable than any single crop. We have not pursued this issue or extended the calculation of relative variability to other periods.

While no single regime has the lowest variability of output growth in all countries, fluctuating exchange rates have the highest variability of output growth only in the United Kingdom and Italy. The data suggest that countries that follow medium-term predictable policies, like Japan, have been able to lower variability and uncertainty under fluctuating rates, while countries that follow less predictable policies— notably the U.S., the U.K., and Italy—have not. In the latter countries, policy actions shift more frequently from stimulus to restraint, increasing variability and uncertainty.

The U.K., the U.S., and Italy shifted in the late 1970s or early 1980s from inflationary to disinflationary policies. The policy change was sharp and sudden, and the U.S., U.K., and Italy suffered a relatively severe recession followed by a relatively brisk recovery. In contrast, Japan experienced a comparable (or higher) rate of inflation in 1974 and 1975 as it, like Germany, maintained more gradual and persistent policies.

Italy, like Denmark, has a fixed but adjustable exchange rate with respect to countries in the European Monetary System and fluctuating rates against the pound, the dollar, and the yen. Variability of output and growth in Italy under fluctuating rates differs considerably from the experience of Denmark, however.

The contrasting experiences under the fluctuating rate regime suggest that differences in policy action and in the perceived degree of commitment to a stable policy are an important source of the difference in outcome. Fluctuating exchange rates do not enhance or prevent variability. They provide an opportunity to increase stability. Some countries have benefited from the opportunity, but others have not.

The results for prices and inflation show a similar, mixed pattern. Again, no regime dominates in all countries. Data for variability of prices and inflation are shown in table 4.8.

Table 4.8   **Mean Absolute Error for Prices and Inflation (in percentages)**

Country	Classical Period			Bretton Woods			Fluctuating Rates		
	(1)	(2)	(3)	(1)	(2)	(3)	(1)	(2)	(3)
Denmark	1.9	1.8	1.2	2.4	1.9	1.2	1.8	1.7	1.1
Germany	3.2	3.0	1.9	2.0	1.7	0.9	0.9	0.8	0.6
Italy	2.8	2.5	1.2	1.9	1.5	0.9	2.9	2.7	2.1
Italy[a]							2.5	2.3	1.8
Japan[b]	3.9	3.3	1.6	2.2	1.7	0.9	2.7	2.4	1.3
Japan[c]				1.9	1.5	0.8	1.9	1.8	1.1
Sweden	3.0	2.9	2.2	2.7	2.2	1.1	1.8	1.7	1.0
U.K.	1.8	1.6	1.0	2.0	1.6	0.9	4.6	4.3	2.1
U.S.	2.2	1.8	0.9	2.3	2.3	1.2	1.9	1.8	1.0

Note: (1) = price level; (2) = rate of price change; (3) = maintained inflation.
[a]Omits 1974.
[b]Includes 1879–97 under bimetallism, with 1898–1913 on the gold standard.
[c]Omits one large outlier: 1965 under Bretton Woods, and 1975 under fluctuating rates.

One of the claimed advantages of the gold standard is the reduced variability of long-run anticipated inflation. The annual data, like the quarterly data for the United States in Meltzer (1984), give little support to this claim. For most countries the variability of maintained inflation (table 4.8, column 3) is as high or higher under the gold standard than under Bretton Woods or the fluctuating rate regime. There is no evidence that the gold standard fostered long-term price stability as that term is used here.[11]

Generally, prices and rates of price change have smaller forecast errors in one of the postwar regimes. The United Kingdom is, again, the exception since price level forecast errors are lowest there under the gold standard. For the United States, forecast errors are lowest under fluctuating rates, not under the Bretton Woods system.

The three regimes differ in the sources of price variability. The average MAE for the seven countries in the classical period is higher (2.7) than under Bretton Woods (2.3) or fluctuating rates (2.4). Each type of error, ε, γ, and ρ, is largest on average in the classical period. Transitory errors in level are smallest under fluctuating rates; fluctuating rates appear to buffer transitory shocks. Permanent shocks to growth are relatively more important under fluctuating rates than under Bretton Woods, reflecting the experience of Italy and the United Kingdom. That experience suggests, however, that under the fluctuating rate system countries were less successful in buffering shocks to the perceived permanent rate of inflation than transitory shocks to the price level. Wage indexation following the oil shocks most likely contributed to this result for Italy in the 1970s.

William Poole has suggested to us that we provide estimates for individual commodity prices to see whether our estimates of anticipated long-term variability under the gold standard are biased or misleading. Table 4.9 reports the results for metals, chemicals, and wool prices under the three regimes. In all three cases, the lowest variability is under the Bretton Woods regime. For metals prices, variability is highest under the gold standard, but for chemicals and wool, variability is highest under fluctuating rates. The relatively high variability of chemical prices in recent years reflects, to some degree, the effects of petroleum prices on petrochemical prices, but this does not explain the relatively high variability of wool prices. Of particular interest is the variability of sustained inflation. Although the results in table 4.9 draw on only a small part of the available data, they give no reason to believe that the computations based on price index numbers (table 4.8) give a misleading or biased view of the variability of unanticipated changes in prices and sustained inflation under the gold standard.

Recent work in monetary economics investigates the types of shocks that dominate fluctuations in output. Much of this work relies on quarterly changes in the United States in recent years, a period that includes major changes in oil prices. The shocks to output and prices estimated here provide some relevant information for other countries over a longer time and under different regimes.

Table 4.10 shows the contemporaneous correlation between unanticipated changes in output and prices under the three monetary regimes. A positive correlation between shocks suggests the possible dominance of shocks to aggregate demand. The reason is that unanticipated changes in aggregate demand shift the aggregate demand curve along an unchanged, positively sloped, short-run supply curve, so output and prices rise and fall together. Unanticipated shifts in aggregate supply along a negatively sloped aggregate demand curve induce a rise in prices and a decline in output, or a fall in prices and a rise in output.

The correlations are subject to different interpretations. Taken as evidence of the type of shock, however, they show that neither demand

Table 4.9	Mean Absolute Error for U.S. Commodity Prices in Three Regimes (in percentages)								
	Classical Period			Bretton Woods			Fluctuating Rates		
Commodity	(1)	(2)	(3)	(1)	(2)	(3)	(1)	(2)	(3)
Metals	9.38	7.74	3.73	2.24	1.81	0.98	5.25	1.73	3.16
Chemicals	3.11	2.66	1.65	1.26	1.09	0.55	10.57	8.46	5.50
Wool	15.63	14.44	8.53	13.71	10.30	3.78	21.78	11.84	6.38

Note: (1) = price level; (2) = rate of price change; (3) = maintained rate of price change.

Table 4.10   Correlations: Price Level and Output Forecast Errors

Country	Classical Period	Bretton Woods	Floating Rates
Denmark	0.28	−0.88	−0.74
Germany	0.02	−0.34	−0.51
Italy	−0.00	−0.39	−0.21
Japan	−0.13	−0.18	−0.74
Sweden	0.12	−0.86	0.04
U.K.	−0.01	−0.85	−0.29
U.S.	0.20	0.15	−0.66

or supply shocks dominate the contemporaneous correlations in all countries or under all regimes. The classical period shows no fixed pattern. The correlations are relatively small in all countries and are consistent with a mixture of supply and demand shocks. Such a pattern would arise from a mixture of productivity shocks in various countries and gold movements in response to changes in relative productivity and relative demand. Under Bretton Woods, the correlations are negative except in the United States, where the pattern is similar to that found for the classical period. The pattern under fluctuating rates is similar to that under Bretton Woods, with differences for individual countries, but the same mix of relatively high negative correlations in three or four countries and less clear-cut results in the remainder.

If we accept the evidence from the correlations, searching for the dominant type of shock is not likely to prove fruitful. This is not surprising. There is little reason to believe that shocks to aggregate demand or to aggregate supply dominate fluctuations of output and prices. Economic theory gives no reason for presuming that one or another type of shock dominates under all regimes.

A system of fluctuating rates permits countries to reduce shocks to aggregate demand from abroad. If under Betton Woods there were a mix of aggregate demand shocks from abroad and domestic or international shocks to supply, the shift to fluctuating rates would heighten the relative importance of supply shocks by eliminating (or reducing) the influence of aggregate demand shocks. The relatively strong oil shocks and the change in regime could then produce the observed change in the correlations for countries like Japan and the United States following the change in regime.

4.5 Interaction Between Shocks

Prices and output are part of an interactive system in which shocks to one variable affect forecasts for that variable and others in the economic system. Also, shocks to one variable induce shocks to other variables or to the same variable at a later date. The MSKF estimates ignore these interactions. In this section we discuss some efforts to go beyond the univariate system to explore interaction across countries and between shocks within a country.

To study the interactions, we use VARs to relate the shocks estimated using the MSKF. The VARs form a system of linear regressions of equal lag length relating, for example, the current price shock (or output shock) to lagged values of price and output shocks in the same country or in a foreign country.[12]

The VARs relating shocks to output and prices in the same country yield results not unlike the contemporaneous correlations. There is no dominant pattern. Some interactions between price and output shocks are negative, some are positive, but most are not significant by the usual standards.

We investigated the effect of introducing the interrelation between prices and output in the home country and in the country with the dominant currency—the U.K. in the classical period and the U.S. under the Bretton Woods system. Again, no consistent patterns were found, perhaps because the number of degrees of freedom becomes relatively small, particularly in the postwar regimes. To investigate this possibility, we computed the matrix of simple correlations between price shocks across countries for each type of shock and, separately, the simple correlation between output shocks. There are seven countries, so there are twenty-one correlation coefficients for each type of shock. The number of degrees of freedom differ in the different regimes, with the largest number for the gold standard and the smallest number for fluctuating rates.

Table 4.11 shows the number of correlations that are at least twice the computed standard error of the transformed correlation,

$$\sigma_z = \frac{1}{\sqrt{n-3}} \, ,$$

where n is the number of observations and

$$z = \frac{1}{2} \ln \frac{1 + r}{1 - r}$$

for correlation r. For prices, the number of correlations shown is largest under Bretton Woods and smallest under the gold standard. For output, the number of correlations in the table is highest under fluctuating rates. The latter may reflect the common oil shocks in the 1970s. Whatever the reason, it is clear that fluctuating rates did not prevent unanticipated shocks from affecting prices and output in several countries. Moreover, the effects on prices and output are found for permanent and transitory shocks.

Table 4.11   Correlations by Type of Shock and by Regime

	Gold Standard			Bretton Woods			Fluctuating Rates		
	ε	γ	ρ	ε	γ	ρ	ε	γ	ρ
Output									
Positive	1	2	1	6	6	6	7	9	9
Negative	3	2	2	0	0	0	0	0	0
Prices									
Positive	2	3	3	10	8	11	7	9	7
Negative	1	1	0	0	0	0	0	0	0

A notable difference between the gold standard and other standards is the finding of correlated negative shocks to output and prices. For the gold standard this is consistent with, and supportive of, the conclusion reached by Easton (1984) using deviations from trend of output. One plausible explanation is that under the gold standard, gold flows worked to expand output in one country and contract it in another, as the price-specie mechanism implies. This mechanism may have been strong enough to overcome the effects of common shocks arising from gold discoveries, technical changes in gold production, and changes in the demand for gold. Closer examination shows that both of the negative correlations for permanent output shocks involve the United Kingdom.[13] As noted earlier, this suggests that the United Kingdom may have succeeded in lowering output variability under the gold standard by allowing the London market to serve as an international financial market.

There are no similar findings for the United States under Bretton Woods. In fact, there are no correlations involving U.S. output in table 4.11 for the Bretton Woods period. For the price level and inflation correlations the situation is very different: five of the eleven correlations for ρ include the United States. Only Italy shows a relatively small correlation with the United States. It appears that the MSKF finds the expected interrelation between shocks to the maintained U.S. inflation rate and shocks to maintained inflation in other countries under fixed exchange rates. In contrast, only two of the eight correlations between permanent shocks to the price level under Bretton Woods involve the United States. It appears that one-time price level changes, estimated by γ, did not diffuse internationally to the same degree as did persistent inflation under Bretton Woods, estimated by ρ.

Many of the papers in Bordo and Schwartz (1984) report mainly null results for interactions under the gold standard, similar to the results we obtained from VARs using annual observations. These findings are puzzling. The relation of prices in different countries under fixed exchange rates has been reported for centuries. The problem may be the quality of the data, as some authors suggested, or the use of annual rather than quarterly data, or the relatively small number of degrees of freedom available.

To investigate the effect of using quarterly data, thereby increasing the number of degrees of freedom, we used available quarterly data for the United States and the United Kingdom under the gold standard. Gordon (1982) developed quarterly values of output and prices for the U.S.; Friedman and Schwartz (1963) provide quarterly data for the U.S. monetary base; and Capie and Webber (1985) constructed quarterly data for the U.K. monetary base. To study interaction under the gold standard, we estimated VARs relating shocks to the monetary base in the U.S. (BUS), the monetary base in the U.K. (BUK), U.S. real GNP and price deflator (RUS and PUS), for the period mid-1891 to mid-1914. Shocks were computed using the MSKF program separately on each of the series. The results of the VARs are shown in table 4.12 for four lags.

The quarterly data suggest statistically significant interactions between shocks to nominal and real values in the United States and the

Table 4.12   **Vector Autoregressions for the U.S. and U.K. (4 lags, 1891:2 to 1914:2)**

Dependent Variable	Variable	Sum of Lag Coefficients	Significant Level	R^2	DW
BUS	BUS	−1.77	*	0.34	2.0
	RUS	0.02	0.98		
	PUS	0.51	0.02		
	BUK	−0.23	0.03		
RUS	BUS	0.67	0.61	0.22	2.1
	RUS	−0.60	0.01		
	PUS	0.77	0.02		
	BUK	−0.05	0.25		
PUS	BUS	−0.41	0.52	0.12	2.0
	RUS	0.11	0.42		
	PUS	−0.53	0.11		
	BUK	0.33	0.72		
BUK	BUS	0.66	0.35	0.25	2.0
	RUS	0.00	0.21		
	PUS	−0.46	0.01		
	BUK	−0.43	0.05		

Note: BUS = total shock to U.S. monetary base; RUS = total shock to U.S. real GNP; PUS = total shock to deflator; BUK = total shock to U.K. monetary base. Quarterly U.S. data from RUS and PUS are from Gordon (1982); U.S. base from Friedman and Schwartz (1963); U.K. base from Capie and Webber (1985). DW = Durbin-Watson statistic.

*Less than 0.005.

United Kingdom. A main channel of interaction relates current and lagged values of shocks to the monetary bases in the United States and the United Kingdom with current and lagged values of shocks to prices and output.

Lagged shocks to the U.S. price level have a positive effect on the (unanticipated) U.S. base and a negative effect on the U.K. base of approximately the same magnitude after four quarters. An unanticipated increase in U.S. prices induces a transfer of base money (gold) from the U.K. to the U.S.; an unanticipated decline in U.S. prices induces an (unanticipated) outflow of gold. The lagged effect of the lower U.K. base reinforces the effect of higher prices on the U.S. base.

Past unanticipated prices have a positive effect on U.S. output; price and output shocks are positively related in the output equation, a pattern suggestive of demand shocks. Allowing for the lagged effects suggests a much stronger and more reliable relation between shocks to prices and output than is shown by the contemporaneous correlations. A 1 percent (unanticipated) increase in the price level raises output by 0.77 percent within four quarters.

The relatively strong and significant interaction between unanticipated prices and money poses two problems. First, the response of unanticipated money to unanticipated prices is opposite to the textbook description of the gold standard, where higher U.S. prices induce a flow of gold (base money) from the United States to the United Kingdom or other countries. We investigated whether the four-quarter response reversed at longer lags. For values up to twelve lags, the effect of PUS on BUK changes to a positive (and statistically significant) sum, but the numerical value is small. Second, the estimates suggest that a change in unanticipated prices moves the system away from a purchasing power parity equilibrium, at least for a time.

Further, the large (-1.77) and statistically significant influence of lagged BUS on current BUS, and the smaller effect (-0.43) of lagged BUK on BUK suggests that stabilizing interaction under the gold standard may have depended much more on internal dynamics and capital movements and interest rates than on the price and output changes emphasized by price-specie-flow theories. The estimated responses of BUS and BUK to RUS are small and nonsignificant (0.02 and 0.00, respectively) and, as noted, the responses to PUS reinforce rather than stabilize BUS and BUK for periods up to three years.

On the financial side, we find that an unanticipated shift in gold or capital from the U.K. to the U.S. raises BUS and lowers BUK. Presumably, interest rates rise in the U.K. and fall in the U.S., but the lagged effects of BUS work to reverse the unanticipated increase in the U.S. monetary base and to offset the lagged effects of BUK on BUS. The lagged effects of BUK on current BUK reinforce the stabilizing properties of lagged BUS on current BUS.

The stabilizing effects of lagged own values of the unanticipated impulses may have been reinforced by the effects of price, output, and money anticipations. We have not investigated these channels. Further, our results come from a study of incomplete bilateral adjustment. We do not have quarterly data on prices and output in the United Kingdom, and we neglect changes in third countries that were part of the trade and payments system. For these reasons, our findings are, at most, suggestive of the way the gold standard may have worked in practice.

4.6 Conclusion

As Schwartz (1984, 11) notes, there are several hypotheses but little empirical evidence about the transmission of changes under the gold standard. Our study of unanticipated money, prices, and output begins to fill part of the gap and suggests that, at least for the United States and the United Kingdom, base movements played a dominant role in the international transmission of impulses. Price shocks as measured here had no role in achieving stability; the lagged effects of unanticipated price impulses appear to have reinforced expansive or contractive influences on output and money.

There are many explanations of the difference between the operation of the gold standard in the classical period before World War I and its operation during the interwar period. Our findings suggest that increased management of capital flows under the gold exchange standard may explain part of the difference. The data for the United States and United Kingdom suggest that capital movements, operating as unanticipated changes in the monetary base, were a main force stabilizing the system following price changes. Price and output impulses either had weak short-term stabilizing properties or worked to reinforce prior impulses. Price movements helped to stabilize the U.S.-U.K. system only, if at all, after a period of years. To the extent that central bank management reduced interwar capital movements, it reduced the stabilizing effects of lagged unanticipated values of the U.S. and U.K. monetary bases, thereby giving greater weights to the effects of past (unanticipated) price impulses.[14]

A main aim of this study has been to compare the welfare properties of alternative monetary arrangements. The three monetary regimes we considered were the classical regime, when leading countries were on the international gold standard; the Bretton Woods regime; and the current fluctuating exchange rate regime. We used four criteria: rate of output growth, rate of inflation, and the stability of prices and of output growth. To compute variability of prices, output, inflation, and real growth, we relied on estimates from a multistate Kalman filter. The filter computes values for unanticipated levels and rates of change of prices and output for each year, and allocates the unanticipated changes to three types of shock: permanent changes in the growth rate, permanent changes in level, and transitory changes in level.

We analyzed data for seven countries that differed in size, in the relative importance of trade, and in institutions. The countries were Denmark, Germany, Italy, Japan, Sweden, the United Kingdom, and the United States. Some countries established a link to gold very early in the nineteenth century. Some, like Italy, remained on the gold standard for only a brief period. We started the classical period about 1870, when several countries committed to maintain a fixed gold value of their currency. The classical period ends with the start of World War I, when most of the countries in our sample left the gold standard.

No single system dominated on all the welfare criteria. We do not attempt to weight the criteria to arrive at an overall judgment. Instead, we consider each criterion in turn.

The rate of inflation was lowest, on average, under the gold standard. The rate of growth was highest in most countries under the Bretton Woods system. The variability of prices and of output growth was highest for most countries under the gold standard. The main exception was the U.K.

There are well-known problems in making intertemporal comparisons, so the evidence of increased variability under the gold standard should be treated cautiously. One explanation, unrelated to the monetary standard, was the greater variability of agriculture and its greater relative importance in earlier periods. Some attempts to calculate the relative variability of industrial and agricultural production gave limited support to this proposition. For prices, the limited evidence for the United States did not support the hypothesis, but the limited evidence from individual commodity prices was difficult to interpret.

Some countries experienced greater stability under Bretton Woods, some under fluctuating exchange rates. We have found no evidence that the move to fluctuating exchange rates generally increased variability of output, prices, growth, or inflation. On the contrary, some countries achieved greater stability under fluctuating rates than under the alternative regimes. We conjecture that this result reflects the operation of credible, medium-term policies working either directly, or by stabilizing expectations, on the demand for money or velocity.

Using quarterly data for the United States from 1890 to 1980, Meltzer (1984) found that short- and long-term variability of prices and output was higher under the gold standard than in the postwar years. The annual data for the seven countries broadly support the same conclusion. In Meltzer, evidence of the much discussed long-term stability of prices under the gold standard comes mainly from ex post data showing that eventually the price level reverted to the value reached a half century or a century earlier. In contrast, our conclusion is based on a measure of long-term price anticipations. The latter seems to us a more relevant measure of stability or uncertainty.

A byproduct of our work was some evidence on the type of shocks affecting the economies of the seven countries. We have found that experience differed under different regimes and between countries. No dominant pattern emerged. The search for a uniform cause of fluctuations would appear to be a misplaced effort.

Our results were subject to several limitations. The statistical model we use to compute impulses or shocks does not allow for mean reversion, an important part of the case for the gold standard. The gold standard provided a rule under which many felt confident that government policies would remain limited in scope. When governments adopted policies leading to temporary departures from gold or to devaluation, gold often provided an available means of protection for individuals. Although our statistical procedure is adaptive, it does not fully reflect these welfare-enhancing attributes of the classical gold standard.

There are other limitations. The forecasts and measures of shocks were based on data for periods prior to the period of the forecast, but the data on which we rely were not available at the time. And, as is well known, data for the nineteenth century are not entirely reliable. Further, we have not attempted to hold constant other relevant factors affecting output and prices, including weather, changes in output mix, and changes in nonmonetary policies.

Despite these and other limitations, there is sufficient uniformity in our results to support two propositions. First, short- or long-term anticipations about prices and output were less stable under the gold standard than under the monetary arrangements of the past thirty-five years. Second, a fluctuating exchange rate regime does not impose greater uncertainty and instability. Some countries were able to reduce uncertainty about prices and output under the fluctuating exchange rate regime, both absolutely and relative to Bretton Woods and to the classical gold standard.

Appendix
Data Sources

EUROPEAN COUNTRIES: Data on prices and output before World War I are from Mitchell (1976). Postwar data are from OECD, various issues. German industrial and rye production from 1875 to 1913 is from Mitchell (1976, 355–56, 241, 254).

JAPAN: Data for output from 1878 to 1913 are Okhana's estimates of real income. Price data are for 1873–1913. Both series are from Bank of Japan (1966). Postwar data are from OECD, various issues.

UNITED STATES: Data for output and prices before World War I are Net National Product (Kendrick) and implicit GNP deflator (Kendrick) from U.S. Department of Commerce (1966). Industrial production is Frickey's index, 1889–1913, the U.S. Department of Commerce series (1960, 13), and the Federal Reserve index of industrial production, 1950–85. Metals prices and chemical prices are from Warren and Pearson to 1890 and the Bureau of Labor Statistics after 1890; see Commerce (1960), series E7, E9, E20, and E22 extended to 1985 using Bureau of Labor Statistics data. Corn production from 1889 to 1913 is from Commerce (1960), series K266.

Notes

1. There were suspensions of the gold standard and, in some countries, devaluations against gold even in the classical gold standard period. See Eichengreen (1985, 6) for a list of countries that devalued. Mussa (1986) compares variability of ex post real exchange rates under fixed and fluctuating exchange rates in the postwar era.

2. Expansion of trade under fixed exchange rates achieved by increasing variability of prices and output is not a clear welfare gain. Further, evidence on the relation between exchange rate regimes and the volume of trade is, at best, mixed.

3. The periods are given in table 4.2 below. All end in 1913.

4. For expositional purposes, we take the optimal rate of inflation to be zero.

5. Schwartz (1981) finds a negatively sloped gold supply curve for the postwar period, so the mechanism has not worked the same way in all periods.

6. A more complete discussion is in Bomhoff (1983, chapter 4) and Kool (1983).

7. Testing the data for each country using standard Box-Jenkins identification techniques indicates that second differencing is required to achieve stationarity in almost all cases.

8. We use last period's actual value as this period's forecast.

9. The computations of ϵ, γ and ρ begin in 1952, so there are twenty-one years of fixed rates and thirteen years of fluctuating rates.

10. The correlations are discussed more fully below.

11. The random walk in the anticipated growth rate does not incorporate mean reversion, as noted earlier.

12. While the VARs help to compensate for our neglect of interactions between variables, they introduce a different problem. The estimates are no longer "true" forecasts. Estimates for a particular period now depend on events that occur later in the sample period.

13. The two countries are Denmark and Italy. The negatively correlated price shocks are for the United Kingdom and Germany.

14. Rich (1984) found that price movements worked to stabilize the U.S.-Canada bilateral system only over relatively long periods.

References

Bank of Japan, Statistics Department. 1966. *Hundred year statistics of the Japanese economy.* Tokyo: Bank of Japan.
Bomhoff, E. 1983. *Monetary uncertainty.* Amsterdam: North-Holland.
Bordo, M. 1981. The classical gold standard: Some lessons for today. *Federal Reserve Bank of St. Louis Review* 63 (May): 2–17.
———. 1986. Explorations in monetary history: A survey of the literature. *Explorations in Economic History* 23: 339–415.
Bordo, M., and A. J. Schwartz. 1984. *A retrospective on the classical gold standard, 1821–1931.* Chicago: University of Chicago Press.
Capie, F., and A. Webber. 1985. *A monetary history of the United Kingdom, 1870–1982.* Vol. 1, *Data, sources, methods.* London: Allen and Unwin.
Commission on the Role of Gold in the Domestic and International Monetary Systems. 1982. *Report to the Congress.* Vol. 1. Washington, D.C.
Cooper, R. 1982. The gold standard: Historical facts and future prospects. *Brookings Papers on Economic Activity* 1:1–45.
Easton, S. T. 1984. Real output and the gold standard years, 1830–1913. In Bordo and Schwartz (1984, 513–38).
Eichengreen, B. 1985. Editor's introduction. In *The gold standard in theory and history,* ed. B. Eichengreen, 1–35. New York: Methuen.
Friedman, M., and A. J. Schwartz. 1963. *A monetary history of the United States, 1867–1960.* Princeton: Princeton University Press.
Gordon, R. J. 1982. Price inertia and policy ineffectiveness in the United States, 1890–1980. *Journal of Political Economy* 90:1087–1117.
Harrison, P. J., and C. F. Stevens. 1971. A Bayesian approach to short-term forecasting. *Operational Research Quarterly* 22:341–62.
Holt, C. C. 1957. *Forecasting seasonals and trends by exponentially weighting moving averages.* Pittsburgh: Carnegie Institute of Technology.
Klein, B. 1976. The social costs of the recent inflation: The mirage of steady "anticipated" inflation. *Carnegie Rochester Conference Series on Public Policy* 3:185–212.
Kool, C. J. 1983. Appendix 1. In Bomhoff (1983, 227–46).
Meltzer, A. H. 1984. Some evidence on the comparative uncertainty experienced under different monetary regimes. In *Alternative monetary regimes,* eds. C. D. Campbell and W. R. Dougan, 122–53. Baltimore: Johns Hopkins University Press.
———. 1985. Variability of prices, output and money under fixed and fluctuating exchange rates: An empirical study of monetary regimes in Japan and the United States. *Bank of Japan Monetary and Economic Studies* 3 (3):1–46.
———. 1988. On monetary stability and monetary reform. In *Toward a world of economic stability,* eds. Y. Suzuki and M. Okabe. Tokyo: University of Tokyo Press.
Mitchell, B. 1976. *European historical statistics, 1750–1970.* New York: Columbia University Press.

Mussa, M. 1986. Nominal exchange rates and the behavior of real exchange rates: Evidence and implications. *Carnegie Rochester Conference Series on Public Policy* 25:117–214.

Rich, G. 1984. Canada without a central bank: Operation of the price-specie-flow mechanism, In Bordo and Schwartz (1984, 547–75).

Rockoff, H. 1984. Some evidence on the real price of gold, its costs of production, and commodity prices. In Bordo and Schwartz (1984, 613–44).

Schwartz, A. J. 1981. Gold output. Memo to the members of the Gold Commission, September.

———. 1984 Introduction. In Bordo and Schwartz (1984, 1–20).

———. 1986 Alternative monetary regimes: The gold standard. In *Alternative monetary regimes*, eds. C. D. Campbell and W. R. Dougan, 44–72. Baltimore: Johns Hopkins University Press.

U.S. Department of Commerce, Bureau of the Census. 1960. *Historical statistics of the United States, Colonial times to 1957*. Washington, D.C.: GPO.

U.S. Department of Commerce, Bureau of the Census. 1966. *Long-term economic growth, 1860–1965*. Washington, D.C.: GPO.

Comment   William Poole

I enjoyed reading the Meltzer-Robinson (hereafter, MR) paper,[1] and learned a lot from it. There are two aspects to this work. First, MR provide a compact summary of inflation and output data for seven countries and a commentary on the principal issues. Second, they provide a detailed analysis of their data using the multistate Kalman filter.

My concerns about the Kalman filter in the context of this paper involve the small number of observations and the quality of the data. It appears that MR estimate a substantial number of parameters from relatively few observations. The maximum number of observations during the classical period is 44 for the United Kingdom; the Bretton Woods and floating rate periods taken together contain 36 observations. The results must depend heavily on the a priori specification. For the Bretton Woods and floating rate periods, the Kalman filter forecasts and forecast errors are calculated from 23 and 13 observations, respectively. Given that the floating rate period has only 13 observations, I would be a little more cautious in drawing general conclusions about floating rates than are MR. As for the quality of the data, MR do develop a strong case by examining a number of different countries and several different series for some countries.

Tables 4.7 and 4.8 provide the basic findings of the paper. Although the results are not uniform across countries and across periods, in

William Poole is a professor of economics and the director of the Center for the Study of Financial Markets and Institutions at Brown University, Providence, Rhode Island.

general the classical period had somewhat higher variability of output forecast errors from the Kalman filter than the Bretton Woods and flexible exchange rate periods. I read table 4.8 as essentially a draw in comparing price forecast errors during the classical period and the post–World War II periods. These tables do not provide support for arguing the superiority of the gold standard.

Table 4.6 shows that the Kalman filter forecasts have means and standard deviations that are close to those of the actual data, indicating that the Kalman filter forecasts and the actual data have similar statistical properties. I would have expected the standard deviations of the Kalman filter forecasts to be significantly lower than those of the actual data, on the grounds that efficient forecasts cannot pick up the random component in the levels of the data. The results in table 4.6 arise because the levels data are nonstationary, or approximately so; levels disturbances account for a small part of the standard deviations of these series. Note 7 reports that second differencing is required to achieve stationarity, and table 4.5 shows that for Germany the Kalman filter and random walk models are essentially the same for both the Bretton Woods and flexible rate periods. My guess is that repeating table 4.5 for the other countries would yield similar results.

In table 4.5 the Kalman filter forecasts are more accurate than random walk model forecasts only for the classical period. The reason, no doubt, is that the classical period has two distinctive subperiods divided by 1896, as table 4.1 shows. The Kalman filter adjusts its forecasts when going from one subperiod to the next, which the random walk model cannot do.

MR focus attention on errors from Kalman filter forecasts, and they argue that the errors are likely to be related to welfare costs, However, they note that stability of output levels does not enhance welfare. Table 4.7 should be read in conjunction with table 4.3. For most countries, growth was high and more stable during the Bretton Woods period than during either the classical or floating rate periods.

In many applications the purpose of using a filter is to obtain efficient forecasts. Efficient forecasts may be relatively little affected by errors in the data; one of the purposes of any filtering technique is to deal effectively with data errors. But in the MR application, the name of the game is to estimate the forecast errors themselves. Data errors are included in these estimates, and surely the nineteenth-century data have larger errors than the post–World War II data. Also, price indexes after World War II include many more goods which tends to make these series less variable than nineteenth-century series constructed from relatively few goods.

The fact that the mean absolute errors in tables 4.7 and 4.8 are of the same order of magnitude for the gold standard and floating rate periods suggests that the "true" errors—that is, the forecast errors' net of data errors—may well have been smaller during the gold standard era. However, table 4.9 does not support this hypothesis for several U.S. commodity price series, which are presumably of reasonably consistent quality over time.

Data construction may also have something to do with the results in table 4.10 which reports correlations between price and output forecast errors. There is a striking difference between the correlations for the classical era and the post–World War II era. I think it is correct that data on GNP or GDP after World War II start with nominal magnitudes, which are than split into real and price parts. Thus, errors in the price data create equal and opposite errors in the quantity data and could explain, in part, the negative correlations in table 4.10 for the Bretton Woods and floating rate periods. Moreover, when the implicit deflator is used as the price variable, cyclical changes in the composition of constant dollar GNP tend to create a negative correlation between the deflator and constant dollar GNP. Were the data for the classical era constructed in about the same way, or might a difference in construction explain the arithmetically larger correlations for the classical period?

Negative serial correlation of price changes has been an important part of the case for the gold standard, but table 4.4 does not support the case. Before I accept the fine detail of these results, I need to know more about the data. We know that constructing annual data by averaging monthly data induces a spurious positive serial correlation of changes. There is also the issue of the extent to which nineteenth-century data were constructed using interpolations. Nevertheless, data construction is surely not responsible for the fact that the classical period consisted essentially of a long deflation followed by a long inflation. The case for negative serial dependence cannot be built on such evidence for there are only two observations: one deflation, followed by one inflation.

Let me now turn to table 4.12 and the discussion surrounding it. The interactions across countries is an interesting and important topic, but I am uneasy with the story MR try to extract from vector autoregressions. Note that MR apply the VARs to the shocks estimated from the Kalman filter. It is certainly possible that the Kalman filter forecasts, which represent the systematic part of the individual series, display relationships across countries that exactly fit the classic gold standard mechanisms.

The VARs may be telling us that the forecast errors computed from the Kalman filter are higher than they should be. MR note that the Kalman filter ignores interactions across variables. If table 4.12 is read as suggesting that there are indeed some interactions of modest statistical significance, then the calculated Kalman forecast errors discussed earlier in the paper may not be a reliable guide to comparing variability across countries and exchange rate regimes. However, because the VARs do not identify highly significant interactions it is reasonable to conclude that the forecast errors defined by the univariate Kalman filter approximate the errors that economic agents would actually make in practice.

I question MR's interpretation of table 4.12. For example, they are concerned about the positive effect of prices on the base as reported in the first VAR in table. But in the VAR context, the price disturbance cannot be interpreted ceteris paribus. The price disturbance initially raises BUS, but lagged BUS lowers BUS. Moreover, in the VAR for PUS, lagged BUS reduces PUS. Without simulating the system, it is impossible to see how all this will work out. MR suggest as much in their comment that capital flows and interest rates may have played an important role. It would have been possible to include interest rates in the VAR, but I would not hazard a guess as to the result or how to interpret the result once I saw it.

MR conclude that the short- and long-term variability of both output and prices was higher under the gold standard than during the postwar years. To support this conclusion it would be helpful if MR would report results in tables 4.7 and 4.8 for the Bretton Woods and fluctuating rates periods combined. To my taste there are too few observations under floating rates to have great confidence in statistical results for this period. As MR note when discussing the average rate of inflation under floating rates, it is misleading to attribute the economic ills of the 1970s to the floating rate system; these ills were, in part, left over from Bretton Woods.

My suspicion is that MR's conclusion on variability is correct for output, but probably not for prices. Table 4.8, as it stands, is essentially a draw, but the inflation section of table 4.3 leaves the gold standard a clear winner. The two gold standard subperiods defined in table 4.3 each delivered average inflation rates closer to zero than did the Bretton Woods and floating rate periods. Economic welfare depends on the average inflation rate as well as on inflation forecast errors, perhaps because in practice economies do not fully adjust to ongoing inflation.

MR do not attempt to weight the price and output results to arrive at an overall welfare judgment. There is reason, however, to emphasize the price results. The argument is not that price stability is more important than output stability, but that we are comparing alternative monetary systems rather than alternative output systems, such as central planning versus the market. The monetary system is the primary determinant of price performance, but perhaps only a minor determinant of output performance. There is certainly a substantial amount of evidence that output growth and inflation are, at best, very weakly related.

There is another way to put this point. If the gold standard did not deliver price stability, then the argument is over. But it is reasonable to conclude that the gold standard did deliver price stability in greater measure than other approaches tried since 1914. The stability was not as great as the gold enthusiasts would have us believe, but for the reasons I have discussed, the stability was probably greater than MR have concluded.

I agree with MR that the case for mean reversion of the price level under the gold standard is not strong, at least in terms of a strict interpretation of that hypothesis. The first part of the classical period involved deflation and the second part involved inflation. If the claim is that the deflation caused an increase in gold production and the subsequent inflation, then these data by themselves contain too few observations to test the hypothesis. The mean reversion hypothesis should not be taken literally anyway. There is no reason whatsoever to believe that the equilibrium relative price of gold is a constant.

But the case for the gold standard does not rest on the fact that inflation from 1896 to 1913 cancelled out deflation from 1873 to 1896. Either of these periods taken separately exhibited satisfactory price performance by today's standards. The average rate of inflation or deflation was relatively low. The year-to-year variability appears high by today's standards, but that is at least partly illusory. Some of the greater variability of the inflation rate in the nineteenth century reflects the relatively narrow scope of available price indexes, while some of the apparent smoothness of postwar inflation reflects an ex post rather than an ex ante calculation of the average inflation rate. That is the point of MR's Kalman filter analysis, and it shows up in the results reported in table 4.8.

I agree with MR's skepticism that long-term price predictability promotes investment in durable capital. Most of us believe that a less predictable price level must surely lead to a less efficient allocation of resources, but the methods available to hedge price surprises seem extensive enough to keep the costs relatively low. Distributional effects, which seem to be fairly random across income classes, are greater and they are probably the source of much of the political dissatisfaction caused by unstable prices. Issues of equity and political stability are outside the scope of the MR paper, but given their broad overview of the subject, brief mention of these issues seems in order.

MR comment that the costs of maintaining long-term price predictability include those arising from returning to an established parity, as with Britain in 1821 and 1925. There are economic costs in these cases, but MR emphasize that there are benefits to wealthowners in the form of protection from confiscatory actions of government. I would add that there are also broad political benefits for any government that wants to maintain a reputation for reliability. A government cannot break its economic commitments without raising questions about its reliability in other areas, such as its reliability as a treaty partner.

Finally, we should be careful to select appropriate criteria upon which to judge the gold standard. Early in the paper MR argue that, "[i]n place of the long-term commitment to a fixed nominal exchange rate of domestic money for gold, countries could have made a commitment to a stable expected price level." Given the state of knowledge of monetary economics in the nineteenth century, the gold standard *was* the logical arrangement to achieve a stable expected price level. Although the gold standard is, I believe, no longer a suitable monetary system, the fact that reputable economists and not just cranks believe that the gold standard is worthy of serious consideration even today is a tribute to the system.

Note

1. The Meltzer-Robinson paper was revised several times after the conference, as was my discussion. I regard my interchange with the authors as unusually fruitful, and wish to thank them for being so responsive to my comments and for their useful suggestions on my written discussion. However, the standard disclaimer applies: errors in my discussion are my responsibility (and errors in their paper are their responsibility).

General Discussion

McCALLUM doubted the finding of long-run inflation unpredictability under the gold standard. In terms of an ARIMA formulation, this disbelief amounts to skepticism that inflation rates were not covariance stationary—that it was necessary to second difference the log of the price level. He presented evidence suggesting that second differencing was not necessary. He described the results of some ARIMA calculations, estimating (0,3,2) models and also very simple models—(0,1,1) and (1,1,0)—that use first differences of the log of the price level for five countries excluding Italy, which was not on the gold standard, and Japan, for which he did not have the data. In all these cases, very simple first-difference models outperformed the second-difference models in the sense that, basically, they are equivalent in terms of explanatory power. So there is no advantage to the more general specification. Thus, at the level of an ARIMA analysis, according to McCallum, it is just not the case that there seems to be any evidence in favor of the second-difference formulation, which the Meltzer-Robinson setup represents. Furthermore, he conjectured that second differencing the data would be as inappropriate for Kalman filter models as he found it to be for the ARIMA models.

Finally, he pointed out that estimation of an ARIMA (0,2,2) model, as in equation (8) of the paper, revealed that for four out of five countries the sign of the second moving average coefficient was opposite to that predicted by the model.

MELTZER responded that, based on a comparison of ARIMA models on line to the multistate Kalman filter model on line, in most cases, the multistate Kalman filter had lower standard errors of forecast than the other models. [These results are reported in the published version of the paper.] He also pointed out that the calculations should not be interpreted as a statement about the gold standard but about the performance of the gold standard *relative* to other standards.

STEIN suggested looking at the variation of output around capacity output as a measure of the ability of different regimes to adjust to monetary shocks. He doubted the Meltzer-Robinson conclusion that price predictability was any better under floating rates than in previous periods, citing a paper by Robert Barro in the *Journal of Business* (1986) that showed interest rates to be poor predictors of inflation, particularly after 1971.

B. FRIEDMAN pointed out that the Kuznets-type of GNP estimates used in the study were based on the components of GNP that were likely to be the most variable. He suggested the use of Christina Romer's new industrial production and GNP estimates. He also wondered whether sectoral shifts in the composition of economic activity over time would be in the direction of dampening fluctuations—that the greater degree of variability during the gold standard period may be due, in part, to the higher share of agriculture relative to manufacturing and services in total production during that period. [The published version of the paper finds this not to be the case.]

WOOD wondered how evidence that long-term bond yields exhibited much greater stability under the gold standard than in the past thirty-five years could be reconciled with the conclusion of the paper that price unpredictability was higher under the gold standard than in the recent period, particularly bearing in mind the stability of the real rate of interest that Friedman and Schwartz reported in *Monetary Trends*.

MELTZER responded that looking at the actual movements of interest rates cannot tell you much about unanticipated variability.

KOCHIN made the point that an investor in 1910 would have been trying to predict the price level in 1919, not the conditional predicted price level *assuming* that the world gold standard would persist to 1919. In fact, in 1919 the world was off the gold standard.

For ten-year forecasts of the price level, the chance of going off the gold standard was always significant. All transitions off the gold standard are ignored in this study since data off the gold standard was excluded.

Moreover, comparing periods when the world was on the gold standard with those when it was not, biases the case in favor of the gold standard because it is a system which, when there is a big shock such as World War I, the world will abandon. The paper thus compares one data set where the shocks are excluded with another where the shocks are included.

MELTZER responded that the Kalman filter gives an on-line forecast, and to the extent that such factors entered into people's heads, it should affect the permanent shock or the rho component. To the extent that it is there and is systematic, it is taken out as anticipated.

B. FRIEDMAN suggested that the authors include measures of the actual variability of monetary growth, inflation, and real output growth as a benchmark for comparison to the forecast errors. [The final draft of the paper incorporates this suggestion.]

WHITE suggested that, in order not to bias the historical comparison between the gold standard and fiat money regimes, one would also want to include fiat money episodes that have blown up, for example, the interwar period.

CHOUDHRI made the point that the difference between the standards may be due to measurement errors or real shocks. But these errors or shocks might be country specific, due, e.g., to Japan, so that an interesting test might be to compare the variance of errors across countries.

CARLINER suggested that the variability of prices and output over time might depend on common forces affecting all countries, such as improvements in the technology of financial systems or the shift out of agriculture.

LAIDLER doubted that, during the gold standard period, agents could satisfactorily predict prices and output in the way the paper assumes they were doing. The historical data used today were not available to them at the time. This, he argued, is an example of a problem that is always present when one uses historical data. We know much more about what is going on in historical time series than did the agents whose behavior generated them.

MELTZER responded that such a line of criticism pertains to all historical research. He pointed out that the data available to agents, at least for the 1920s, were not that different from what are available today.

5 The International Transmission of Inflation Afloat

Michael R. Darby and James R. Lothian

Almost eleven years ago to the day, Anna Schwartz and we began a detailed study of inflation under the Bretton Woods system and in the years that immediately followed its breakdown. At the time, the consensus among economists and in a sizable portion of the financial community was that floating exchange rates, though perhaps not a panacea, certainly were to be welcomed rather than avoided.[1] The conclusions we reached were very much in accord with that line of reasoning. The United States—the reserve currency country under Bretton Woods—embarked on a policy of generally accelerating monetary expansion. The fixed exchange rates in force under the system facilitated the spread of the inflation that resulted.

The actual transmission of inflation, however, was a drawn out process, not the quick adjustment period envisioned in many of the theoretical models. In summarizing the results of the research carried out under the project, we characterized the process as one of "lagged adjustment to lagged adjustment" (Darby and Lothian 1983, 510).

Michael R. Darby is Assistant Secretary of the United States Treasury for Economic Policy. James R. Lothian is Visiting Professor, New York University, Graduate School of Business Administration.

The authors especially wish to thank Cornelia McCarthy, who provided both excellent research assistance throughout the project and a number of valuable suggestions, and James Girola, who assisted in the analysis and investigation of the reaction functions. They also would like to thank Dallas S. Batten, and participants in the UCLA Workshop in Monetary Economics, the New York University Seminar in International Business, and the NBER conference in honor of Anna J. Schwartz, for their comments; Barbara Podesta, Michelle B. Price, and Mario Yrun for their assistance; and the Earhart Foundation for partial support. The views expressed in this paper are those of the authors and ought not be construed as necessarily representative of the position of the United States Treasury or of any of the individuals or institutions cited above.

Anna, in her historical overview of the period (1983, 25), pointed to the reason why:

A variety of measures, adopted in countries with over- or under-valued currencies to stave off devaluation or revaluation, affected the channels of international transmission of price change. Surplus countries tried to avoid price increases, deficit countries price decline, both as external consequences of their balance-of-payments positions. Intermittently, depending on cyclical conditions, countries in both categories took steps to right payments imbalances.

She went on to conclude that if Bretton Woods was not a textbook-type example of a fixed exchange rate world, neither was the period that followed a classic example of a floating exchange rate world. Instead, "it was a managed system, with substantial official intervention . . . [in which] countries have continued to hold foreign exchange reserves" (1983, 44).

Now, as doubts about the efficacy of floating rates continue to mount, we return, so to speak, to the scene of the crime, not to begin a new project on international transmission with Anna but to present some further evidence on the subject. We examine the behavior of policy variables and other important economic variables across a sample of twenty OECD countries under both exchange rate regimes, and derive a series of test equations to evaluate the extent of the long-run differences in monetary policy behavior between the two systems. We then go on to examine the correspondence between shorter-term movements in economic variables in the various countries under the two systems. We conclude with a discussion of policymakers' reaction functions.

The results of the longer-term analysis are clear-cut: Policymakers gained a considerably greater degree of long-run independence under floating rates. The cross-country variability of nominal variables—average rates of inflation, of monetary growth, and of interest—generally increased dramatically under floating rates. Moreover, the relationship between nominal money stocks and other variables in these countries changed in the way that one would expect given long-run policy independence under floating rates.

The results of the examination of shorter-term behavior are more mixed. Nevertheless, they do not support the notion that short-run linkages common to fixed rates remained fully intact under floating rates. Over such time frames, too, there appear to have been important changes. To the extent that these linkages have remained the same, moreover, one important reason is the tendency for the monetary authorities of various countries to react in the same way to developments abroad. In a number of important instances, their attempts to maintain exchange-rate and interest-rate stability appear to have served as a continued channel of monetary transmission from the United States.

5.1   Theoretical Considerations

To illustrate the potential differences in economic behavior under regimes of fixed and floating exchange rates, let us begin by considering a simple two-country quantity theoretic model. Such a model is implicit in Friedman's (1953) well-known defense of floating rates. It forms the nucleus of the monetary approach to the balance of payments advanced by Harry G. Johnson and others in the early 1970s, and it underlies much of the earlier theorizing on the subject.

The model, as it pertains to the domestic economy, takes the form of a demand for money function, a monetary equilibrium condition, and a purchasing power parity relation.

The demand for money function is of the form

(1) $$m^* = L(y,i,u) + p ,$$

where m^* is the percentage rate of growth of the desired quantity of nominal cash balances demanded, y is the percentage rate of growth of real income, i is the rate of change of the nominal rate of interest, p is the rate of inflation, and u is a portmanteau variable included to represent other factors such as the degree of financial sophistication.

The purchasing power parity relation is of the form

(2) $$p = p' + e ,$$

where a prime signifies the reserve-currency country, and e is the percentage change in the exchange rate—the price in domestic currency of a unit of the reserve currency.

In the fixed exchange rate case, e is zero and p will take whatever value is consistent with p'. In equilibrium, the growth rate of the nominal quantity of money supplied will equal the growth rate of the nominal quantity of money demanded:

(3) $$m = m^*.$$

Combining (3) with (1) and recalling the discussion in connection with (2), we have

(4) $$m = L(y,i,u) - p'.$$

With p' given, the nominal stock of money is proximately determined by the quantity of real cash balances demanded.

Interest rates in this world of long-run equilibrium and fixed exchange rates are assumed to change by the same absolute amount in the domestic economy and in the reserve-currency country. By definition, exchange rates are fixed. If they are expected to remain so, then interest parity implies equality of levels of nominal interest rates among countries. Note that since actual and anticipated rates of inflation within each country are equal on these assumptions, the Fisher relationship implies that real interest rates are also equal in the two countries.

In a floating exchange rate world, equations (1), (2), and (3) and the reserve-country analogues of (1) and (3), are combined into a three-equation system in which the rate of change of the exchange rate is determined by the difference in the growth rates of the excess supplies of money $(m - L)$ in the two countries, and each country's inflation rate is determined by the rate of growth of its excess supply of money alone. We can write these equations as:

(5) $$e = m - L(y,i,u) - m' + L'(y',i',u'),$$

(6) $$p = m - L(y,i,u),$$

(7) $$p' = m' - L'(y,i,u).$$

Again, these are to be viewed as long-run equilibrium equations.

Unlike the fixed rate case, there is no necessary connection between growth rates of the supply of, and the demand for, money. Money supply is a variable determined by domestic policy considerations. An increase in the growth rate of the demand for money with no change in the growth of supply would result in a decrease in the rate of inflation. Variations in L affect m only if policymakers choose to stabilize p.

In further contrast to the fixed rate case, nominal interest rates are free to vary among countries. Full interest rate parity is consistent with the differences in the levels of interest rates equal to the percentage rate of increase of the exchange rate. This independence of nominal interest rates does not correspond, of course, to a similar independence of real interest rates which may be even more harmonized as the capital-control impedimenta of fixed exchange rates have been removed.[2]

One of the issues during the Bretton Woods era was how accurately equation (4) described the situation faced by a nonreserve country *in the short run*. Put differently, the question of interest was the degree to which a non-reserve-currency country could affect its money supply and price level over such periods. There was much less debate as to whether such a country could, in the absence of a change in the exchange rate, do so in the long run.

Similar questions have arisen since the advent of floating rates. One difference is that in many of these discussions, particularly in the financial press, little or no distinction has been made regarding the time dimension of the problem. The long run is implicitly viewed as identical in most respects with the short run, with the rise in inflation in the industrialized world near the start of this decade being interpreted as evidence of no change in the transmission properties of the system. Other proponents of the view that flexible exchange rates have not worked as expected argue that exchange rates have tended to move perversely, relative to their purchasing power parity values, and, therefore, have served to transmit fluctuations from one country to another rather than to limit their spread, and that via "ratcheting effects" have themselves been a cause of inflation.[3]

The alternative view is that these intercountry linkages, while perhaps important in the short run, have been of little consequence in the long run. Central banks, according to this argument, may have followed targets of the interest-rate or exchange-rate variety that reduced their degree of short-run monetary control, but those targets were changed often enough and by sufficient amounts that the degree of long-run control was substantial. Purchasing power parity, though not a good predictor of exchange rate movements over shorter time periods, held tolerably well over longer periods. (See Davutyan and Pippenger 1985, and Lothian 1986.)

One test of these competing sets of hypotheses is to examine the long-run variability among countries of money supply growth, of inflation, and of interest rates during the two periods.[4] Increases in the variability of all three during the floating rate period are consistent with the hypothesis that floating rates have increased the autonomy of the various domestic monetary authorities. If the variability has not increased, however, it is difficult to draw any firm conclusion: under Bretton Woods, actual exchange rates did change and exchange controls and the like were used to offset market pressures that otherwise would have led to exchange rate changes. Policy dependence may, therefore, have been less than complete. Correspondingly, under floating rates some monetary authorities may have geared their policies to maintaining interest rate equality with other countries or may have pursued nearly identical domestic inflation targets.

Fortunately, there are several ways of distinguishing between these two states of the world. If equations like (4) and (6) present reasonably accurate alternative long-run descriptions, then under fixed exchange rates we should observe a significant positive one-for-one relationship between the quantities of real cash balances demanded and nominal cash balances supplied in different countries, and under floating exchange rates, little or no relationship. Correspondingly, under fixed rates we should observe no relation between the quantity of real cash balances demanded and the price level, and under floating rates, a zero or negative relation.

The regression coefficient of real money growth in the regression of nominal on real money growth should be unity, and the standard error of estimate for the regression should be relatively low. Under floating rates, we should see very nearly the reverse. The regression coefficients should be much lower in value, and zero in the case in which each country's monetary authorities pursued money supply targets that were independent of growth in the real quantity of money demanded. By the same token, the standard error of estimate should be much higher, reflecting both the lower regression coefficient and the hypothesized higher (cross-country) standard deviation of nominal money growth.[5]

The discussion of interest rate behavior among countries under the two regimes also suggests a further relationship that we can exploit. Under fixed exchange rates, observed variations in inflation rates among countries are likely to be smaller and more heavily dominated by transitory elements than under floating rates. Differences in actual inflation rates are, therefore, less likely to provide useful information about future inflation rates than in a regime of floating exchange rates. As a result, the relationship between average levels of bond yields and of inflation rates is likely to be looser under fixed exchange rates than under floating rates. But, as we point out below, this is not the only possible interpretation of such a difference in the relationship. Accordingly, we place considerably less weight on these results.

5.2   Empirical Results: Longer-Term Relationships

The data we use to compare the two regimes are for twenty OECD countries over the period 1956 to 1986. For all twenty countries there are annual figures for money supply (M1 except for Sweden, where data availability dictated using a broader definition), a cost of living index, and real income (GNP or GDP, depending upon the country). For a subsample of fourteen countries, data for government bond yields are also available. The sources of almost all of these data were the publications and companion computer tapes of the International Monetary Fund.[6]

5.2.1   Cross-Country Variability

Evidence on variability is contained in figures 5.1 and 5.2. Figure 5.1 is for the entire twenty countries. Figure 5.2 is for the subsample of fourteen countries. In both figures we have plotted yearly cross-country standard deviations of rates of monetary growth and of inflation.[7] Figure 5.2 also includes a plot of the yearly cross-country standard deviations of bond yields.

Both measures of variability plotted in figure 5.1 show substantial increases beginning in the early 1970s and becoming fully manifest in the mid-1970s, with the increase in the variability of the rate of inflation

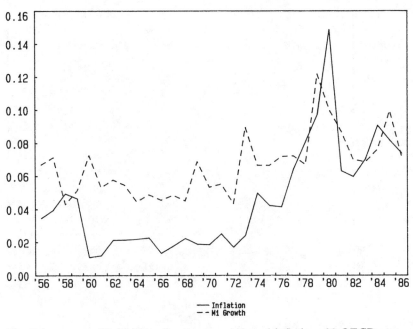

Fig. 5.1   Variability of money growth and inflation; 20 OECD countries; 1956–1986. *Source:* International Monetary Fund. *Note:*
Figures are standard deviations of annual data for each
country.

being particularly dramatic.[8] Figure 5.2 shows sizable increases in inflation and in interest rate variability at approximately the same time
as the increases depicted in figure 5.1, but no overall uptrend in the
variability of actual money supply growth. Taken as a whole, therefore,
these data are consistent with the hypothesis that national policies have
become more autonomous. The one seeming anomaly is the variability
of money supply growth under the floating exchange rate regime in the
subsample. Further evidence on this issue, and on the variability question in general, is presented in table 5.1.

In this table we list standard deviations of country-average data for
both the fixed rate and floating rate periods in their entireties.[9] These
standard deviations were computed for the variables shown in the
figures and for three additional variables—real income growth, growth
in the excess supply of M1, and real M1 growth. The excess supply of
money variable was defined as the difference between actual M1 growth
and the estimated rate of growth of the real quantity of money demanded.[10] The fixed rate period encompassed the years 1956–73; the

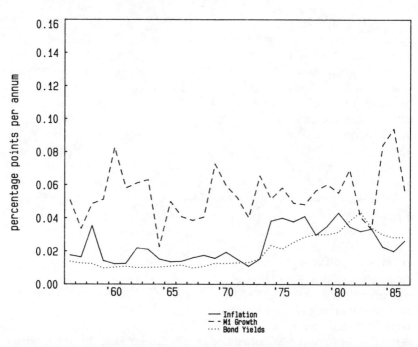

Fig. 5.2   Variability of money growth, inflation, and bond yields; 14 OECD countries; 1956–86. *Source:* International Monetary Fund. *Note:* Figures are standard deviations of annual data for each country.

Table 5.1   **Economic Variability under Fixed and Floating Exchange Rates, 1956 to 1986**

	Twenty Countries		Fourteen Countries	
	Fixed	Floating	Fixed	Floating
Standard deviation of				
M1 growth	0.038	0.060	0.036	0.031
Inflation	0.014	0.067	0.008	0.028
Bond yields	N.A.	N.A.	0.010	0.027
Excess M1 growth	0.022	0.065	0.019	0.035
Real income growth	0.014	0.009	0.015	0.010
Real M1 growth	0.032	0.022	0.033	0.017
Correlation of				
M1, real M1 growth	0.929	0.142	0.978	0.469

Notes: Standard deviations are of country averages of annual data for the periods 1956–73 and 1974–86, respectively. Rates of growth were computed as changes in the logarithms of the variables. Bond yields were expressed in decimal form.

floating rate period, the years 1974–86. Table 5.1 also lists the correlation coefficient across countries for nominal and real money growth.

With the exception of M1 growth in the smaller sample, all of the nominal variables shown in the figures—M1 growth, bond yields, and inflation—show a marked increase in variability in the floating rate period. By way of contrast, real income growth becomes less variable in both samples under floating rates. We believe that this reduction in cross-country variability of real output growth reflects a natural convergence as the postwar recoveries previously added different magnitudes to normal growth rates according to the relative extent of destruction suffered.

As real output growth rates converge, so do our implied estimates of growth in real money demand. Over such substantial periods our estimates of the real quantity of money demanded do not differ substantially from the actual growth in real money; this explains the decline in variability of real M1 growth for both samples in the floating versus the fixed periods.

It seems paradoxical that the variability of inflation goes up sharply in the smaller sample even though variability of M1 growth actually declines. One way to look at this phenomenon is to note that the variability in excess M1 growth—the difference between nominal M1 growth and our estimate of the growth of the real quantity of M1 demanded—increases.

Another way to analyze it is in terms of the usual formula for the variance of an algebraic sum: By definition, inflation is the difference between nominal and real money growth. Hence the variance of inflation is the sum of the variances in nominal and real M1 growth minus twice their covariance. In the fourteen-country sample, the sum component must decrease since both variances individually decrease. The increase in the variance of inflation is a result of the offsetting covariance term falling much more sharply, as the correlation coefficient between nominal and real money falls from approximately unity to less than half. An even sharper fall is evident in the twenty-country sample.

We interpret this as showing that in the long run, under fixed exchange rates, foreign monetary authorities did not vary money growth substantially from that required by growth in real money and world prices. That is, neither revaluations nor measurement problems caused substantial variations among inflation rates, and the monetary authorities allowed nominal money growth to reflect differences in real money growth.

Under floating exchange rates, nominal money growth appears to have been chosen largely independently of variations in real money demand. In one sense, this independence (especially apparent for the twenty countries) is surprising since it suggests that foreign monetary authorities have selected nominal money targets with inflation being a residual, rather than selecting target trend inflation rates and then choosing M1 growth trends which would achieve those targets. We turn next to further evidence in support of this interpretation.

5.2.2 Real Money Growth, Nominal Money Growth, and Inflation

Table 5.2 lists summary statistics from regressions of money supply growth and inflation on the growth of real money balances for both samples.[11] For the fixed rate period we see that cross-country differences in trend growth rates of nominal money supply are essentially explained one-for-one by differences in growth in real cash balances in both cases. The R^2's are 0.86 and 0.95 in the large and small samples, respectively, and the regression coefficients have values insignificantly different from one. For the floating rate period, in contrast, the R^2's are low, the standard errors considerably higher, and the regression coefficients are not significantly different from zero at the 0.95 level.

Now, turn to the duals of the above relationships, the regressions of inflation on real cash balances. During the fixed rate period, as the theory suggests, we observe no significant relationship between the two variables. During the floating rate period, we observe negative relationships between the two—again, as the theory suggests, provided

Table 5.2   **Regressions of Money Growth and Inflation on Real Money Growth for Country-Average Data**

Dependent Variable	Period	Constant	$m - p$	$\bar{R}^2$	SEE
20 Countries					
m	1956–73	0.037	1.102	0.856	0.014
		(6.315)	10.658		
p	1956–73	0.037	0.102	0.001	0.014
		(6.315)	0.989		
m	1974–86	0.110	−0.381	0.034	0.061
		(7.956)	(0.607)		
p	1974–86	0.110	−1.381	0.168	0.061
		(7.956)	(−2.200)		
14 Countries					
m	1956–73	0.035	1.067	0.953	0.008
		(10.191)	(16.239)		
p	1956–73	0.035	0.067	0.003	0.008
		(10.191)	(1.018)		
m	1974–86	0.081	0.832	0.155	0.028
		(9.039)	(1.838)		
p	1974–86	0.081	−0.168	−0.071	0.028
		(9.039)	(0.371)		

Note: Absolute values of t-statistics are beneath the coefficients in parentheses.

that monetary authorities switch from an exchange rate to a money growth policy. For the larger sample, this negative relationship is statistically significant; for the smaller, it is not.

One additional point about these results that deserves mention is the problem of measurement error. One set of regressions related nominal M1 growth to real M1 growth—the difference between nominal M1 growth and inflation. The other related inflation to real M1 growth. Measurement errors in nominal money will, therefore, bias the coefficient in a regression of nominal money growth on real money growth toward 1.0. Measurement errors in prices will bias the coefficient in a regression of inflation on real money growth toward −1.0.

Bias, however, does not appear to be the explanation for the differences that we actually observe between the two periods. To see this, consider the situation in which both m and p contain measurement errors. In this instance, the estimated coefficient will be a weighted average of the true coefficient, and the ratio of the error in nominal money growth to the sum of that error and the error in inflation. The weights, respectively, will be the share of the variance of the true value of $m - p$ in its total variance (including both types of error) and one minus that share.[12]

Suppose that in each period the true value of the coefficient in the relation linking nominal and real money growth rates is zero, that is, in both periods monetary authorities determine nominal money growth without regard to its inflationary implications. To obtain our estimates of near unity and close to zero, the variance in the measurement error of nominal money would have to almost completely dominate the total variance of real cash balances under fixed rates, and be an exceedingly small fraction of the total variance under floating rates. The total variance, however, fell from the one period to the next. The variance of the measurement error would, therefore, have to fall by a multiple— close to two, in the case of the full sample, and five, in the case of the smaller sample—of the decline in the total variance. This is totally implausible.

Alternatively, suppose that the true coefficient is unity in both instances, that both regimes behave like the classic fixed rate model. To produce our pattern of estimates, two things would have to happen. The decline in the variance of real money growth would have to be due totally to a decline in the systematic portion of the variance. At the same time, the ratio of the variance of the error in nominal money to the sum of the errors in prices and nominal money would have to become exceedingly small. Both developments, the latter particularly, appear unlikely. By themselves, therefore, measurement errors do not appear capable of accounting for the overall pattern of estimates that we obtained.

5.2.3   Bond Yields

In table 5.3, we report estimates separately for each period of the relationships between the average level of bond yields in each country and both the average rate of money growth and the average rate of inflation. For the fixed rate period there is a positive, but statistically insignificant, relationship between bond yields and inflation, and a positive and barely significant relationship between bond yields and money growth. For the floating rate period, in contrast, both relationships are highly significant.

These results are consistent with the explanation advanced earlier that revolves around differences in the conduct of policy and hence in the longer-term inflation process under the two exchange rate regimes. With completely fixed exchange rates, intercountry differences in rates of inflation will be transitory. Permanent differences require continuously changing exchange rates. Under floating exchange rates, intercountry inflation differentials can exist indefinitely. Hence, the distinction between permanent and transitory components of the inflation rate becomes less relevant. Provided that there were no other factors which changed between the two periods and which affected the ability of current and past rates of inflation and monetary growth to proxy anticipated future rates of inflation, we can view the estimated relationships as a further indication of the essential differences between the two regimes.

One factor that, in principle, could be important is the generally greater variability of nominal variables under floating rates. In the presence of measurement errors, this would produce higher correlations during that period. In practice, however, this cannot be the full explanation since variations in money growth across the fourteen countries do not increase, yet the correlation of money growth and bond yields does.

Table 5.3   **Regressions of Bond Yields on Inflation and Money Growth for Country-Average Data**

Period	Constant	m	p	$\bar{R}^2$	SEE
1956–73	0.050	0.130		0.155	0.010
	(8.025)	(1.842)			
1956–73	0.041		0.506	0.087	0.010
	(3.105)		(1.496)		
1974–86	0.037	0.772		0.770	0.013
	(3.250)	(6.665)			
1974–86	0.037		0.854	0.742	0.014
	(3.240)		(6.190)		

Notes: The dependent variable was the level of government bond yields, expressed as a decimal. Absolute values of *t*-statistics are beneath the coefficients in parentheses.

Another possible explanation for these results is that there was simply a very long adjustment lag. Market participants, for whatever reason, adjusted extremely slowly to high and rising inflation. Consequently, during the fixed rate period when inflation first started its worldwide rise, bond yields remained relatively low. Only as the process continued into the floating rate era did the adjustment, including necessary institutional and regulatory changes, become more complete. While a lag of this length seems somewhat implausible, this explanation cannot be ruled out.

5.3   Empirical Results: Shorter-Term Relationships

The long-run relationships appear to have changed in a way that is consistent with the simple theoretical analysis, although we were surprised by the lack of stronger evidence that central bank nominal money targets were influenced by their inflationary implications. Now we present evidence of several sorts on the short-run links among the countries and how they fared with the change in the exchange rate regime.

5.3.1   Relationships Between U.S. and Foreign Variables

This evidence is summarized in a series of tables reporting the results of annual regressions of the form

$$x_i = a + bx_{us},$$

where x_i is variable x in country i and x_{us} is its counterpart in the United States. The variables were alternatively nominal M1 growth, real M1 growth, inflation, real output growth, and the level of the government bond yield. In each instance, the regressions were run with contemporaneous values of the variables for both the fixed and floating periods as defined above. There was also some experimentation with lags and with different time periods. Tables 5.4 through 5.8 contain the results of these regressions.

At first glance, these results appear to run totally counter to those already presented. They seem to imply less independence, rather than more, under floating. Consider the inflation rate comparisons reported in table 5.4.

Under floating rates, the correlation between U.S. and foreign inflation rates is actually higher. This is true on average and for a sizable number of cases viewed individually. In going from fixed to floating, the median R^2 for these regressions rises from 0.21 to 0.28. Correspondingly, in 14 of the 19 individual inflation comparisons, the R^2 either rises or stays very nearly constant. Viewed from this perspective, inflation rates appear to have been more similar across countries under floating rates.

Table 5.4   Regressions of Foreign on U.S. Inflation

Country	1956 to 1973					1974 to 1986				
	a	b	$\bar{R}^2$	SEE	DW	a	b	$\bar{R}^2$	SEE	DW
Australia	0.014 (1.541)	0.693 (2.474)	0.23	0.0195	1.06	0.075 (4.031)	0.325 (1.337)	0.06	0.0280	0.90
Austria	0.025 (3.634)	0.383 (1.809)	0.12	0.0147	1.02	0.026 (2.144)	0.380 (2.379)	0.28	0.0184	0.70
Belgium	0.013 (2.103)	0.628 (3.400)	0.38	0.0128	0.71	0.045 (2.331)	0.355 (1.417)	0.08	0.0288	0.47
Canada	0.005 (1.160)	0.832 (6.296)	0.69	0.0092	0.90	0.033 (3.099)	0.661 (4.783)	0.65	0.0159	1.31
Denmark	0.034 (3.032)	0.585 (1.713)	0.10	0.0237	1.15	0.037 (3.325)	0.737 (5.104)	0.68	0.0166	1.32
Finland	0.050 (3.299)	0.296 (0.640)	−0.04	0.0321	1.17	0.052 (2.395)	0.659 (2.314)	0.27	0.0327	0.48
France	0.036 (2.470)	0.420 (0.948)	−0.01	0.0308	2.41	0.042 (3.616)	0.743 (4.896)	0.66	0.0175	0.71
Germany	0.016 (2.576)	0.445 (2.285)	0.20	0.0135	0.51	0.008 (0.983)	0.446 (4.038)	0.56	0.0127	0.76
Greece	0.004 (0.264)	0.928 (2.273)	0.20	0.0284	0.97	0.153 (5.380)	0.306 (0.823)	−0.03	0.0428	0.86

	a	b								
Italy	0.024	0.448	0.03	0.0247	0.65	0.076	0.914	0.56	0.0262	1.15
	(2.090)	(1.262)				(4.366)	(4.016)			
Japan	0.027	0.737	0.15	0.0256	0.90	−0.003	0.915	0.24	0.0478	0.48
	(2.214)	(1.997)				(0.108)	(2.205)			
Netherlands	0.020	0.829	0.33	0.0189	1.58	0.015	0.548	0.35	0.0233	0.51
	(2.238)	(3.046)				(0.962)	(2.710)			
Norway	0.021	0.789	0.28	0.0197	2.08	0.065	0.288	0.09	0.0223	1.36
	(2.276)	(2.782)				(4.378)	(1.490)			
Portugal	0.009	1.174	0.53	0.0181	1.26	0.189	0.114	−0.08	0.0415	1.37
	(1.099)	(4.518)				(6.871)	(0.315)			
Spain	0.063	0.195	−0.05	0.0348	1.22	0.101	0.532	0.16	0.0335	0.97
	(3.878)	(0.389)				(4.525)	(1.830)			
Sweden	0.028	0.523	0.21	0.0155	1.46	0.058	0.444	0.39	0.0174	1.84
	(3.855)	(2.341)				(5.038)	(2.938)			
Switzerland	0.014	0.671	0.23	0.0188	0.62	0.009	0.417	0.24	0.221	0.73
	(1.637)	(2.475)				(0.595)	(2.169)			
Turkey	0.062	0.757	−0.02	0.0668	0.90	0.207	1.701	0.05	0.1533	0.96
	(1.997)	(0.788)				(2.032)	(1.277)			
U.K.	0.014	0.976	0.45	0.0175	1.23	0.024	1.220	0.48	0.0403	0.95
	(1.764)	(3.876)				(0.901)	(3.484)			

Note: The symbols a and b represent the intercept and slope coefficient; t-statistics are beneath in parentheses.

Table 5.5   Regressions of Foreign on U.S. Money Growth

Country	1956 to 1973					1974 to 1986				
	a	b	$\bar{R}^2$	SEE	DW	a	b	$\bar{R}^2$	SEE	DW
Australia	0.014	0.974	0.15	0.0525	2.08	0.099	−0.110	−0.09	0.0660	2.32
	(0.609)	(1.977)				(1.864)	(0.172)			
Austria	0.055	0.705	0.24	0.0298	1.58	0.051	0.033	−0.09	0.0675	3.02
	(4.366)	(2.524)				(0.950)	(0.051)			
Belgium	0.016	1.028	0.33	0.0360	1.49	0.068	−0.225	−0.06	0.0400	1.60
	(1.078)	(3.046)				(2.110)	(0.580)			
Canada	0.021	1.113	0.18	0.0550	1.59	0.006	1.169	0.09	0.0817	1.87
	(0.913)	(2.157)				(0.086)	(1.476)			
Denmark	0.071	0.570	0.10	0.0360	2.05	0.145	−0.145	−0.09	0.0849	2.10
	(4.652)	(1.690)				(2.136)	(0.176)			
Finland	0.043	1.408	0.22	0.0625	1.76	0.236	−1.535	0.21	0.0770	2.39
	(1.638)	(2.402)				(3.818)	(2.056)			
France	0.095	−0.038	−0.06	0.0455	1.24	0.190	−1.296	0.62	0.0294	2.04
	(4.945)	(0.090)				(8.061)	(4.541)			
Germany	0.072	0.319	0.00	0.0354	1.55	0.066	0.060	−0.09	0.0458	1.76
	(4.772)	(0.959)				(1.799)	(0.135)			
Greece	0.138	−0.038	−0.06	0.0470	1.65	0.238	−0.961	0.43	0.0315	2.36
	(6.925)	(0.087)				(9.401)	(3.144)			

	a	b								
Italy	0.108 (5.767)	0.800 (1.945)	0.14	0.0439	1.46	0.156 (3.910)	−0.179 (0.371)	−0.08	0.0498	0.79
Japan	0.152 (5.310)	0.469 (0.743)	−0.03	0.0674	1.92	0.085 (2.177)	−0.209 (0.443)	−0.07	0.0485	1.69
Netherlands	0.021 (1.272)	1.372 (3.849)	0.45	0.0380	1.18	0.096 (2.259)	−0.224 (0.438)	−0.07	0.0528	1.83
Norway	0.026 (2.191)	1.315 (5.103)	0.60	0.0275	1.95	0.134 (2.422)	−0.366 (0.547)	−0.06	0.0689	2.01
Portugal	0.063 (2.404)	0.713 (1.223)	0.03	0.0622	1.08	0.231 (3.232)	−1.319 (1.363)	0.07	0.0652	2.25
Spain	0.104 (4.685)	0.859 (1.749)	0.11	0.0524	1.40	0.140 (3.776)	−0.132 (0.295)	−0.08	0.0461	0.91
Sweden	0.053 (5.448)	0.665 (3.083)	0.33	0.0230	1.78	0.119 (3.544)	−0.346 (0.855)	−0.02	0.0418	1.83
Switzerland	0.053 (2.609)	0.529 (1.169)	0.02	0.0483	0.96	0.013 (0.216)	0.252 (0.346)	−0.08	0.0753	2.23
Turkey	0.154 (5.401)	0.088 (0.140)	−0.06	0.0671	1.22	0.276 (4.143)	0.526 (0.652)	−0.05	0.0832	1.55
U.K.	−0.007 (0.381)	1.358 (3.349)	0.38	0.0433	2.23	0.072 (1.947)	0.732 (1.632)	0.12	0.0462	2.64

Note: The symbols a and b represent the intercept and slope coefficients; t-statistics are beneath in parentheses.

Table 5.6   Regressions of Foreign on U.S. Bond Yields

Country	1956 to 1973					1974 to 1986				
	a	b	$\bar{R}^2$	SEE	DW	a	b	$\bar{R}^2$	SEE	DW
Australia	0.028 (7.559)	0.538 (7.067)	0.74	0.0038	1.18	00.040 (1.872)	0.793 (3.825)	0.53	0.0158	0.62
Belgium	0.030 (6.613)	0.682 (7.525)	0.77	0.0046	1.73	0.014 (2.111)	0.900 (14.296)	0.94	0.0048	1.55
Canada	0.007 (2.785)	1.044 (19.859)	0.96	0.0026	1.07	0.013 (1.911)	0.963 (14.406)	0.95	0.0051	1.54
Denmark	-0.001 (0.214)	1.606 (13.780)	0.92	0.0059	1.21	0.063 (2.262)	0.851 (3.122)	0.42	0.0208	0.72
France	0.019 (3.605)	0.859 (8.010)	0.79	0.0054	0.53	0.006 (0.449)	1.072 (8.247)	0.85	0.0099	1.22
Germany	0.044 (6.047)	0.545 (3.700)	0.43	0.0074	0.97	0.047 (2.535)	0.318 (1.750)	0.15	0.0139	0.58
Italy	0.042 (5.291)	0.529 (3.297)	0.37	0.0081	1.00	0.017 (0.620)	1.299 (4.879)	0.66	0.0203	0.94
Japan	0.072 (43.728)	-0.016 (0.477)	-0.05	0.0017	1.87	0.069 (3.655)	0.078 (0.424)	-0.07	0.0141	0.51
Netherlands	-0.001 (0.299)	1.197 (12.604)	0.90	0.0048	0.73	0.054 (3.399)	0.339 (2.174)	0.24	0.0119	0.43
Norway	0.029 (8.500)	0.472 (6.914)	0.73	0.0034	1.05	0.020 (0.776)	0.819 (3.205)	0.44	0.0195	0.53
Sweden	0.014 (2.987)	0.912 (9.614)	0.84	0.0048	1.09	0.035 (3.142)	0.746 (6.871)	0.79	0.0083	0.90
Switzerland	0.005 (1.625)	0.734 (11.094)	0.88	0.0033	1.01	0.048 (3.188)	0.006 (0.044)	-0.09	0.0112	0.53
U.K.	0.005 (1.167)	1.349 (16.160)	0.94	0.0042	1.60	0.134 (5.577)	-0.069 (0.294)	-0.08	0.0179	0.42

Note: The symbols a and b represent the intercept and slope coefficients; t-statistics are beneath in parentheses.

Table 5.7   Regressions of Foreign on U.S. Real Money Growth

Country	1956 to 1973					1974 to 1986				
	a	b	$\bar{R}^2$	SEE	DW	a	b	$\bar{R}^2$	SEE	DW
Australia	0.014 (1.059)	0.262 (0.493)	−0.05	0.0528	1.95	−0.008 (0.404)	0.069 (0.194)	−0.09	0.0717	1.99
Austria	0.041 (5.442)	0.559 (1.893)	0.13	0.0294	1.60	−0.001 (0.079)	0.347 (1.113)	0.02	0.0628	3.32
Belgium	0.014 (1.652)	1.193 (3.694)	0.43	0.0321	1.92	−0.021 (2.507)	0.288 (1.907)	0.18	0.0304	1.86
Canada	0.020 (1.588)	1.536 (3.061)	0.33	0.0499	1.81	0.009 (0.355)	1.112 (2.576)	0.32	0.0870	1.94
Denmark	0.039 (3.701)	0.365 (0.878)	−0.01	0.0414	2.04	0.041 (1.546)	0.578 (1.217)	0.04	0.0957	2.20
Finland	0.034 (1.753)	0.472 (0.616)	−0.04	0.0762	1.44	0.021 (0.873)	−0.290 (0.681)	−0.05	0.0859	2.19
France	0.043 (2.945)	0.374 (0.648)	−0.04	0.0574	1.75	−0.003 (0.355)	−0.136 (0.932)	−0.01	0.0294	2.15
Germany	0.050 (4.867)	0.535 (1.323)	0.04	0.0403	1.02	0.028 (2.131)	0.383 (1.630)	0.12	0.0474	1.73
Greece	0.103 (9.275)	0.406 (0.925)	−0.01	0.0437	2.19	−0.008 (0.465)	−0.333 (1.030)	0.00	0.0651	1.29
Italy	0.101 (9.085)	0.018 (0.042)	−0.06	0.0436	1.17	−0.001 (0.072)	0.463 (1.634)	0.12	0.0571	1.13

(*continued*)

Table 5.7 (continued)

Country	1956 to 1973					1974 to 1986				
	a	b	$\bar{R}^2$	SEE	DW	a	b	$\bar{R}^2$	SEE	DW
Japan	0.116 (7.052)	0.647 (0.995)	0.00	0.0647	2.07	0.004 (0.259)	0.589 (2.417)	0.29	0.0491	2.54
Netherlands	0.016 (1.515)	1.352 (3.207)	0.35	0.0420	1.13	0.022 (1.830)	0.403 (1.889)	0.18	0.0430	2.33
Norway	0.027 (3.192)	0.551 (1.671)	0.10	0.0328	1.19	0.019 (0.932)	0.153 (0.414)	-0.07	0.0744	1.97
Portugal	0.049 (3.604)	-0.113 (0.209)	-0.06	0.0536	1.01	-0.069 (3.440)	-0.704 (1.560)	0.12	0.0695	2.13
Spain	0.063 (4.880)	0.525 (1.031)	0.00	0.0507	1.73	-0.010 (0.821)	0.265 (1.169)	0.03	0.0456	1.39
Sweden	0.030 (4.401)	0.603 (2.258)	0.19	0.0266	1.87	0.003 (0.288)	-0.065 (0.322)	-0.08	0.0394	2.04
Switzerland	0.037 (2.623)	0.271 (0.480)	-0.05	0.0561	0.77	-0.009 (0.390)	0.524 (1.235)	0.04	0.0855	1.89
Turkey	0.072 (4.169)	0.169 (0.248)	-0.06	0.0677	1.45	-0.011 (0.296)	0.306 (0.485)	-0.07	0.1268	1.69
U.K.	-0.008 (0.671)	1.069 (2.276)	0.20	0.0467	2.34	0.011 (0.710)	1.163 (4.407)	0.61	0.0532	2.42

Note: The symbols a and b represent the intercept and slope coefficients; t-statistics are beneath in parentheses.

Table 5.8 Regressions of Foreign on U.S. Real Income Growth

Country	1956 to 1973					1974 to 1986				
	a	b	$\bar{R}^2$	SEE	DW	a	b	$\bar{R}^2$	SEE	DW
Australia	0.038 (3.451)	0.372 (1.317)	0.04	0.0231	1.91	0.020 (3.465)	0.356 (2.149)	0.23	0.0155	2.07
Austria	0.064 (7.387)	−0.416 (1.880)	0.13	0.0181	2.32	0.020 (3.067)	0.157 (0.846)	−0.02	0.0174	2.66
Belgium	0.039 (4.119)	0.115 (0.470)	−0.05	0.0200	1.24	0.014 (1.803)	0.116 (0.512)	−0.07	0.0213	3.12
Canada	0.026 (3.220)	0.640 (3.024)	0.32	0.0173	1.75	0.017 (2.864)	0.619 (3.605)	0.50	0.0160	1.27
Denmark	0.030 (3.446)	0.444 (1.983)	0.15	0.0183	2.49	0.010 (1.400)	0.424 (1.962)	0.19	0.0202	2.44
Finland	0.046 (2.506)	0.094 (0.197)	−0.06	0.0389	1.41	0.030 (4.214)	−0.148 (0.713)	−0.04	0.0195	1.09
France	0.047 (9.129)	0.232 (1.756)	0.11	0.0108	2.08	0.016 (3.222)	0.211 (1.429)	0.08	0.0138	1.94
Germany	0.058 (3.528)	−0.147 (0.349)	−0.05	0.0346	1.81	0.005 (1.169)	0.586 (4.495)	0.62	0.0122	2.41
Greece	0.070 (6.115)	−0.063 (0.214)	−0.06	0.0242	2.39	0.014 (1.413)	0.451 (1.559)	0.11	0.0270	1.86
Italy	0.059 (5.726)	−0.129 (0.484)	−0.05	0.0218	1.05	0.011 (1.255)	0.386 (1.477)	0.09	0.0244	2.49

(*continued*)

Table 5.8 (continued)

Country	1956 to 1973					1974 to 1986				
	a	b	$\bar{R}^2$	SEE	DW	a	b	$\bar{R}^2$	SEE	DW
Japan	0.080 (5.686)	0.452 (1.250)	0.03	0.0296	1.51	0.027 (4.916)	0.397 (2.448)	0.29	0.0152	1.35
Netherlands	0.047 (3.441)	0.083 (0.236)	−0.06	0.0287	1.60	0.008 (1.372)	0.380 (2.173)	0.24	0.0163	1.91
Norway	0.030 (4.391)	0.356 (2.005)	0.15	0.0145	2.09	0.034 (5.903)	0.336 (2.017)	0.20	0.0156	1.35
Portugal	0.046 (4.504)	0.449 (1.712)	0.10	0.0214	1.98	0.023 (1.883)	0.201 (0.572)	−0.06	0.0328	1.67
Spain	0.053 (3.668)	0.230 (0.619)	−0.04	0.0303	1.50	0.020 (3.623)	0.069 (0.438)	−0.07	0.0148	1.37
Sweden	0.038 (4.965)	0.013 (0.064)	−0.06	0.0163	1.63	0.018 (2.957)	−0.010 (0.058)	−0.09	0.0162	1.49
Switzerland	0.039 (3.625)	0.105 (0.376)	−0.05	0.0229	1.56	−0.004 (0.293)	0.322 (0.904)	−0.02	0.0333	1.93
Turkey	0.049 (3.997)	0.218 (0.688)	−0.03	0.0260	2.18	0.047 (3.679)	−0.111 (0.299)	−0.08	0.0348	1.36
U.K.	0.017 (2.195)	0.367 (1.830)	0.12	0.0164	1.93	0.002 (0.380)	0.518 (2.863)	0.37	0.0169	2.18

Note: the symbols a and b represent the intercept and slope coefficients; t-statistics are beneath in parentheses.

The inference, however, does not follow. Underlying it is a common confusion, confusion between a ratio and an absolute amount. The R^2 is, so to speak, the proportion of the glass that is full. The R^2 tells us very little when the size of the glass—the variability of the dependent variable and hence the total sum of squares, the denominator of the ratio—has changed.

This is the case throughout our sample. Temporal variations in inflation, nominal money growth, and bond yields in the United States and most foreign economies were generally much greater in the floating rate period than in the fixed. A higher R^2 can, therefore, be consistent with more residual variation and more slack in the relationships under floating rates—the empty portion of the glass being larger—or the converse.[13] What we want to look at instead are direct measures of the slack, the standard errors of estimate of the regressions. In most cases, these are substantially greater during the floating rate period. The median for the inflation rate regressions is 0.025 under floating versus 0.019 under fixed. In the individual inflation regressions, we see increases in 14 of the 19 instances.

Very much the same thing holds for nominal money growth and for bond yields—increases in the median standard errors in going from fixed to floating (from 0.044 to 0.053 for money; from 0.005 to 0.014 for yields) and in the standard errors of most of the relationships viewed individually (15 of 19 for money; 12 of 13 for yields). Two major differences between these relationships and those for inflation are the much lower correlations in both periods for money, and the declining, but still high, second-period correlations for yields. Another is the much larger residual variability in the money relationships than in the other two sets of relationships.

Comparing one period with the other, we see a pattern in the real money regressions largely similar to those described for the three nominal variables. Standard errors under floating are generally much higher than under fixed. Median figures are 0.047 and 0.065, respectively, and in only four individual instances (Belgium, France, Japan, and Spain) do we see a decline. At the same time, however, the R^2's in several of these regressions are higher under floating than in the comparable nominal money regressions, and in five of these cases there is a statistically significant relationship at close to, or better than, the 0.95 level. Canada and the United Kingdom, in particular, stand out. For both countries, we see an approximate one-to-one relationship with the United States under floating. The close, long-term correspondence of velocity behavior documented by Milton Friedman and Anna Schwartz (1982) for the United States and the United Kingdom has therefore continued to hold. Canada, evidently, has also become part of the process.

The real money regressions, thus, point to some continued non-monetary transmission abroad from the United States under floating, while the bond-yield regressions point to capital-market transmission in particular, but those channels apparently were neither ubiquitous nor dominant.[14] Noticeably absent under both exchange rate regimes are the significant negative relationships between U.S. and foreign real money growth that would signal currency substitution as suggested in Brittain (1981).

The closest we come to observing stronger relationships under floating are those reported in table 5.8 for real income growth. Standard errors of estimate on average decline under floating (from a median figure of 0.022 to one of 0.017), are lower or approximately the same in over half of the individual comparisons, and decline markedly in the case of Austria, Germany, Japan, the Netherlands, and Spain. And in the first four instances, as well as in the cases of Canada, Norway, and the United Kingdom, the R^2 is also noticeably higher. In the other countries, no similar tendencies are apparent.[15]

This last set of results is not inconsistent with the theoretical proposition of increased independence under floating. The independence posited by theory is of nominal magnitudes rather than real magnitudes. To the extent that floating is accompanied by removal of barriers to trade and investment, international interdependence of real variables could increase.

In addition to removal of such barriers, two other real factors that could be influencing the real-income results is the convergence of trend real growth rates noted above and common oil-price shocks. Neither, however, can completely explain the results. Other comparisons we have made using first differences of real growth rates produce largely similar results to these reported for the growth rates themselves; although such differencing should largely eliminate trend effects. By the same token, oil-price shocks should have affected all of the relationships. This is obviously not the case.

The other possibility is that monetary factors are playing a role here, that domestic monetary policy remains linked under floating exchange rates—albeit less loosely over the longer run and to greatly varying degrees among countries—and that common monetary shocks in many countries have led to common real fluctuation. We explore this question further immediately below.

5.3.2 Monetary Authorities' Reaction Functions

The weight of the evidence in the *International Transmission* volume supported the view that foreign monetary authorities exercised considerable short-run monetary control under both fixed and (the then new) floating exchange rates. The long-run harmonization of inflation rates documented in section 5.2 above came about because of the persistent pressures of reserve flows on money growth whenever price-level divergences became significant. Such a Humean reserve-flow mechanism worked slowly and with lags, but the cumulative effects were clearly overwhelming in the long run. Since monetary authorities have been neither maintaining a clean float nor totally eschewing intervention, an interesting issue is whether this Humean reserve-flow channel still leads to international transmission of monetary impulses. The question is whether or not the effects on the money supply of official intervention are sterilized.

We address this question here, as in *International Transmission,* by examining whether reserve flows scaled by high-powered money have a significantly positive effect on money growth in a reaction function which also allows for response to inflation and the pace of economic growth. We had hoped to analyze it analogously to the approach followed in the earlier volume, to apply a consistent functional form to quarterly data for each country in the period since 1974. Unfortunately, we soon confronted data and modelling problems nearly as severe as those reported in the earlier study. Rather than take on that task at this juncture, and without the good counsel of Anna and our other colleagues, we instead report some exploratory results which we trust will be persuasive as to the value of pursuing these issues further.

Table 5.9 summarizes the results of what Leamer (1978) has termed specification searches for the thirteen countries for which quarterly data were available. A variety of lag structures were examined in an attempt to find a compact, minimal standard error of estimate representation of the data. Significance levels must, therefore, be viewed with considerable skepticism. For 11 of the 13 countries, plausible reaction functions were estimated in which monetary authorities tighten if real output or prices grow rapidly and do not fully sterilize the effects of intervention on money growth, at least in the long run. The Australian and French equations were not successfully fitted.

The results suggest that exchange-market intervention has continued to provide some degree of monetary linkage among these countries. The greater variability of inflation across countries since 1973 apparently reflects the quantitatively greater importance of money-growth versus exchange-rate goals, not the complete elimination of Humean reserve flows due to the exclusive pursuit of sterilized intervention. A surprising result is the apparent influence of reserve changes on American money growth. This differs sharply from the results reported in chapter 16 of our 1983 volume.

The difference is evidently due to our inclusion here of data for the latter part of the 1970s and for 1980. One of the major factors—perhaps *the* major factor—influencing Federal Reserve policy at that time was

Table 5.9 Money Supply Reaction Functions Quarterly Data, 1974–86

Country (Period)	Constant	Coefficients or Coefficient Sums			rho	$\bar{R}^2$	SEE	DW
		r/h	y_T	p				
Austria	0.04	1.71	−1.13	−3.72	0.40	0.686	0.029	1.88
(74Q1–86Q2)	(2.99)	(3.46)	(9.80)	(3.83)	(3.05)			
Australia	0.05	0.05	−3.40	−1.35	−0.10	0.020	0.049	2.06
(74Q1–86Q1)	(2.94)	(0.63)	(1.34)	(1.92)	(0.73)			
Canada	0.22	2.76	−7.22	−9.72	−0.06	0.212	0.092	2.00
(74Q1–86Q3)	(4.19)	(1.55)	(3.18)	(3.75)	(0.41)			
Finland	0.05	0.18	−1.63	−1.08	−0.72	0.160	0.042	2.08
(77Q1–86Q2)	(2.63)	(1.65)	(2.31)	(1.71)	(6.47)			
France	0.04	0.01	−2.73	−0.88	−0.60	−0.006	0.040	2.13
(74Q1–86Q2)	(2.15)	(0.08)	(1.06)	(5.28)	(5.28)			
Germany	0.04	0.52	−1.68	−3.03	−0.81	0.452	0.026	1.66
(74Q1–86Q4)	(9.56)	(3.71)	(3.31)	(6.65)	(9.84)			
Italy	0.06	1.63	−2.31	−1.11	−0.51	0.159	0.049	2.05
(74Q1–86Q3)	(4.39)	(2.76)	(1.93)	(2.79)	(4.21)			
Japan	0.02	1.25	−2.87	−0.99	−0.62	0.118	0.039	2.07
(74Q1–86Q4)	(3.36)	(2.48)	(2.64)	(2.57)	(5.67)			
Spain	0.05	0.37	−3.38	−0.87	−0.72	0.234	0.044	1.80
(74Q1–84Q4)	(2.94)	(3.44)	(2.82)	(1.72)	(6.91)			
Sweden	0.03	1.50	−0.38	−1.51	0.53	0.129	0.037	2.12
(76Q1–85Q2)	(1.47)	(2.23)	(2.02)	(1.93)	(3.84)			
Switzerland	0.01	0.69	−0.77	−1.36	−0.41	0.529	0.031	1.90
(74Q1–85Q4)	(1.35)	(5.43)	(2.26)	(2.38)	(3.09)			
United Kingdom	0.05	0.09	−1.61	−0.68	−0.14	0.172	0.024	1.85
(74Q1–86Q4)	(7.54)	(2.53)	(3.11)	(3.04)	(1.01)			
United States	0.04	0.56	−0.73	−1.19	−0.71	0.350	0.019	1.73
(74Q1–86Q4)	(7.04)	(2.13)	(2.46)	(4.28)	(7.36)			

Source: IMF, *International Financial Statistics.*

Notes: Figures in parentheses are absolute values of t-statistics. All regressions were run using the Cochrane-Orcutt method to take account of first-order autocorrelation. The dependent variable was the change in the logarithm of M1. The symbols r/h, y_T, and p represent the three independent variables: scaled reserves—the ratio of the change in the level of central bank holdings of foreign reserves to the level of high-powered money at the start of the period; (transitory) real income growth—the difference between the change in the logarithm of real GNP and the slope coefficient from a regression of logarithm of real GNP on time during the previous twenty quarters; and inflation—the change in the logarithm of the cost of living index. The specific variants of all three were determined empirically for each country separately and took the forms noted below.

Austria: r/h was the sum of lags 0 to 11 constrained to a uniform distribution; y_T was the sum of lags 1 to 3 constrained to a uniform distribution; p was the sum of lags 2 and 3.

Australia: r/h was the contemporaneous value; y_T was the sum of lags 1 to 20 constrained to a Pascal distribution; p was lag 2.

Canada: r/h was the sum of lags 0 to 20 constrained to a Pascal distribution; y_T was the sum of lags 2 to 5 constrained to a first-degree polynomial with a tail constraint; p was the sum of lags 2 to 5 constrained to a first-degree polynomial with a tail constraint.

Finland: r/h was the sum of lags 0 to 20 constrained to a Pascal distribution; y_T was the sum of lags 3 to 6 constrained to a uniform distribution; p was lag 3.

France: r/h was lag 2; y_T was the sum of lags 0 to 12 constrained to a Pascal distribution; p was lag 3.

Germany: r/h and y_T were the sums of lags 0 to 20 constrained to a Pascal distribution; p was the contemporaneous value.

Italy: r/h was the sum of lags 0 to 12 constrained to a first-degree polynomial; y_T was the sum of lags 0 to 8 constrained to a first-degree polynomial; p was lag 1.

Japan: r/h and y_T were the sums of lags 0 to 20 constrained to a Pascal distribution; p was lag 1.

Spain: r/h was the contemporaneous value; y_T was the sum of lags 0 to 16 constrained to a Pascal distribution; p was lag 4.

Sweden. r/h was the sum of lags 0 to 20 constrained to a Pascal distribution; y_T was the sum of lags 4 to 6; p was lag 2.

Switzerland: r/h was the sum of lags 0 to 20 and y_T the sum of lags 0 to 12, both constrained to Pascal distributions; p was the contemporaneous value.

United Kingdom: r/h was the contemporaneous value; y_T was the sum of lags 2 to 5 constrained to a uniform distribution; p was lag 3.

United States: r/h was lag 2; y_T was the sum of lags 0 to 20 constrained to a Pascal distribution; p was lag 3.

the combination of a falling dollar, a balance of payments deficit, and resultant pressures from policymakers abroad. When the impact of a change in reserves is allowed to vary between the intensive intervention period (defined as 1978 fourth quarter to 1981 first quarter) and the rest of the period, only the intervention-period effect appears to matter. The separate coefficients estimated in a regression that is otherwise nearly identical to the one reported in table 5.9 for the United States was 1.29 with a t value of 2.99 for scaled reserves during the intervention period, and 0.18 with a t value of 0.59 for the same variable during the remainder of the period.

5.4 Conclusions

The principal finding of this paper is that flexible exchange rates have indeed been accompanied by greater long-run monetary policy independence. Across the sample of twenty OECD countries that we have examined, nominal variables have behaved differently under flexible exchange rates than under fixed. The differences, moreover, are exactly the sort that theory suggests under the two regimes.

Inflation rates, nominal bond yields, and monetary policy became more variable under floating rates, and the positive, longer-term covariance between nominal and real rates of money growth that was necessarily a hallmark of the fixed rate system became weak or virtually nonexistent.

This does not mean, however, that we interpret our findings as indicating that the world became less interdependent across the board or that policymakers in one country actually operated without regard to policy and other developments abroad. On the contrary, both actual observation of what went on in this period and a number of the empirical findings reported in the paper—most notably the continued substantial or rising correlations between bond yields in the United States and abroad, and the apparent continued relationship between the scaled balance of payments and monetary growth in most major countries— suggest that interdependence of capital markets, in particular, increased and that central bankers often hesitated to go it completely alone. The Humean monetary channel of transmission, though greatly weakened, did not entirely cease to exist, while other channels may have strengthened.

If long-run independence increased, then how can we explain the two waves of inflation that shook most of the industrialized world in the middle and late 1970s, as well as the disinflation and now apparently increasing inflation in many countries during this decade?

The first episode of inflation, as our earlier work with Anna Schwartz indicated, is best understood as a lagged response to coordinated expansive monetary policies in place under Bretton Woods, with the initial oil-price shock lending a helping hand. The second bout, we believe, can be explained by vestiges of the same type of process. Policymakers, according to our results, in most instances continued to react to balance-of-payments inflows and outflows. In many instances, too, the desire for stability of either interest rates or exchange rates, and sometimes both, continued to exert a powerful attraction. Central bankers' reactions evidently were much more sporadic, and the coordinated movements in domestic monetary policies were, therefore, much more attenuated than under fixed exchange rates.[16] Hence, we find a continued commonality in the movements of inflation rates internationally, but a much greater disparity around the averages.

Now let us turn to several puzzling questions. One is the reason for the differences in the year-to-year relationships estimated for money growth and for inflation. Our inclination is to attribute this difference to lags and the generally more random nature of fluctuations in money supply growth than in inflation rates. An additional factor that may be operating is the shift in the demand for money in the United States in the 1980s. It has very likely drastically reduced the accuracy of actual U.S. money growth as an indicator of excess money growth and thus affected the estimated relationships between it and foreign money growth.

The other two puzzles have to do with the underlying causes of monetary policy behavior. For the United States, as we have pointed out, balance-of-payments considerations emerge in our estimated reaction functions as an influence on policy over this sample period, at least for the Carter intervention era. These results stand in contrast to those reported in *International Transmission* for a much more abbreviated set of observations under floating, which exclude the Carter years.

In addition, for all twenty countries taken as a whole, the data point to monetary growth targets apparently being chosen independently of their inflation consequences. This may reflect the existence of a multiplicity of policy goals in most countries, or perhaps merely the statistical dominance of several countries in which growth in the demand for money was ignored by policymakers, being viewed as of only secondary importance.

Notes

1. The most often cited statements on the subject are Milton Friedman's classic article, ''The Case for Flexible Exchange Rates'' (1953), and Harry G. Johnson's sequel article of a decade and a half later, ''The Case for Flexible Exchange Rates: 1969.'' With regard to Friedman's article it is important to

note that his argument is not that a system of floating rates will provide a country with complete insulation from economic developments abroad, but that there will "be little of no effect through purely monetary channels" (p. 200).

2. In the presence of the Darby (1975) effect and differential tax effects in different countries, the implications for real rates of the "no arbitrage profits" assumption become difficult to determine. Those difficulties are beyond the scope of this paper.

3. See, for example, Williamson (1983, 1985) and the list of references cited in the concluding chapter of the former.

4. A potential problem with examining money growth rates alone is that the behavior of the real quantity of money demanded may differ among countries because of differing rates of real growth, differences in income elasticities, or differences in the behavior of the portmanteau variable. Friedman (1971), Lothian (1976), and Michael Bordo and Lars Jonung (1987) all contain discussions of differing demand-for-money behavior among countries.

5. We can express the standard error of estimate, SEE, as

$$\text{SEE} = [(S_m - bS_{m-p})df]^{1/2},$$

where S_m is the standard deviation of nominal money growth, S_{m-p} is the standard deviation of real money growth, b is the regression coefficient, and df is a correction for the difference in degrees of freedom.

Since df is constant from one period to the next and S_{m-p} should not necessarily change, we can ignore both terms. An increase in SEE in going from fixed to floating will, therfore, require an increase in S_m, a decrease in b, or some appropriate algebraic combination of changes in the two.

6. In a considerable number of instances we encountered breaks in these data, and in several cases, missing observations. Breaks were corrected by interpolation. Publications of the OECD and the *Economist* Intelligence Unit provided most of the missing data. In the case of Portugal we omitted 1986.

7. These standard deviations are of the individual yearly observations about the mean for all countries in that year. For example, for 1956, the first year within the fixed rate period, a standard deviation like the ones plotted in the figures is computed as

$$(\sum_{i}^{n} (x_{i11} - \bar{x}_{.11})^2/(n - 1))^{1/2},$$

where x_{ijt} is variable x in country i ($i = 1, \ldots, n$) in period j ($j = 1,2$) in year t ($t = 1, \ldots, Tj$), and $\bar{x}_{.11}$ is the mean of the observations for all n countries in year 1 of period 1.

8. We have divided the exchange rate periods at 1973, the year during which the Bretton Woods system of fixed-rate parities broke down totally. The break in the behavior of most of the variables plotted in the figures actually comes later. Dummy variable regressions run on these standard deviations generally confirm this impression. The dummy that minimized the standard errors of such regressions necessarily maximizes the regressions (or between-period) sum of squares. This generally occurs for a dividing line between the two periods of 1976.

A relatively late break of this sort, moreover, makes sense. Given an approximate two-year lag between changes in money and prices, the monetary excesses of the early 1970s would not be felt fully in prices until 1974–75. As inflation neared its peak, most countries' monetary authorities could have been expected to reduce their domestic rates of monetary growth, as most in fact did. Not until 1976 or 1977, therefore, would any large divergences in policies among countries begin to become manifest.

9. Using the same notation as in note 7, we can, for example, write the standard deviation for the first (the fixed rate) period as

$$(\sum_{i=1}^{n} (\bar{x}_{i1.} - \bar{x}_{.1.}) / (n - 1))^{1/2},$$

where $\bar{x}_{i1.}$ is the mean of all of the yearly observations for country i in period 1, and $\bar{x}_{.1.}$ is the mean of the yearly observations for all n countries in period 1.

10. The estimates were derived from regressions for the two periods combined of country-average data for each of the periods. For each sample, we regressed the rate of growth of real M1 on the rate of growth of real income and on a measure of the change in the cost of holding money—the change in the government bond yield for the fourteen countries and the average acceleration in inflation for the twenty.

11. The one regression is a linear transformation of the other. The slope coefficient in the regression of nominal on real money growth is equal to one plus the slope coefficient in the regression of inflation on real money growth.

12. Express each variable as the sum of a true value and an error:

(a) $$m = m^* + \epsilon$$
(b) $$p = p^* + \eta$$

where an asterisk now designates a true value. Assume that the errors are independent of one another and of the true values, and that all variables are in the form of deviations from their means. Assume that

(c) $$m^* = \beta (m - p)^*.$$

The coefficient b in a regression of m on $(m - p)$ is

(d) $$b = \frac{E[m (m - p)]}{\sigma^2_{m-p}},$$

$$= \frac{E\{(m^* + \epsilon) [(m - p)^* + \epsilon - \eta]\}}{\sigma^2_{m-p}},$$

$$= \frac{E[m^* (m - p)^* + \sigma^2_{\epsilon}]}{\sigma^2_{(m-p)^*} + \sigma^2_{\epsilon} + \sigma^2_{\eta}}.$$

Substituting from (c) into (d) we have:

(e) $$b = \frac{\beta \sigma^2_{(m-p)^*} + \sigma^2_{\epsilon}}{\sigma^2_{(m-p)^*} + \sigma^2_{\epsilon} + \sigma^2_{\eta}}.$$

We rewrite this in turn as:

(f) $$b = \beta w + (1 - w)\lambda,$$

where

$$w = (\sigma^2_{(m-p)^*}) / (\sigma^2_{(m-p)^*} + \sigma^2_{\epsilon} + \sigma^2_{\eta}),$$

and

$$\lambda = \sigma_{\epsilon}^2 / (\sigma^2_{\epsilon} + \sigma^2_{\eta}).$$

The estimated coefficient is therefore a weighted average of the true coefficient and the ratio of the variance of the error in money growth to the sum of the variances of the errors in money growth and inflation. The weights are the share of the variance of the true value of $m - p$ in the total variance (inclusive of the two errors) and one minus that share.

13. For example, the standard deviation of the yearly U.S. inflation rate increased from 0.017 in the fixed rate period to 0.033 in the floating rate period. Those figures translated into sums of squared deviations from the period means of 0.0048 and 0.0169, respecitvely.

If we use these as an index and, in effect, view the regressions as reversed, we can calculate what a given correlation under fixed would have to increase to under floating to keep the standard error constant. For a fixed-rate-correlation coefficient of 0.50—roughly the median for the period—the corresponding figure under floating rates turns out to be 0.67. This is almost 35 percent higher than the initial figure and well above the actual period median.

14. Regressions run using first differences of bond yields show higher correlations under floating rates than under fixed. The median R^2 is 0.15 in the floating rate case and 0.34 in the fixed rate case. For all of the countries viewed individually, except Canada, for which the R^2 is constant, we also see an increase under floating. Consistent with the level results, however, standard errors of estimate in these regressions also generally rise. Hence, while long-run differences in the levels of interest rates among countries increased under floating, the shorter-run correspondence of their direction of movement apparently did also. See Krol (1986) and Swanson (1987) for further evidence in this regard.

15. Marianne Baxter and Alan Stockman (1987), also using multicountry data, find mostly lower correlations between foreign and U.S. quarterly indexes of industrial production during the floating rate period when the data are in the form of logarithmic first differences, but higher correlations in a number of instances when the data are in the form of deviations from semilogarithmic trends. Since the latter are apt to be smoother series and thus more akin to the annual (real income) data we use, we do not believe that there is any glaring contradiction between our results and theirs.

16. Canada, Germany, and Japan provide interesting examples of how the links between policies actually operated. For Canada, the Bank of Canada's attempts to stabilize spreads between Canadian and U.S. interest rates appears to have been the principal force. (See Bordo, Choudhri, and Schwartz 1987, and Gregory and Raynauld 1985.)

In Germany and Japan, in contrast, examination of data for the balance of payments and for high-powered money indicates that intervention in the foreign exchange market was the major infuence. In both countries, the official settlements balance went into substantial surplus, and growth rates of high-powered money increased considerably in 1978. The two were in line with the much increased balance-of-payments deficits in 1977 and 1978, and the roughly parallel acceleration in high-powered money in 1978 in the United States. The strong relationship of policies in both countries to policy in the United States in these years is further brought out in a series of contributions of Bundesbank and Bank of Japan officials in Meek (1983).

This correspondence between monetary conditions in Germany and Japan with those in the United States was more episodic in nature than continual and, as a result, weaker than for Canada versus the United States. As the annual regressions reported above indicate, the correlations of M1 growth in both countries with M1 growth in the United States were low for the floating period as a whole. Other regressions that we ran using annual growth rates of high-powered money tell a similar story: R^2's of 0.11 for both Germany and Japan vs. the United States.

Batten and Ott (1985) report results derived from an analysis of the relative effects of weekly U.S. M1 innovations on forward exchange rates and foreign interest rates consistent with this description of intercountry differences in the relationships with the United States.

References

Batten, Dallas S., and Mack Ott. 1985. The interrelationship of monetary policies under floating exchange rates. *Journal of Money, Credit and Banking* 17 (February): 103–10.

Baxter, Marianne, and Alan C. Stockman. 1987. For what does the exchange rate system matter? University of Rochester. Typescript.

Bordo, Michael D., Ehsan U. Choudhri, and Anna J. Schwartz. 1987. Money growth variability and money supply interdependence under interest rate control: Some evidence from Canada. *Journal of Money, Credit and Banking* 19 (May): 181–98.

Bordo, Michael D., and Lars Jonung. 1987. *The long run behavior of velocity: The international evidence.* Cambridge: Cambridge University Press.

Brittain, Bruce. 1981. International currency substitution and the apparent instability of velocity in some Western European economies and in the United States. *Journal of Money, Credit and Banking* 13 (May): 303–24.

Darby, Michael R. 1975. The financial and tax effects of monetary policy on interest rates. *Economic Inquiry* 13 (June): 266–76.

Darby, Michael R., and James R. Lothian. 1983. Conclusions on the international transmission of inflation. In *The international transmission of inflation,* Michael R. Darby, James R. Lothian, and Arthur E. Gandolfi, Anna J. Schwartz, and Alan C. Stockman. Chicago: University of Chicago Press.

Davutyan, Nurhan, and John Pippenger. 1985. Purchasing power parity did not collapse during the 1970s. *American Economic Review* 75 (December): 1151–58.

Friedman, Milton. 1953. The case for flexible exchange rates. In *Essays in positive economics,* ed. Milton Friedman. Chicago: University of Chicago Press.

———. 1971. Government revenue from inflation. *Journal of Political Economy* 79 (July/August): 846–56.

Friedman, Milton, and Anna J. Schwartz. 1982. *Monetary trends in the United States and the United Kingdom.* Chicago: University of Chicago Press.

Gregory, Allan W., and Jacques Raynauld. 1985. An econometric model of Canadian monetary policy over the 1970s. *Journal of Money, Credit and Banking* 17 (February): 826–35.

International Monetary Fund. *International financial statistics.* Various issues and companion computer tapes.

Johnson, Harry G. 1969. The case for flexible exchange rates: 1969. *Federal Reserve Bank of St. Louis Review* 51 (June): 12–22.

Krol, Robert. 1986. The interdependence of the term structure of Eurocurrency interest rates. *Journal of International Money and Finance* 5 (June): 245–53.

Leamer, Edward E. 1978. *Specification searches: Ad hoc inferences with nonexperimental data.* New York: John Wiley and Sons.

Lothian, James R. 1976. The demand for high-powered money. *American Economic Review* 66 (March): 56–68.

———. 1985. Equilibrium relationships between money and other economic variables. *American Economic Review* 75 (September): 828–35.

———. 1986. Real dollar exchange rates under the Bretton Woods and floating-rate regimes. *Journal of International Money and Finance* 5 (December): 429–48.

Meek, Paul, ed. 1983. *Central bank views on monetary targeting.* New York: Federal Reserve Bank of New York.

Schwartz, Anna J. 1983. The postwar institutional evolution of the international monetary system. In *The international transmission of inflation,* eds. Michael R. Darby, James R. Lothian, and Arthur E. Gandolfi, Anna J. Schwartz, and Alan C. Stockman. Chicago: University of Chicago Press.

Swanson, Peggy E. 1987. Capital market integration over the past decade: The case of the U.S. dollar. *Journal of International Money and Finance* 6 (June): 215–26.

Swoboda, Alexander K. 1983. Exchange rate regimes and U.S.-European policy interdependence. *International Monetary Fund Staff Papers* (March): 75–102.

Williamson, John. 1985. On the system in Bretton Woods. *American Economic Review* 75 (May): 74–79.

———. 1983. *The exchange rate system.* Washington, D.C.: Institute for International Economics, September.

Comment   Alan C. Stockman

Michael Darby and James Lothian have written a useful paper presenting evidence on the international transmission of inflation under alternative exchange rate systems. Their evidence is consistent with the hypothesis that policymakers gained independence for monetary policy under floating exchange rates in the long run. They also study the short-run links between inflation across countries, comparing statistical relations in pegged and floating exchange rate systems, which they associate with the time periods 1956–73 and 1974–86.

Darby and Lothian first discuss long-run relations in growth rates of prices, nominal money, and real money across countries. They argue that the adoption of floating exchange rates permitted a greater degree of monetary independence in the long run. Darby and Lothian present two types of evidence for this claim.

First, they look at the cross-country variances of average rates of growth of prices and money in the two periods. They find greater

Alan C. Stockman is an associate professor of economics and Director of Undergraduate Studies at the University of Rochester.

variance across countries of average inflation and bond yields (and, in their larger twenty-country sample, of average nominal money growth) in the floating period. They also find a smaller cross-country variance in average real income growth and real money growth in the floating period. The interpretation of these findings given in their paper is straightforward: nominal money and prices were constrained for each country in the long run under pegged exchange rates.

Second, Darby and Lothian show that the correlation across countries between average nominal money growth and average real money growth fell substantially from the pegged to the floating period. They argue that this is the expected result if pegged rates constrained monetary policy and prices in the long run, while floating exchange rates granted some monetary independence. Under pegged rates, an exogenous increase in the nominal money supply cannot be sustained in the long run (without a devaluation), while an increase in real money demand requires a higher nominal money supply because the domestic price level is constrained by the world price level. Given the world price level, then, real and nominal money move together in the long run. Under floating rates, on the other hand, an increase in the nominal money supply raises the price level and affects real money holdings only insofar as it raises expectations of inflation and nominal interest rates (and would be expected to reduce rather than raise real money demand); an exogenous increase in real money demand lowers the price level without necessarily affecting nominal money supply. So under floating rates, the correlation between real and nominal money growth could be smaller than under pegged rates.

This result does not follow unambiguously from theory. Changes in real money demand may be correlated across countries in the long run (just as seasonal changes in money demand are clearly correlated across countries). If so, the correlation between the growth rates of the real and nominal stocks of money could be arbitrarily small under pegged exchange rates (because the world price level would adjust as world money demand changes). Similarly, the correlation between real and nominal money growth could be high under floating rates if changes in the quantity of real money demanded are accommodated by monetary policy (as if, for example, the policymakers are targeting the price level or nominal interest rates with monetary policy).

The long-run relationships that Darby and Lothian seek from the data could perhaps be better investigated by testing for cointegration of nominal money and real money under pegged exchange rates, that is, for the existence of a common trend in both variables. Their argument implies that a common trend in nominal money and real money exists under pegged exchange rates because, under their hypothesis, these variables must move together in the long run. Their argument about the long run allows for any arbitrary short-run behavior of nominal and real money, and the tests for cointegration also permit arbitrary short-run behavior around the common trend. Their argument also implies that this common trend vanished under floating rates as nations took advantage of the long-run monetary independence that floating offered.

Overall, there is likely to be little controversy over the conclusions reached in the paper about long-run relationships. One important policy issue that the evidence presented in the paper is not capable of addressing involves the reasons for higher average inflation in the flexible exchange rate period. In particular, it is possible that the system of floating exchange rates eliminated a constraint on monetary policy that, other things being the same, would have kept money growth and inflation lower had pegged rates been maintained. If so, the benefits from lower money growth and inflation would have to be weighed against the costs due to losses from other policies, such as greater barriers to international trade and financial flows that might also be associated with pegged exchange rates.

The most controversial issues connected with this paper concern the short run. Darby and Lothian argue that there was some short-run independence of monetary policies under pegged exchange rates. They cite the following evidence. First, annual time-series regressions of inflation in each country on inflation in the U.S. have higher standard errors (as well as higher correlation coefficients) in the floating rate period than in the pegged rate period. Darby and Lothian interpret this as a measure of short-run "slack" in the relationships connecting national inflation rates. The same results are obtained from time-series regressions of nominal or real money growth in each country on the corresponding U.S. variable. Darby and Lothian also show that time-series regressions of the growth of real income in each country on U.S. real income growth typically yield lower standard errors and higher correlations in the floating rate period. They interpret this result as reflecting nonmonetary dependencies across countries that may have expanded with the increases in international trade and financial market liberalization that accompanied the floating rate period.

One interesting issue that arises here concerns the interpretation of the short-run and long-run results. Under one interpretation of the notion that countries had some degree of monetary independence in the short run under pegged exchange rates, a country with a pegged exchange rate could increase its nominal money supply and price level in the short run but not in the long run. In that case, we should see some intrinsic dynamics of the exchange-rate-adjusted ratio of price indexes. That is, when countries on pegged exchange rates experience high short-run money growth and inflation rates that exceed world inflation, those experiences should typically be followed by inflation rates that are lower than world inflation (or a devaluation). But there is evidence on exchange-rate-adjusted price ratios that suggests otherwise. There is some evidence that ratios of price indexes across countries, adjusted for exchange rates, are nonstationary random variables—close to random walks—under both exchange rate systems. This is consistent with temporary, serially-independent differences in inflation rates across countries under pegged exchange rates. It suggests that there may have been very little scope for independent monetary policies and inflation, even in the short run, under pegged exchange rates. Factors that caused divergence of relative price levels across countries (and of money stocks, given real money demand) were equally operative in the short run and long run. Highly persistent or permanent changes originating in the real sector of the economy could change equilibrium relative prices (including relative prices of nontraded goods, the terms of trade, and so on), and these changes would seem to be the most likely candidates to explain cross-country differences in the behavior of prices and nominal money.

Short-run effects of monetary policies are unlikely candidates to explain the short-run behavior of prices because one would then expect to see subsequent reversals in price behavior as the economy adjusted to the long run, and this is contrary to the random-walk evidence. It is true that the evidence that exchange-rate-adjusted price ratios are random walks is weak; they may be stationary autoregressive processes with a high degree of persistence, typically taking at least five to ten years to return halfway back to their mean values following a disturbance. But this very high degree of persistence reduces the plausibility of explanations for cross-country differences in price behavior (under pegged rates) that are based on short-run effects of money growth. There are many other plausible explanations. For example, some countries may have experienced greater increases in some years in relative prices of nontraded goods; given international arbitrage in prices of traded goods, this raises the domestic price level and (given real money demand) the nominal money stock. If changes such as these were highly persistent or permanent, then they could explain the evidence on the time-series behavior of relative international price levels.

The result that real income growth is more highly related to U.S. real income growth in the recent floating rate system deserves further study. In recent work, Marianne Baxter and I have studied the behavior of some main macroeconomic and international trade variables under alternative exchange rate systems. We found little evidence that the exchange rate system is connected with the behavior of most of these variables, including real income growth. However, we uncovered some (weak) evidence that output fluctuations became more country-specific and less worldwide in the post-1973 period.

One major problem faced by economists studying the effects of alternative exchange rate systems involves distinguishing effects of the exchange rate system per se from the effects of different time periods under study. This problem can be solved by using cross-sectional information from countries that floated prior to 1973 (such as Canada) and from countries that maintained pegged rates after 1973 (which includes many countries, mainly LDCs) and from mixed arrangements such as the EMS. My casual observations suggest that further study of the long-run relations will support the conclusions reached by Darby and Lothian. The short-run problems are more difficult, as usual.

General Discussion

BRUNNER said that Alan Stockman's remarks reminded him of a study prepared by his group at the University of Bern. They investigated the response of the Swiss National Bank to changes in the Deutschemark–Swiss franc exchange rate, finding a systematically asymmetric response pattern centered around a critical benchmark of 80 francs to DM100. Whenever the Deutschemark rate approached the benchmark and threatened to move lower, the National Bank raised the growth rate of the monetary base. Improvements of the Deutschemark rate did not systematically induce a retardation of the Swiss monetary base.

Brunner also commented on the concept of the reaction function. Its formulation usually involves a relation between money stock (or bank credit) and a selection of economic determinants presumed to guide policy action. This relationship, however, meshes the structure of the money supply process with the response of policy variables to the state of the economy. It is not an informative formulation and may lead to false inferences. A long lag of the dependent variables behind the selected guide variables has generally been attributed to a recognition lag, when it actually results from a misinterpretation by the authorities of their own actions. But the notion of a reaction function suffers from an even more fundamental flaw, at least for the U.S. A detailed study of Federal Reserve policymaking reveals that there is no such thing as a stable reaction function. Policymakers find it politically inadvisable to tie themselves to a regular pattern. Their responses to various conditions change over time and the weights attached to specific aspects of the state of the economy shift. He concluded that the search for a stable reaction function is futile and yields little insight into our policymaking procedures.

DARBY responded that reaction functions do play a role in describing the average behavior of policymakers but not as a guide or a reference point. In response to a point raised in Stockman's comment, Darby attributed the fact that the standard deviation of industrial production sometimes rose in the floating rate period—whereas he and Lothian found that the standard deviation of GNP tended to fall in the same period—to the greater short-run variability of the relative prices of tradables versus nontradables. Because industrial production is largely the production of tradables, more variability in shifts between the tradable and nontradable sectors is observed despite the fact that at the same time—because there is less variation in money and output—less variability occurs in real GNP.

MCCALLUM made the point that Brunner's view of reaction functions does not imply that policymakers do not have stable preferences, rather, it implies that they will not tell us what they are.

BRUNNER agreed that he does not deny stable preferences, but suggests that we need to be careful in understanding to what the preferences apply. In his judgment they do not apply to the usual variables selected (inflation, unemployment, etc.) but to more fundamental political objectives (e.g., the range of admissible actions and the level of public criticism or approbation). These objectives, expressed by a utility function, yield, together with some political constraints, a shifting and unpredictable response to the usually emphasized variables. According to him, the work by Alex Cukierman and Allan H. Meltzer gets closest to the reality of the problem.

LOTHIAN, MELTZER, and MCCALLUM made the point with respect to the Federal Reserve's reaction function that although the Fed has always tried to peg the federal funds rate, it has varied its target rate in different periods in response to different conditions. Thus, according to Meltzer, they responded differently when they wanted to disinflate in 1979 than when they wanted to expand in 1976, or in 1986 when they wanted to drive down the nominal exchange rate.

O'DRISCOLL argued that it is not clear that there is not a set of stable constraints. Particularly in a fiat money regime, it is not clear that the central bank can resist shifting political forces.

LAIDLER expanded on Stockman's point about the importance of distinguishing between a break in the time series and a break in the exchange rate regime in evaluating the correlations between nominal and real money balances in table 5.2. According to him, the period 1956 to 1973 was characterized by relatively low money growth, low inflation and interest rates, and stable real growth, in contrast to the subsequent period characterized by high inflation and interest rates, and wide swings in real output.

Laidler also suggested that an application of Hayek's model of competing monies to central bank behavior in a flexible exchange rate regime leads to the implication that market mechanisms such as currency substitution would, over time, discipline central banks to produce greater exchange rate stability. He asked whether Darby and Lothian observed such a tendency in their data.

LOTHIAN responded that their data showed no evidence of currency substitution in the form of a negative correlation between real cash balances in one country and in another. He agreed with Laidler that central banks learn over time, but doubted if this was by the Hayekian mechanism. Instead he stressed the importance of political forces, giving as an example the disinflation of 1980. In response to Laidler's comment on the break point of the data, Lothian argued that the demarcation between periods chosen may have biased the case somewhat against their findings.

DARBY pointed out that much of the increase in trade volume and integration of capital markets that has occurred since 1973 is regime related. Since the advent of floating rates, governments no longer have the excuse of pressure on international reserves to maintain exchange and capital controls.

MELTZER addressed the question of whether the Hume mechanism or some other adjustment mechanism is dominant. He argued that, in retrospect, both are dominant depending on the period and the nature of the shocks in that period. For example, the response to real shocks, if they were dominant, may induce an increase in productivity in country A which sends capital flowing to it from country B. Eventually country B's income will increase in the form of repatriated return on investment, but that may take a very long time. In this particular example, most of the adjustment is in the capital market, but for another kind of shock, the adjustment may occur mainly in some other market. Both adjustments operate in different proportions under different regimes.

LOTHIAN agreed with Meltzer. According to him, the story that emerges from both the tests and the more descriptive part of their paper is that the Humean mechanism continued to be of considerable importance under floating rates.

M. FRIEDMAN distinguished two different meanings of fixed exchange rates. Fixed rates resulting from unified currencies, in which case central banks have no role. And fixed rates that are pegged rates, in which case central bankers are very important. Under pegged rates, he stated, exchange rate problems always come up and central bankers are the ones to turn to when you run into exchange rate problems. Moreover, he felt that the self-interest of central bankers would be better served by a fixed exchange rate regime than by a floating rate regime, because a fixed rate regime gives them greater independence from domestic political forces. Central bankers can always point to external pressures to explain why they cannot accommodate the politicians.

Friedman then amplified Laidler's point that central banks have been going through a very important learning process about how to live in a world of floating exchange rates. According to him, although there is evidence of learning by central banks, this does not mean that they do not make mistakes. Nineteen seventy-one marked the introduction of an historically unprecedented monetary system in the world. It was the first time that all countries were on a pure fiat currency standard, hence it is not surprising to him that it took them some time to settle down and figure out how to handle it. In the process, they produced a worldwide inflation in the 1970s. Friedman stated that his belief that the central banks have settled down is shown by the widespread disinflation policies in 1979, and by the reluctance that Japan and Germany have recently demonstrated to yield to pressures coming from the United States to inflate.

BORDO pointed out that central banks are opposed to actually creating unified currency areas, but at the same time they frequently engage in working out exchange rate arrangements—for example, recent initiatives at policy coordination—which will preserve their important role.

STEIN characterized a fixed exchange rate regime as one where, for a period of time, the exchange rate does not change, but then when it changes, it does so by a discrete amount. In other words, he characterized the fixed exchange rate period as a series of step functions. Under fixed rates, inflation rates can frequently diverge among countries while exchange rates are held fixed, but then when countries find that their price levels are way out of line, there will be a discrete adjustment in exchange rates. The process will then repeat itself. Stein asked whether continuity was better than discontinuity.

DARBY agreed with Stein's characterization of the fixed rate regime. This was the view expressed by him, Lothian, Gandolfi, Schwartz, and Stockman in the *International Transmission of Inflation* volume. In his paper with Lothian, he viewed the key question as whether or not the fixed rate system was fundamentally different from the flexible rate period in terms of variability of inflation. That is, were the pegs more binding than the current transient goals, such as they are. He viewed their evidence as saying that in the recent period the transient goals were much less binding than the pegs were previously. Although they did find large changes under Bretton Woods, the variance in the average rate of change was less. There was in fact more harmonization under the Bretton Wood system for nominal variables than under floating rates.

Anna J. Schwartz:
An Appreciation

Karl Brunner
Milton Friedman

A Life of Scholarship   Karl Brunner

The scholarly enterprise shares in full measure all human foibles, flaws, and frailties. The disinterested and objective pursuit of knowledge offers an ideal against which we may assess reality. Anna Schwartz should be viewed in the context of this reality in order to appreciate her scholarly life and her work.

The divisions in monetary and macro analysis deepened over the postwar period, occasionally producing some acrimony, signs of intolerance, and an unwillingness to seriously explore opposite views. Anna Schwartz has maintained throughout her life a remarkable scholarly attitude. She suffers, however, no fuzzy ambivalences. Ideas and beliefs are clearly presented and firmly argued. In this way, over the decades she has contributed her share to a continued civil and meaningful discussion in the profession. Her scholarship is also marked by deliberate care and attention to language and detail. The empirical work characterizing her scholarly pursuits over fifty years reflects a strong sense of thoroughness and concern for accuracy. We also note her attention to substantive issues. All her work reveals a pronounced attention to the actual problems of our world.

She was only twenty years old in 1936 when for five years she joined a project in collaboration with A. D. Gayer and W. W. Rostow. This project explored "The Growth and Fluctuation of the British Economy, 1790–1850." This project set an important pattern for the life work of

Karl Brunner is the Fred H. Gowen Professor of Economics and the Director of the Bradley Policy Research Center at the University of Rochester.

Anna Schwartz. Immense care was invested in the assembly of important statistical data which would provide us with useful information. She developed a major skill in this line of research which enriched the basis for any relevant monetary analysis. This line is visible in her longtime collaboration with Milton Friedman on the classic volume *A Monetary History of the United States* (1963) and the subsequent volume exploiting United States and British data, *Monetary Trends in the United States and the United Kingdom* (1982). In recent years her attention returned to British monetary history when she was a consultant for a project at the City University of London. There have been other contributions to the statistical basis of monetary analysis. All these efforts leave an intellectual heritage in monetary theory which benefits the profession. The collection of data, moreover, is integrated with an analysis interpreting the events. That work and the ensuing discussions widened both our historical knowledge and our grasp of major aspects of monetary analysis.

The role of international monetary regimes has off and on attracted her attention. *A Monetary History* contains an excellent history of the international gold standard. This theme recurred on several occasions in recent years. The disarray in our financial arrangements challenges us to explore the nature of regimes which lower ominous threats of permanent and unstable inflation, avoid persistent and erratic deflation, lower long-term price uncertainty and short-run monetary uncertainty. Anna Schwartz has examined on repeated occasions experiences under the historical gold standard in order to determine the lessons we can learn for the future. Her brief appearance in public service in 1981–82 as staff director of the United States Gold Commission also channeled her attention for some time to these questions. Her skills developed over many years of demanding empirical research, and her willingness and ability to cooperate and interact with other people made her a successful staff director of the Gold Commission. And the Commission's report she wrote remains a useful document for all students of the gold standard and for the broader issue bearing on the choice of an international regime.

The detailed examination of important historical episodes in the United States and the United Kingdom unavoidably directed attention to the role of monetary institutions and monetary policy. Anna Schwartz increasingly recognized the flaws of a monetary regime operating without an anchor in a floating, discretionary manner. The unnecessary debacle of the 1930s and the drift into long-term inflation beyond 1966 reveal the fundamental failure of our policymaking institutions. This does not preclude phases or episodes of adequate performance under a discretionary policy, exemplified by the postwar period until 1966. The flaw built into the discretionary policy pursued over the decades by our authorities involves its basic unreliability and uncertainty. We have no reason to expect that major inflations or deflations will be avoided. Nor can we expect that pervasive short- and long-run uncertainties about monetary evolution will vanish. Recognition of this problem shaped Anna Schwartz's approach to monetary policy. Her concern also motivated her to join the Shadow Open Market Committee at its beginning in September 1973. She is one of four founding members who still actively participate in "the Shadow's" activities. Her contributions to the semiannual meetings are most valuable. As a member of the subcommittee drafting the final statement, she plays a particularly sensitive and important role.

Anna Schwartz may look back over a lifetime of scholarship with few regrets and much satisfaction. This volume honoring her scholarly dedication attests to the profession's recognition of her work and achievement. Fate may be generous and offer, beyond the past fifty-two years, more opportunities to a fine scholar to pursue a lifelong, deep commitment.

Collaboration in Economics   Milton Friedman

I have thought a great deal about what, if anything, I could say on the occasion of this conference that I have not already said, and there isn't much. So I thought I would talk a bit about the problems of collaboration. That is a subject on which Anna and I both have a great deal of experience. We have collaborated with one another for over thirty years. It has been a remarkable experience, certainly on my part. During those thirty years, I do not recall any kind of personal acrimony or altercation, even though we had many differences of opinion about individual items. From my point of view, it was an almost perfect example of collaboration. Anna did all the work and I got a lot of the credit. How much more can you ask than that? That led me to think about the more general topic of collaboration, which I think is interesting, in part, because I have been very much impressed that the extent of collaboration, the number of papers in professional journals which are signed by two or three or four persons, is very sharply on the increase. I do not know why that is happening. I wish that one of you would construct a theory of the determinants of collaboration.

Milton Friedman is a senior research fellow of the Hoover Institution.

Historically, collaboration is a very rare thing in economics, especially in economic theory.

In the great period of British development of economics in the nineteenth century, I can think of only one example of a truly collaborative enterprise, and that has a peculiar story attached to it. I suspect that few of you know the story about the *Economics of Industry* by Alfred Marshall and Mary Paley Marshall. Mary Paley Marshall was the daughter, or granddaughter, or niece, or some other relative of the Archbishop Paley. She was one of the first students at one of the first women's colleges opened at Cambridge. Newnham, I believe. At that time they did not permit classes with both men and women. They had to have separate classes for men, and separate classes for women. The various professors would go to the women's colleges and tutor or give classes for the women. Alfred Marshall was dragooned into giving lectures in economic theory at Newnham College. Mary Paley, who attended Marshall's lectures, found what he was saying interesting. She was an ambitious young lady who had good connections, so she contracted with Macmillan to write a textbook in economics based on what Marshall had been teaching.

My wife, Rose, and I decided long ago that that is the main reason he ever married her—to keep her from publishing the book under her own name. But he did succeed in marrying her and the book was published as *Economics of Industry* under the joint authorship of Marshall and Marshall. It is a very well written, very good book. I have always thought that some of Alfred Marshall's later work would have been much improved if Mary Paley had played a larger role in it. The book went through two editions. After the *Principles of Economics* came out under his own name, he suppressed the Marshall and Marshall, bringing out a condensation of the *Principles* under his own name which he entitled *Economics of Industry*, in order to kill the earlier volume. As Austin Robinson said in his review of Mary Paley's autobiography, "the happiest days of her life were before she met Marshall and after he died."

I do not like to recommend that as a good example of collaboration. However, I have had a lot of personal experience with collaboration. I counted some ten different people with whom I have collaborated at one time or another, and Anna would have a much longer list if she counted up the number of people with whom she has written joint articles. I was going to say that one way to have good collaboration is to collaborate at a distance. Anna and I were seldom in the same place, and that has great virtues. It forces you to write down what you are doing, or what the differences of opinion are, or to communicate in words, and you are much less likely to have disagreements. But after I thought about that, I had second thoughts. Because I could not have been in closer contact with the other woman in my life, who is also a major collaborator of mine. So I must conclude that my experience yields no general rule except that you collaborate with the right women. And I have to pat myself on the back for having done very, very well in that department in both cases. In connection with the more popular works Rose and I have written, people are always coming up and asking how we collaborate, and I always say: Well, I write one sentence and then I give the pen to her and she writes the next sentence. I assure you, neither Rose and I nor Anna and I ever did it that way.

It has been a real joy and pleasure to collaborate with Anna over these years, because I always knew that everything she did was going to be done right. It was going to be precise, it was going to be accurate, it was going to be thoughtful. Moreover, both of us were prepared to change our views or to change what we had done or written if the other provided evidence that we were wrong or that there was a better way. In general, collaboration is a very intimate kind of thing. It only works if people have real confidence in one another, and respect one another's integrity and one another's competence. I certainly can say that I have been very fortunate indeed in that respect.

There are a few other people in this room with whom I have collaborated at one time or another. In fact, I am reminded of that famous story they used to tell about Seymour Harris. He was being introduced by somebody who said, "Now I don't have to introduce him. Those of you who have not read his books have written them." I do believe, however, that the general subject of why collaboration in economics has multiplied so much is a serious subject that deserves some thought. In the natural sciences, as opposed to our discipline, the collaboration is often spurious. The person who gets the money, as the head of an institute or a research group, may attach his name to every paper that comes out of that research group.

One person who had a great influence on Anna and me in our work on monetary history, and indeed, was responsible in the first place for our embarking on *A Monetary History,* was Walter W. Stewart. He had been director of research at the Federal Reserve Board in the twenties, and at the time Anna and I started on our monetary project at the National Bureau, he was at the Institute for Advanced Study in Princeton. He was also a director of the Bureau, and Arthur Burns suggested that I talk with him about our monetary studies. He persuaded me, and Anna, with her economic history background, reinforced his suggestion, that it was important to have a historical background before we got started on a primarily statistical study.

I have found the process of collaboration a very useful way to combine different gifts. Anna is an historian and I am not. And our talents have complemented one another. We each have been able to make independent contributions. There is very little else one can ask of those with whom one works.

I want to close by saying only that I am very grateful to Anna for having had the privilege of working with her for so long; I am grateful to all of you people for joining me in celebrating her achievements. I have here the first published copy of a book that I want to give to Anna. It contains a collection of her articles. It is not a festschrift. It is a collection of things she herself has written, so she cannot blame anybody else for it. Michael Bordo and I do take the responsibility for having put it together. Michael has been another one of the many people with whom Anna has so fruitfully collaborated. And beyond that, my wife thought that she ought to have some roses to celebrate this occasion.

Appendix: Publications of Anna J. Schwartz

1940 British share prices, 1811–1859. *Review of Economics and Statistics* (May): 78–93.

1947 *Currency held by the public, the banks, and the treasury, monthly, December 1917–December 1944.* Technical Paper 4. National Bureau of Economic Research. (With E. Oliver)

The beginning of competitive banking in Philadelphia, 1782–1809. *Journal of Political Economy* (October): 417–31.

An attempt at synthesis in American banking history. *Journal of Economic History* (November): 208–16.

1953 *The growth and fluctuation of the British economy, 1790–1850.* 2 vols. Oxford: Clarendon Press. 2d ed.: Sussex, Harvester Press, 1975. (With A. D. Gayer and W. W. Rostow)

1960 Gross dividend and interest payments by corporations at selected dates in the 19th century. In *Trends in the American economy in the nineteenth century*, 407–45. Studies in Income and Wealth 24. New York: National Bureau of Economic Research.

1963 Money and business cycles. *Review of Economics and Statistics* supp. (February): 32–64. (With Milton Friedman)

A monetary history of the United States, 1867–1960. Princeton, N.J.: Princeton University Press. (With Milton Friedman)

1969 The definition of money. *Journal of Money, Credit and Banking* (February): 1–4. (With Milton Friedman)

Short-term targets of some foreign central banks. In *Targets and indicators of monetary policy,* ed. K. Brunner, 27–65. San Francisco: Chandler.

Why money matters. *Lloyds Bank Review* (October): 1–16.

1970 *Monetary statistics of the United States.* New York: Columbia University Press. (With Milton Friedman)

1972 The Aliber, Dewald, and Gordon papers: A comment. *Journal of Money, Credit and Banking* (November): 978–84.

1973 Secular price change in historical perspective (pt. 2). *Journal of Money, Credit and Banking* (February): 243–69.

1975 How feasible is a flexible monetary policy? In *Capitalism and freedom, problems and prospects,* ed. R. T. Selden, 262–93. University Press of Virginia. (With Phillip Cagan)

Has the growth of money substitutes hindered monetary policy? *Journal of Money, Credit and Banking* (May): 137–59. (With Phillip Cagan)

Monetary trends in the United States and the United Kingdom, 1878–1970: Selected findings. *Journal of Economic History* (March): 138–59.

1976 Comments. In *Conference on monetarism,* ed. Jerome Stein, 43–49. The Hague: North-Holland.

Comments. In *Financial innovation,* ed. William L. Silber, 45–51. Lexington, Mass.: Heath.

1977 Issues in monetary economics and their impact on research in economic history. In *Research in economic history,* ed. R. E. Gallman, 81–129. Greenwich, Conn.: Johnson Associates. (With M. D. Bordo)

Policies for research in monetary economics. In *The organization and retrieval of economic knowledge,* ed. M. Perlman, 281–93. New York: Macmillan.

1978   Comments on papers by Fourcans, Fratianni, and Korteweg. In *Carnegie-Rochester Conference Series on Public Policy,* eds. K. Brunner and A. H. Meltzer, 193–201. Vol. 8. The Hague: North-Holland.

1979   The banking reforms of the 1930's. In *Regulatory change in an atmosphere of crisis: The current-day implications of the Roosevelt years,* ed. Gary M. Walton, 93–99. New York: Academic Press.

Clark Warburton: Pioneer monetarist. *Journal of Monetary Economics* (January): 43–65. (With M. D. Bordo)

1980   Money and prices in the nineteenth century: An old debate rejoined. *Journal of Economic History* (March): 61–67. (With M. D. Bordo)

1981   Understanding 1929–1933. In *The Great Depression revisited,* ed. Karl Brunner, 5–48. Boston: Martinus Nijhoff.

A century of British market interest rates, 1874–1975. The Henry Thornton Lecture, The City University, Centre for Banking and International Finance, London. (January)

Money and prices in the nineteenth century: Was Thomas Tooke right? *Explorations in Economic History* 18:97–127. (With M. D. Bordo)

1982   The effect of the term structure of interest rates on the demand for money in the United States. *Journal of Political Economy* (February): 201–12. (With Milton Friedman)

Interrelations between the United States and the United Kingdom, 1873–1975. *Journal of International Money and Finance* 1 (April): 3–19. (With Milton Friedman)

Monetary trends in the United States and the United Kingdom: Their relation to income, prices, and interest rates, 1867–1975. Chicago: University of Chicago Press. (With Milton Friedman)

Report to the Congress of the Commission on the Role of Gold in the Domestic and International Monetary Systems. Vol. 1. (March).

Reflections on the Gold Commission *Report* (pt. 1). *Journal of Money, Credit and Banking* (November): 538–51.

1983   International debt, insolvency, and illiquidity. *Journal of Economic Affairs* (April). (With K. Brunner et al.)

The importance of stable money: Theory and evidence. *Cato Journal* 3 (May): 63–82. (With M. D. Bordo)

The international transmission of inflation. Chicago: University of Chicago Press. (With M. R. Darby et al.)

1984   *A retrospective on the classical gold standard, 1821–1931*. Chicago: University of Chicago Press. (With M. D. Bordo)

Introduction. In *A retrospective on the Classical Gold Standard, 1821–1931*, eds. M. D. Bordo and A. J. Schwartz. Chicago: University of Chicago Press.

Comments on the paper by Alan Budd, Sean Holly, Andrew Longbottom and David Smith. In *Monetarism in the U.K.* eds. Brian Griffiths and Geoffrey E. Woods, 129–36. New York: Macmillan.

International lending and the economic environment. *Cato Journal* 4 (September).

Currents and countercurrents in political and economic thought: A comment on the Fellner paper. In *Carnegie-Rochester Conference Series on Public Policy*, eds. K. Brunner and A. H. Meltzer, 253–57. Vol. 21. The Hague: North-Holland.

1986   Real and pseudo-financial crises. In *Financial crises and the world banking system*, ed. Geoffrey E. Wood. New York: Macmillan.

Comments on "The open economy: Implications for monetary and fiscal policy" by Dornbusch and Fischer. In *The American business cycle: Continuity and change*, ed. R. J. Gordon, 504–10. Chicago: University of Chicago Press.

Has government any role in money? *Journal of Monetary Economics* (January): 37–62. (With Milton Friedman)

"The failure of the Bank of United States: A reappraisal": A reply. *Explorations in Economic History* (April): 199–204. (With Milton Friedman)

Alternative monetary regimes: The gold standard. In *Alternative monetary regimes*, eds. C. Campbell and W. Dougan. Baltimore: Johns Hopkins University Press.

Sustained recovery and trade liberalization: How the transfer problem can be solved. In *The international debt problem—Lessons for the future*, ed. H. Giersch, 133–44. J. C. B. Mohr (Paul Siebeck) for Institut für Weltwirtschaft des Universität Kiel.

1987   The behavior of money stock under interest rate control: Some evidence for Canada. *Journal of Money, Credit and Banking* 19, no. 2 (May). (With M. D. Bordo and E. U. Choudhri)

The search for stable money: Essays on monetary reform. Chicago: University of Chicago Press. (With J. A. Dorn)

Prospects of an international monetary constitution. *Contemporary Policy Issues* (April): 16–30.

The lender of last resort and the federal safety net. *Journal of Financial Services Research* 1:77–111.

Money in historical perspective. Chicago: University of Chicago Press.

1988   Banking school, currency school, free banking school. Arthur D. Gayer. Thomas Joplin. Sir Henry Parnell. In *The new Palgrave dictionary of economics.* 4 vols. New York: Stockton Press. (v. 1, 182–86; v. 2, 488–89, 1037–38; v. 3, 793).

Bank runs and deposit insurance reform. *The Cato Journal* 7 (Winter): 589–94.

Financial stability and the federal safety net. In *Restructuring banking and financial services in America,* eds. W. S. Haraf and R. M. Kushmeider. Washington, D.C.: American Enterprise Institute.

1989   Comment on Barry Eichengreen's "Trade deficits in the long run". Federal Reserve Bank of St. Louis (forthcoming).

Comments on Thomas Rymes's, "The theory and measurement of the nominal output of banks, sectoral rates of saving and wealth in the national accounts." In *The measurement of saving, investment, and wealth,* eds. R. E. Lipsey and H. S. Tice. Studies in Income and Wealth, v. 52. Chicago: University of Chicago Press (forthcoming).

Transmission of real and monetary disturbances under fixed vs. floating rates. *The Cato Journal* (forthcoming). (With M. D. Bordo)

International debts: What's fact and what's fiction. *Economic inquiry* (forthcoming, January).

Systemic risk and financial restructuring. *Proceedings of a conference on bank structure and competition,* 11–13 May 1988. Federal Reserve Bank of Chicago (forthcoming).

Book Reviews

English bank note circulation 1694–1954, by Emmanuel Coppieters. Review, *Journal of Political Economy* (August 1956): 353–54.

The origins of Hamilton's fiscal policies, by Donald F. Swanson. Review, *Kyklos* 18 (1964): fasc. 3, pp. 517–19.

The greenback era, by Irwin Unger. Review, *Political Science Quarterly* December 1965): 625–27.

Commercial bank behavior and economic activity, by Stephen M. Goldfield. Review. *Kyklos* 20 (1967): fasc. 2, pp. 539–40.

Commercial bank cooperation: 1924–31, by Stephen V. O. Clarke. Review, *Kyklos* 21 (1968): fasc. 1, pp. 161–63.

Statistics of the British economy, by. F. M. M. Lewis. Review, *Kyklos* 21 (1968): fasc. 2, pp. 392–94.

The Jacksonian economy, by Peter Temin. Review, *Journal of Economic History* (June 1970): 476–79.

Sovereignty and an empty purse: Banks and politics in the Civil War, by Bray Hammond. Review, *Journal of Economic Literature* (March 1972): 74–75.

The international economy and monetary movements in France, 1493–1725, by Frank C. Spooner. Review, *Journal of European Economic History* (Spring 1974): 252–55.

The banking crisis of 1933, by Susan E. Kennedy. Review, *Journal of Monetary Economics* (January 1975): 129–30.

The world in depression, 1929–1939, by Charles P. Kindleberger. Review, *Journal of Political Economy* (February 1975): 231–37.

Domestic monetary management in Britain, 1919–38, by Susan Howson. Review, *Journal of European Economic History* 5, no. 2 (1976): 500–503.

Money and empire, by Marcello de Cecco. Review, *Journal of Modern History* (September 1977): 490–91.

The Bank of England, 1891–1944, by R. S. Sayers. Review, *Journal of Economic Literature* (September 1977): 945–47.

The Golden Constant: The English and American experience, 1560–1976, by Roy W. Jastram. Review, *Journal of Economic History* (September 1978): 784–86.

Growth and fluctuations, 1870–1913, by W. Arthur Lewis. Review, *Journal of European Economic History* 8 (1979): 504–6.

The collected writings of John Maynard Keynes. Vol. 21: *Activities 1932–1939: World crisis and policies in Britain and America,* edited by Donald Moggridge. Review, *Journal of Economic Literature* (September 1983): 12–14.

The floating pound and the sterling area, 1931–1939, by Ian Drummond. Review, *Journal of European Economic History* 13 (1984): 668–70.

The development and operation of monetary policy, 1960–1983, a selection of material from the *Quarterly Bulletin* of the Bank of England. Review, *The Banker* (February 1985): 100–101.

World inflation since 1950: An international comparative study, by A. J. Brown. Review, *Economic History Review* (November 1986): 670–72.

The gold standard in theory and history, edited by Barry Eichengreen. Review, *Journal of Economic History* (December 1986): 1106–8.

A financial history of western Europe, by Charles P. Kindleberger. Review, *Journal of European Economic History* (forthcoming).

Participants

Rachel Balbach
Centerre Bank, N.A.
P.O. Box 267
St. Louis, MO 63166

George J. Benston
School of Business
Emory University
Rich Building
Atlanta, GA 30322

George H. Borts
Department of Economics
Brown University
P.O. Box Q
Providence, RI 02912

Michael D. Bordo
College of Business Administration
University of South Carolina
Columbia, SC 29208

Charlotte F. Boschan
Senior Economist
Citibase
P.O. Box 966
New York, NY 10268

Karl Brunner
Graduate School of Management
University of Rochester
Taylor Hall 24
Rochester, NY 14627

Phillip Cagan
Department of Economics
Columbia University
New York, NY 10027

Forrest H. Capie
City University Business School
Barbican Centre, Frobisher Crescent
London, EC2Y 8HB, England

Geoffrey Carliner
Executive Director
National Bureau of Economic
   Research
1050 Massachusetts Avenue
Cambridge, MA 02138

Ehsan U. Choudhri
Department of Economics
Carleton University
Ottawa, Ontario K15 536
Canada

Michael R. Darby
Assistant Secretary for Economic
   Policy
The Department of the Treasury,
   Room 3454
Washington, D.C. 20220

James A. Dorn
CATO Institute
224 Second Street, SE
Washington, D.C. 20003

Solomon Fabricant
National Bureau of Economic
  Research
269 Mercer Street, 8th Floor
New York, NY 10003

David I. Fand
Department of Economics
Wayne State University
Detroit, MI 48202

Martin Feldstein
President and Chief Executive
  Officer
National Bureau of Economic
  Research
1050 Massachusetts Avenue
Cambridge, MA 02138

Benjamin M. Friedman
Department of Economics
Harvard University
Littauer Center 127
Cambridge, MA 02138

Milton Friedman
Hoover Institution
Stanford University
Stanford, CA 94305

Arthur E. Gandolfi
Citibank, N.A.
399 Park Avenue
New York, NY 10043

Guy-Georges Harregat
Senior Vice President
Credit du Nord
520 Madison Avenue
New York, NY 10022

Robert Hetzel
Federal Reserve Bank of Richmond
100 North 9th Street
P.O. Box 27622
Richmond, VA 23219

Doris Ikle
c/o Office of the Under Secretary of
  Defense for Policy
U.S. Department of Defense
Room 4E830
Washington, D.C. 20301

Levis A. Kochin
Department of Economics
University of Washington
Seattle, WA 98195

David Laidler
Department of Economics
University of Western Ontario
London, Ontario N6A 5C2
Canada

Robert E. Lipsey
National Bureau of Economic
  Research
269 Mercer Street, 8th Floor
New York, NY 10003

James R. Lothian
Graduate School of Business
  Administration
New York University
100 Trinity Place
New York, NY 10006

Alvin L. Marty
City University of New York
33 West 42nd Street
New York, NY 10036

Bennett T. McCallum
Graduate School of Industrial
  Administration
Carnegie-Mellon University
Schenley Park
Pittsburgh, PA 15213

Cornelia McCarthy
2890 Coddington Avenue
Bronx, NY 10461

A. James Meigs
Department of Economics
Princeton University
Princeton, NJ 08544

David I. Meiselman
Virginia Polytechnic Institute
2990 Telestar Court
Falls Church, VA 22042

Allan H. Meltzer
Graduate School of Industrial
    Administration
Carnegie-Mellon University
Schenley Park
Pittsburgh, PA 15213

Geoffrey H. Moore
Center for International Business
    Cycle Research
Graduate School of Business
Columbia University
Uris Hall
New York, NY 10027

Gerald P. O'Driscoll, Jr.
Research Department
Federal Reserve Bank of Dallas
Station K
Dallas, TX 75222

Leif H. Olsen
Leif H. Olsen Associates
49 Locust Avenue
New Canaan, CT 06840

Mark Perlman
Department of Economics
University of Pittsburgh
Pittsburgh, PA 15260

William Poole
Department of Economics
Brown University
Providence, RI 02912

Robert H. Rasche
Department of Economics
Michigan State University
101 Marshall Hall
East Lansing, MI 48824-1038

Saranna Robinson
School of Urban and Public Affairs
Carnegie-Mellon University
Schenley Park
Pittsburgh, PA 15213

Hugh Rockoff
Department of Economics
Rutgers University
New Brunswick, NJ 08903

W. W. Rostow
Department of Economics
University of Texas
Austin, TX 78712

Anna J. Schwartz
National Bureau of Economic
    Research
269 Mercer Street, 8th Floor
New York, NY 10003

Jerome L. Stein
Department of Economics
Brown University
Providence, RI 02912

Alan C. Stockman
Department of Economics
University of Rochester
Rochester, NY 14627

Paul Wachtel
Chairman, Department of
    Economics
New York University
Graduate School of Business
90 Trinity Place
New York, NY 10006

Lawrence H. White
Department of Economics
New York University
New York, NY 10003

Geoffrey E. Wood
Centre for Banking and International
    Finance
City University
Frobisher Crescent, Barbican
London, EC2Y 8HB, England

Name Index

Subject Index

Aggregate demand, 176. *See also* Money demand
Agriculture: bank failures and, 31–32; gold standard and, 181–82
Aldrich Vreeland Act (1908), 21, 27, 38, 43
Alternative monetary standards, 5
Arima model, 176, 200
Asset exchanges, 24–25

Balance of payments: monetary policy and, 52, 231; quantity model and, 205–8
Bank(s), and banking systems: agricultural areas and, 31–32; antebellum competition of, 72–73; banking panics and. *See* Bank panics; bond risks, 32; branches, 45; business cycles and, 83–84; free banking and, 73; money endogeneity and, 119; money-income relationship and, 19; money inelasticity and, 37–38; national bank notes, 38; open market purchases and, 43; regulation of, 45–46. *See also* Central banks; *specific banks*
Banking holiday (1933), 29, 35
Bank of England: credit focus of, 4; gold flows and, 41; as lender of last resort, 94; *Monetary Trends* conference, 95–98; stabilization policy of, 92
Bank of United States, collapse of, 29
Bank panics, 19, 23–37, 40, 120
Bayesian forecasts, 175
Belmont-Morgan syndicate, 54

Bland Allison Act (1878), 54
Bonds: gold standard and, 166, 201; inflation regressions and, 214; money growth and, 214, 225; national bank notes and, 38; news and, 50; riskiness of, 32; WWII bond-price support, 48–49
Box-Jenkins method, 174
Bretton Woods system, 8, 49; commodity prices and, 184; growth rate and, 191; inflation and, 203; interest rate seasonality and, 41; output price interactions and, 187; price movements in, 165, 170; seven countries under, 170–90. *See also* Fixed exchange rate system; Gold standard
Britain. *See* Great Britain
Budget deficits, 50–52, 54
Bureaucracy, theory of, 47
Business cycle, 3, 89; banking panics and, 26, 120; Gayer-Rostow-Schwartz model of, 82–87; gold standard and, 168; interest-rate effect and, 128, 134; monetary effects and, 3, 7, 133–34; money-income relations and, 20; money supply and, 7, 105–6; NBER econometrics and, 18, 97–98; 1920 theories of, 112; unanticipated changes and, 118

Caldwell and Company, 31
Cambridge school, 112
Canada, 5, 46